THE TRANSFIGURATION

OF CHRIST

IN SCRIPTURE AND TRADITION

JOHN ANTHONY McGUCKIN

STUDIES IN THE BIBLE AND EARLY CHRISTIANITY
VOLUME 9

THE EDWIN MELLEN PRESS
LEWISTON/QUEENSTON

Library of Congress Cataloging-in-Publication Data

McGuckin, John Anthony
  The Transfiguration of Christ in Scripture and
tradition.

  (Studies in Bible and early Christianity ; 9)
  Bibliography: p.
  Includes index.
  1. Jesus Christ--Transfiguration. I. Title.
II. Series.
BT410.M34   1987   232.9'56   86-23892
ISBN 0-88946-609-2 (alk. paper)

BT
410
.M34
1987

This is volume 9 in the continuing series
Studies in the Bible and Early Christianity
Volume 9 ISBN 0-88946-609-2
SBEC Series ISBN 0-88946-913-X

All rights reserved. For information contact:

The Edwin Mellen Press   The Edwin Mellen Press
Box 450   Box 67
Lewiston, New York   Queenston, Ontario
USA 14092   L0S 1L0 CANADA

Printed in the United States of America

In Memoriam

FRANCIS McGUCKIN

1916 - 1981

Κυριε μου μεταμορφωσον την μορφην
του σωματος μου εν αγγελικη δοξη.

Acta Philippi 144.

List of Abbreviations

ANCL	Ante Nicene Christian Library (1st series) Oxford
ANF	Ante Nicene Fathers. (2nd series) Michigan
APOT	Apocrypha & Pseudepigrapha of the Old Testament vol.2, Oxford
ATR	Anglican Theological Review
CBQ	Catholic Biblical Quarterly
CC	Corpus Christianorum
CR	The Clergy Review
ET	English Translation
GCS	Die Griechischen Christlichen Schriftsteller
JBL	Journal of Biblical Literature
JTS	Journal of Theological Studies
LF	A Select Library of the Fathers. Oxford.
NPNF	Nicene and Post Nicene Fathers.Series 1,Oxford; Series 2,Michigan
NTS	New Testament Studies
OTM	Oxford Theological Monographs
PG	J P Migne Patrologia Graeca
PL	J P Migne Patrologia Latina
RB	Recherches Bibliques
RHR	Revue de l'Histoire des Religions
SBT	Studies in Biblical Theology. SPCK Monographs.
TDNT	Theological Dictionary of the New Testament, Ed. Kittel/Friedrich
TSK	Theologische Studien und Kritiken
TZ	Theologische Zeitschrift
WBzT	Wiener Beitrage z.Theologie
ZNW	Zeitschrift fur die Neutestamentliche Wissenschaft
ZTK	Zeitschrift fur Theologie und Kirche

ACKNOWLEDGEMENTS

This study has been the result of insights and inspirations gathered from so many friends and theologians of different traditions it would be impossible to number them all. So many faces appear, so many delightful memories of Patristics conferences all over the world. But I would specifically like to record my thanks to **Robert Murray, Michael Richards , Joseph Laishley** , (and the late **Maurice Bevenot**) for so generously communicating their love of Scripture, Church History, and Patristics, in the early years of my studies at Heythrop College, in the University of London. Archpriest **George Dion. Dragas,** of the University of Durham, gave me a shining example of devotion to the Fathers along with the rare pearl of his affection and friendship. Canon **John H. Davies** , of Southampton University, generously read the biblical chapters and offered the advantage of his usual perspicacious comment. And finally **Rose Patricia O'Kelly** typeset the final version of the manuscript. This was an onerous task indeed, fulfilled with typical grace and enthusiasm. To her I must record a special debt of thanks.

PREFACE

He came down,
And veiled his face
With a veil of flesh.
In the brilliance of his light
All Jordan became light.
He was radiant on the mountain
To a small degree,
Yet they the apostle called the 'pillars'
Were shivering,trembling, and aghast.
He granted them a glimpse of his secret glory
To the extent that they could bear.

Ephraem Syrus, Hymn 7.2

I caught my breath
In the chill splendour
And hush of night;
Bowed my heart
Before humanity transfigured,
Touched with immortality.

(Richard Church: Collected Poems.)

TABLE OF CONTENTS

INTRODUCTION

As perhaps befits a study on the Metamorphosis of Jesus, this book is polymorphic in design. Is it a biblical or a patristic study ? Is it meant for professional scholars or for those with a general interest in theological themes ? To answer the first question leads us to analyse a certain problem posed in its very formulation. The present study is an attempt to bridge the fatal gap that has grown up in this present century between dogmatics and biblical exegesis. The necessary specialisation required of the respective disciplines is today so great that it is no wonder that theological students are required to work exclusively in one field or the other to be able to cope with the amount of critical literature being produced. A drawback to this process is that the critical advances in biblical research usually leave the voice of patristic criticism wholly relegated to the sidelines. The Fathers, if they are consulted at all, are drawn in solely on questions about canonicity or authorship.Whether they are seen, even then, as relevant to critical concern,tends to be governed by **a priori** considerations. This procedure may well be justifiable.There is a world of difference between the semitic idioms of theology used in the era of Jesus and his contemporaries, & the Hellenistic modes of exegesis employed by the later Fathers.The writings of the latter, though nearer the time of the biblical era,are not thereby guaranteed to have a deeper understanding of semitic idiom than that possessed by contemporary scholarship. Indeed, often the opposite is the case. Nonetheless, the massive rejection of the patristic voice that has taken place in the modern era is to be lamented,for the nineteenth century ideology that so boldly dissected and separated out the evangelistic allegorisations and the dominical logia, as if they were utterly separate genres, must now be brought into question.The new appreciation of second Temple Judaism's own approach to scriptural exegesis - for example the writings of Qumran, the Aramaic Targumim,or the later rabbinic corpus - has enhanced our understanding of the integral employment of analogy,idiom, and allegorical symbolism within the message of Jesus himself. A new approach to patristic exegesis, and to allegorical interpretation, is called for. This will not be in the old manner of naively equating the patristic meanings with the concerns of the biblical text, but will be an approach that is open to the development of narrative insights in the unfolding history of a story or a text.

In the contemporary theological world this all too frequent divorce between exegesis and dogmatics may well have impoverished the biblicists, but it has certainly impoverished church dogmatics. No longer is it conceivably possible for dogmatists to remain unaware of the results of critical biblical research. The Bultmannian existentialist attempt to dismiss the Jesus of history from the Christological domain has clearly, and rightly, failed. This, however, has left a massive task confronting catholic Christian dogmatics, the task of reconciling the classical Christological understanding of the patristic church (an understanding still 'contemporary' in so far as it is enshrined in catholic cult and spirituality) with the Christological modes of the early biblical writers. In the end one may conclude that the reconciliation is certainly not to be found in terms of homonymity; that patristic and biblical theology are, after all, quite different things. This in no way reduces our urgent responsibility for seeking out some form of dogmatic synthesis in contemporary terms, for churches which still preserve both Scripture and Tradition as normative parts of their own self-identity.

This study is polymorphic, therefore, in being biblical and patristic because it wishes to look at that fascinating divide between the thought-world of the New Testament and that of the later Fathers. It has chosen redaction criticism as its methodology for part 1, and a new translation of the main patristic homilies and a synthetic analysis of their content, as its method for part 2. One single theme was chosen to give inner unity to a task that would otherwise have been so vast it stood in danger of losing itself. While the study's structure, therefore, has a familiar look to it (a theme analysis in the traditional manner) one hopes that its methodological intent might also be breaking some new ground. In a time when great pressure is often applied to university finances,theological study is often cast in the role of the lamb to the slaughter.Even within a theological budget in the faculties,patristics and church history tend to be offered up on the altar of expediency to redeem exegesis and systematics. The signs for a return to a proper holistic view of theological understanding are not auspicious and it is, therefore, a fitting time to call for a necessary widening of our perspectives, not their continuing narrowing into neo-scholastic subject categories that are becoming more and more cramped in their nature and effect.

Our second question concerned the style of the research in this study.Is it critical and professional, or meant as some kind of resource for a wider church readership ? In spite of the dangers of being accused of confusing one's readership I still enjoy the hope that it might serve for both purposes. The preliminary redactive analyses might be hard work for those unused to this type of procedure but the second part of the book collects together, for the first time ever, all the main homilies on the Transfiguration and thus offers the reader a rich source of Lectio Divina from the ancient church, as well as continuing the historical analysis in its own right. The detailed study of Hesychasm lies outside the scope of this book,but it would not be right to treat of the issue of Jesus' Metamorphosis without acknowledging the profound symbolic role it has played in the liturgical and spiritual life of the church. This sense of spirituality is devotional and theological at one and the same time. This union,indeed,is what the Fathers along with all the ancients meant by the very word 'theology'. Lactantius, in the early fourth century diagnosed the sickness of his world (the cultural & metaphysical collapse of the pagan Empire) as rooted in the divorce they had effected between Religion and Wisdom.The believers in God and the philosophers had gone their separate ways to the detriment of each.He saw the religionists in danger of lapsing into uncritical and superstitious bigotry,the intellectuals into relativistic and hopeless cynicism.Perhaps such a separation between the devotional and the

'theological' has opened up in Christianity itself in these days ?
Whether it achieves its end or not, this present study hopes to represent both concerns.In doing so it is attempting to recreate the
authentic patristic method of analysis,using contemporary theological
tools.It represents,then, what the late and lamented Fr.George Flor-
ovsky called for in his term 'neo-patristic synthesis'.

        Finally,if it is not altogether too presumptious of
me (my students insist on telling me that it is), I also hope that
the readers may also simply enjoy their perusal of these assembled
texts.

John A. McGuckin,
Department of Theology,
La Sainte Union College,
Southampton,
England.

THE TRANSFIGURATION

OF CHRIST

IN SCRIPTURE AND TRADITION

PART ONE

CHAPTER ONE

THE FORMATION OF THE TRANSFIGURATION NARRATIVE
A REDACTIVE HISTORY

1.1. The Metamorphosis in traditional commentary.

The patristic exegesis of the narrative of Jesus' transfiguration is
a rich and manifold tradition. One of the major exegetical strands,
that comes from the third century onwards to be the dominant approach, is the interpretation of the wonderful events on the mountain
as an epiphany of the essential deity of Christ. The text is read as
saying that the divine light burst out from its fleshly bonds, and
for an instant the real glory of the Man-God was shown to the disciples in all its radiance, to strengthen and prepare them (as Leo will
tell us, for example) for the oncoming trial of the Passion and death
of their Lord. Clement of Alexandria comments on the episode as
follows:'The Lord who ascended the mountain...laid bare the power
proceeding from him ... he appeared as God in a body of flesh.'[1]
Origen interpreted the light of transfiguration as the symbol of his
divine Logos-nature , and the radiance of his garments as a mystical
allusion to the Holy Scriptures, which were the 'garments of the
Word.'[2]
      Hilary of Poitiers, in one of his more esoteric texts,
asks his readers what they find so amazing in the Transfiguration
narrative, since for him the great wonder is that Jesus was not perm-
anently illumined throughout his entire ministry. Hilary finds, then, the
miraculous element to be one of a constant suppression of visible
glory throughout the earthly life, rather than a brief epiphany on
the mountain. He also finds in the text evidence for his view that
Jesus was possessed of a different type of humanity to ours : 'How
can we judge of that flesh conceived by the Spirit by analogy with
an ordinary human body ? That flesh, that bread, is from heaven;
that humanity is from God. He had a body that could suffer, and
he did suffer, but he did not have a nature which could feel pain.
His body was possessed of a unique nature of its own. It was there-

fore transformed into heavenly glory on the mountain. It put fevers to flight by its touch.It gave new vision by its spittle.When he ate and drank it was a concession to our ordinary habits,not to his own necessities.'[3] Even if we can prescind from the almost Docetic tone of the theology, it is clear that the dominant note of his interpretation is that here we are dealing with a revelation of the essential deity of Christ. Gregory Nazianzen interprets the light of Metamorphosis as the uncreated light of Jesus' godhead : 'Light was that godhead which was shown on the mountain to the disciples,too strong for their eyes.'[4] And finally,in the fifth century Leo is able to learn from the narrative that :'there is no separation of the essence of the Begetter from that of the only-Begotten.The disciples trembled not only at the Father's majesty, but also before that of the Son. In a higher sense they had understood the one deity of each person.'[5]

Hereafter,this high Christological interpretation of the patristic era has a long and honourable lineage descending without pause into the contemporary Orthodox approach. It is also found clearly repeated in the 1952 **Catholic Commentary on Holy Scripture**[6] in the late Alexander Jones' exegesis of Matthew,whose opening remarks on the Transfiguration narrative are as follows : 'The Father had already revealed the divinity of his Son to Peter (Mt.16.17) he now,about one week later,reveals it more publicly.'[7] The Maynooth Professor,J.A.O'Flynn, in the same commentary's exegesis of Mark, which in accordance with catholic attitudes of that time regarded it as dependent on Matthew for most of its information,followed much the same interpretative line ,as we might expect : 'The glory of the divinity which was normally veiled,is allowed to shine forth. Even Christ's garments shared in the radiance proceeding from the glory of his divine person.' [8] Pure patristics this. The catholic approach manifested in the more recent **Jerome Biblical Commentary**[9] is perhaps more aware of the speed of change which has taken place in catholic biblical scholarship in the intervening years.It now takes for granted Markan priority,but it is strangely concerned with 'hedging its bets' when it comes to offering a theological interpretation of the narrative. The straightforward 'historische' reading of the story has gone now, but there is a lot of reticence here. John McKenzie who comments on the Matthaean text goes for a symbolistic or mystical meaning :'The heavily symbolic character of the story indicates that this story,like the story of Jesus' Baptism,is more theological than historical in character.The narrative must rest upon a mystical experience of the disciples,but the experience itself is impossible to reconstruct.'[10] In this 'mystical experience' approach McKenzie is reproducing the line taken by Evelyn Underhill in her study **The Mystic Way**[11],a line favoured also by many of the continental liberal critics, such as Meyer and Harnack,in the early decades of the century.[12] Yet by stressing the 'symbolistic' method of analysis McKenzie also seems to opt for the exegetical approach of Wellhausen[13]Loisy[14] and Bultmann,who read the narrative as one of the purest examples of the mythic form in the whole of the New Testament.[15] In the light of all this I think it is clear that the final version adopted by McKenzie represents a working synthesis of most of the major schools of exegesis.While this might well be normal 'commentary procedure' it is far from being a satisfactory method of interpreting the biblical text,as it might be compared to the firing of a blunderbuss to kill a fly, in the firm hope that one at least of the myriad of pellets will do the job in hand.

In the course of its history outside the perameters of these traditional approaches,the Transfiguration narrative has attracted the following exegetical schools of thought:

(a) The dogmatic-Christological.Witnessed in the patristic writings and reproduced in traditionalist works thereafter which implicitly follow the Fathers. It is usually based on a straightforwardly historical reading of the story.

(b) A visionary-ecstatic phenomenon of an unusual kind;either that of Jesus himself or of Peter.

(c) The narrative as a misplaced or proleptic Resurrection story.[16]

(d) A symbolic narrative designed to illustrate the theology of Parousia.[17]

In his comments McKenzie had dismissed (c) as 'not accepted by the vast majority of NT scholars.' In itself this was a distortion of the **status quaestionis**, for while the majority of scholars found difficulties in accepting any thesis that made the narrative out to be some strange form of Resurrection story (how could such a claim be judged except by comparing the tale with the classical versions of the Resurrection story as already existing in the Gospels and Letters and finding minimal points of comparison)McKenzie had failed to understand that this was not the same as concluding the tale had no bearing at all on Resurrection glory (considered as a theology of Jesus' posthumous exaltation) , and therefore the 'Resurrectionist' school of thought is far more pervasive and well-founded than his comments made out.[18] Moreover he is silent about (a) and eventually opts for an interpretation which creatively combines (b) and (d). So much for J L McKenzie's treatment of Matthew in the **Jerome Biblical Commentary**,but when we turn in the same volume to the commentator of Mark,we find an analysis more or less exactly the same as the version in the 1952 **Catholic Commentary.**[19] Here we have confident statements that the narrative is based on some factual historic experience within the course of the ministry of Jesus. We are given a theological interpretation that connects this episodewith the Christological epiphany of Caesarea Philippi.

These few examples of previous catholic exegesis are simply taken as tide-markers of commonly available scholarship that demonstrate fairly well that the patristic analysis of the transfiguration narrative is still alive and well. While the **JBC**,as is right and proper, is more in tune with modern critical scholarship than any of its predecessors could be, it nonetheless still offers a theological interpretation of the text that is largely drawn from undisclosed patristic premisses.

Let us now turn our attention elsewhere to see if the application of redactive critical principles to the Markan text will allow us to discern the narrative's pre-history.It is important in this respect to work towards an understanding of two major issues: (a) What traditional story came into Mark's hands as his original Jesus tradition, and (b) What redactive changes did he make to his source, and for what theological end? If we can establish insights into these two areas we are well on the way to establishing,if not the meaning of the event,at least the meaning of the narrative as the evangelist himself understood it. If we can do this, then we may then look back to the patristic witness to see what relevance it has, and what relationship survives between such exegesis and the biblical text from which it springs.

1.2.Establishing the Primitive Text.

Our first task in hand is to establish which of our three canonical versions has priority of reading. The general principle of Markan priority (while nothing has materialised of late with sufficient force to challenge it in general terms) does not always work in the case of text units or pericopai,since the versions of pericopai in the alternative Synoptic Gospels may individually have a stronger claim to representing a more primitive state of the tradition.In short, Markan priority does not deny that Mark's redactive alterations to the tradition may leave his text in a less primitive state, as it were, than those who follow him. In redactive studies of this type, each case must be treated on its own merits.The starting point in method is to analyse the synoptic variants.

We find that Matthew's version differs from that of Mark in the following eight details :

(Ma)   The description of Jesus' face 'shining like the sun' is proper to him (Mt.17.2)

(Mb)   The long analogy Mark gives of the fuller's bleach to describe the garments' radiance is not found in Matthew.We have instead the terse analogy:'they became as white as light.(Mt.17.2)

(Mc)   Matthew recounts the order of the prophets' appearance in the traditional biblical manner of Moses followed by Elijah (Mt.17.3). In the first mention of them Mark has them appearing in reverse order, a procedure which is unique in all biblical literature. The second time he mentions them, only a few verses further on, Mark reverts to the traditional order as found in Matthew.

(Md)   Matthew has it that Peter is the sole figure responsible for offering Tabernacles to Christ.He also makes Peter's offer reverently dependent on Christ's approval,and thus does not present Peter (as Mark does) as making some kind of blunder that stands in need of correction. The implied correction of Mk.9.6,then, is not present.

(Me)   Matthew has the proprium that the cloud was a bright one. (Mt.17.5)

(Mf)   Matthew records the awesome fear of the disciples as a result of the theophany through the cloud (Mt. 17.6) whereas Mark recorded the reason for fear as being the appearance of the prophets and the unnatural radiance of their Lord (Mk.9.6).

(Mg)   Matthew has the heavenly voice use exactly the same words as at the baptism in the Jordan. In his text alone, then,the voice goes on to say :'with whom I am well-pleased'. (Mt.17.5) [20]

(Mh)   Matthew's account of the fear of the disciples is told in a much more developed and stylised manner than that of Mark. He also describes Jesus coming to touch their prostrate forms and raise them up (Mt.17.6-7) a detail which is proper to his Gospel.

Luke's version of the tale differs from Mark in the following details:

(La)   Jesus' motive for going up the mountain is recorded by Luke alone who tells us that it was in order 'to pray' (Lk.9.28). In addition he has no mention of the Matthaean and Markan theme that Jesus and the disciples were 'apart by themselves' even though at other times in his Gospel he seems expressly to introduce this same theme in connection with his treatment of Jesus' prayers.

(Lb)   The word 'Metamorphosis' is not recorded as applying to Christ **in toto.** Luke has it that during his prayer his face took on a different appearance (Lk.9.29).

(Lc)   Luke describes the heavenly visitors first of all as 'two men' (repeated again at 9.33) before going on to identify them more precisely as the two prophets, whom he then lists in the traditional order, first Moses, then Elijah.

(Ld)   The most extensive textual difference is Lk.9.31-33a where Luke alone introduces the word 'glory' ($\Delta o\xi\alpha$) and tells the reader the substance of the conversation between Jesus and the prophets: as having something to do with the mystery of his death ($\varepsilon\xi o\delta o\varsigma$) in Jerusalem. He records, as a proprium, the strange sleep that falls on Peter and his companions and their (successful) struggle to see his glory.

(Le)   Luke gives the reason for the awe of the disciples as the theophany from the cloud in which he concurs with Matthew over and against Mark (Lk.9.34).

The difference in Luke 9.28a where Luke alone records 'after eight days' is not a significant textual variant for our purposes. The 'six days' represents semitic idiom, the 'eight days' hellenistic. It is not an indication **per se** of a variation in tradition history in the way the story has been transmitted, though doubtless Luke is responsible for making this amendment himself. All three narratives, however, agree in chronologically relating the Transfiguration back to the starting point of the logion about 'not tasting death' (Mk.9.1 and parallels) which in the Markan redaction stands as the culmination of a series of apocalyptic sayings on the nature of discipleship (Mk. 8.34-38). From this basis, if we assume the premiss of the general priority of Mark's text, it would follow that when Matthew and Luke independently agree together, against Mark, for a detail of the story we therefore have an indication that they have separately retained the prior narrative tradition, and that consequently Mark appears at that point to have made a personal redactive alteration to his source which the others have elected not to follow. When only Matthew , or Luke , has a narrative detail on the other hand we have a **prima facie** case for reading this as their pesonal editorial development, a case that can become fairly conclusive if in that particular narrative detail we can detect a theological motive that is in accord with what has already been established about their individual editorial tendencies. If in the case of a narrative detail preserved by only one of the evangelists apart from Mark no theological motive can be clearly discerned, this may indicate the possible preservation of a pre-Markan stage of the tradition : an interesting example of this can be observed in Luke's detail about the 'two men' who appear from heaven. Our text will deal with this subsequently.

These then are the basic rules of thumb that shall help us analyse the narrative and establish the primary version of the story. Working from these premisses the following five conclusions can be deduced, of which the first four deal with the changes Mark appears to have introduced into the traditional source that came to him :

(a)   Both Matthew and Luke observe the change that came over the face of Jesus. Mark does not. The description in Matthew (shining like the sun) uses apocalyptic idiom to depict the change[21], whereas Luke, avoiding the Markan term 'Metamorphosis' (possibly because it has too overt connotations of the

Hellenistic notion of Theosis [22] (In the manner of the Παλιγεννεσια Πνευματικη familiar in the Mystery Cults) has gone for a more prosaic but none the less conclusive version of the 'changed features'. This argues that the pre-Markan version of the story laid central emphasis on the radiant face of Jesus, but that Mark, for reasons of his own, has elected to shift this narrative emphasis.

(b)   Both Matthew and Luke recount the order of appearance of the prophets in the traditional manner ; that is, first Moses and then Elijah. Mark himself lists them in this order when he has Peter mention them in the course of his offer of tabernacles. It is a small detail but one that can be immensely important, for Mark has evidently made a conscious decision to change their order of appearance in Mk.9.4 against the whole tradition of biblical procedure. In changing their order it is arguable that he has in consequence given slightly more emphasis, or drawn more attention to Elijah rather than Moses. At this point did Mark simply change round the order of appearance for the prophets in a story that already contained them , or is he responsible for adding them to the text in the first place ? There are indications that the latter is the case, for in the Lukan version of the tale we find the heavenly visitors first of all described as 'two men' which is a typical biblical metonym for angels. The added detail - 'they were Moses and Elijah' appears almost as an afterthought. I take this as a sign that his own source had preserved a tradition that recounted an angelic epiphany on the mountain (something to be expected in the narrative of any theophanic event, especially one written in the manner of the Sinai archetype where the Angel of Covenant appeared to Moses [23]) but that he has yielded to the extra information that he discovered in the Markan version of the story, and so reads on from Mark the statement of their identity,which is why it appears as an afterthought in his own version. In this case the original generic reference to angelic presence in theophany has probably been redrafted by Mark's own hand to transform it into an attendance by prophets , and not just any prophets - only these two will do for his purposes.For such a dramatic change in narrative emphasis we must find a correspondingly serious theological motive in Mark's mind. Such a proposed motivation must also be in line with what can be established elsewhere about the style,theology, and purpose of his other redactive alterations throughout his Gospel. Such a motive, I believe, is not hard to discover, and shall be argued shortly. For the moment we can summarise - Luke at this point in the text has preserved a more primitive version of the Transfiguration story which he has subsequently amended in favour of his reading of Mark.In the process he has left some awkward signs of redactive work in his own text at Lk.9.30b.

(c)   In both Matthew and Luke, the apostles (Peter in particular) come out of the story in an enhanced light. In Matthew (who generally tends to glorify Kephas at several other similar junctures) the apostle appears reverent and highly sensible in his comments. In Luke's version the disciples struggle valiantly & successfully against sleep, not ordinary drowsiness but some kind of ecstatic sleep[24], but the redactive detail here is clearly a Lukan device to draw the

Transfiguration narrative into some form of textual parallelism with his version of the Gethsemane story [25]. In Mark alone do we find a thinly veiled edge of criticism in his dealings with Kephas, for the offer of tabernacles is here interpreted as the result of a fear so great that it has made him speak nonsense ('he did not know what to say') and this in turn leads the evangelist implicitly to correct by explicitly excusing him.Mark seems here to be introducing into the original tradition one of his own theological motifs[26].The original text can be taken to have been laudatory of the disciples and probably designed to enhance their position and authority in the early church. Mark seems,then, to be personally reducing that theme by his changes.

(d)   Both Matthew and Luke recount the awe of the disciples as a result of the cloud theophany[27].This is a common and typical theophany-form based upon the Sinai archetype.Mark alone has given the appearance of the prophets as the cause of the disciples' fear.The appearance of angels in the OT frequently causes theophany-dread but there is no precedent for such dread in the presence of returning prophets, especially since Mk.9.13 discounts any possibility of reading the Elijah allusion as a reference to the eschatological prophet of Malachi 4.5. This certain incompatibility is a further sign that Mark has been personally responsible for transforming what were originally angelic attendants into the two prophets. But more to the point he has also relocated the awe of the disciples to relate to this appearance of the prophets rather than to the cloud or the voice of God which follow. He is clearly responsible ,then, for fragmenting what was previously a coherent narrative that laid all its stress on the appearance of God. Mark has been prepared to make such a major redactive inbreak simply in order to place great stress on the appearance of these two prophets whom he has introduced. These figures, we must conclude are obviously central and crucial to his personal theological concerns, and he prefers them as a theological vehicle rather than the Sinai archetype that seems to have lain behind the primitive source.

(e)

All the remaining redactive differences are satisfactorily explained on the basis that Matthew and Luke have also added or omitted details in the normal processes of their personal redactions of Mark's text. Each of these remaining differences in narrative has a fairly obvious relation with what has already been established about their distinctive theological styles and espoused causes. In regard to Matthew, for example, this premiss accounts for the details mentioned above :- Mb,Md,Me,Mg, and Mh. In each case (particularly clearly in the last instance Mh referring to Mt.17.6-7) we witness a typical Matthaean Haggadah of his Markan source. With regard to Luke the same premiss also accounts for the redactive changes set out in La and Ld above , that is Luke's concern with the prayer life of Jesus, and the soteriological root of his whole ministry.

In short, and on the basis of the above analysis,we can perhaps summarise by saying that the most primitive version of the Transfiguration story was designed to do two things : firstly to draw a parallel between Moses' and Jesus' experience of God (and probably their subsequent roles as mediators) based upon a use of the Sinai narrative as literary archetype[29] , and secondly to heighten the authority and validate the status of the 'pillars' of the church who had attended their transfigured Lord[30]. A similar motif can be discerned in the narratives of the Resurrection Δοξα which not only serve as theological comments on the status of the Lord,but also on the status and the authority of his apostolic witnesses.

The original source enshrined, then, an implicit Christology of the prophetic/Mosaic type, and an incipient theology of ecclesiastical governance. The two issues are intimately related,of course,in so far as authority in ancient Christianity (as today for that matter) is designed to validate a certain type of theological thinking as 'orthodoxy'. The Christology of the pre-Markan source would appear to be maintaining a vision of Jesus who is like the New Moses, that eschatological prophet spoken of and promised in Deut.18.15 [31]. Looking at the description of Kephas' homily in Acts 3.18-26,which shows him offering a Christology based on the Moses-Jesus analogy[32] perhaps we would not be far off the mark to presume that Kephas himself was the preacher behind the formation of the primitive version of the Transfiguration homily,which he offered as a haggadah on the Sinai theophany in order to substantiate a prophetic Christology. The form of the narrative would therefore have taken shape and been circulated as a result of his wide ranging homiletic activity in the ancient church. This would also account for the strong presence of the authority motif that is so favourable to Peter in the original version. Following up on this hypothesis we can outline some of the theological implications behind the original source more fully.

When Moses ascended the mountain to be embraced by the Shekinah cloud he was publicly validated before all Israel as the supreme mediator of God's authoritative Torah. On his descent from the mountain, his radiant and transfigured face inspired awe in the people[33]. After his descent Moses engaged in the organisation of Israel as the people of God gathered in community round the Torah,and he shared some of his 'ecclesial' authority with his High

Priest,Aaron. It is not difficult to see an underlying motive for Kephas in this Transfiguration homily in its primitive form, for if Jesus is the New Moses,the new giver of Torah and founder of a new people, then Kephas is his Aaron,the High Priest of that new Israel. The fact that Peter is accompanied in the original homily by James and John,the Boanerges,does not gainsay this centrally Petrine interpretation,as they are clearly subsidiary **dramatis personae,** perhaps fulfilling the roles of Nadab and Abihu to Peter's Aaron[34]. Moreover,if Kephas was delivering such a homily in Mark's church at Rome, in the early sixties of the first century,then the sons of thunder had already been dead for two decades,and thus were in no position to counter his interpretation of their relative authoritative merits. If they had lived, to judge from Mk.10.35-41,then they would probably have had much to say about their own claims to be the authoritative interpreters of Jesus and the inheritors of his leadership over the church community. One such figure who made his own claims to apostolic authority,Paul,also has a dramatic and 'alternative' reworking of the Sinai haggadah in his own homiletic repertoire which rises to the fore after his personal visit to these very 'pillars of the church'.In an excellent and suggestive article B.D.Chilton[35] suggests that Paul composed this alternative haggadic version in a deliberate attempt to revise that tradition in particular (the Sinai Haggadah) which was being used by the 'pillars' to underscore their own apostolic status and theological vision.

1.3. Establishing the Markan Redaction.

If such a Kephas homily stands as the archetype of the Transfiguration story then what do we learn from the Markan manner of redactive alteration ? Whenever the redactor's hand is at work,a theological motive is not far away, and the amazing complexity of the narrative as it now stands in our texts is an eloquent testimony to the fact that much editorial reworking has gone on here.

The fact that Mark deliberately omits reference to the Shekinah light on the face of Jesus,and chooses to speak instead of a thoroughgoing Metamorphosis (a striking Hellenistic word, very rare in the NT[36],signifying radical spiritual transformation) argues that he wished to remove any overtly Sinaitic theme in his version of the narrative, and his main reason for doing this,I suggest, is to remove the Moses-Jesus analogy from centre stage, along with its inherently prophetic Christology. This is a theological motive very much in line with the rest of his Gospel, for he is the champion of a gentile church that sees itself,in the Pauline manner, as freed from the Mosaic Torah by Jesus. The same motive is at play when Mark makes his second great redactive inbreak and identifies the two angelic attendants of the original Sinai Haggadah as Elijah and Moses. In the first place,the actual presence of Moses,now alongside Jesus,actually makes the original point of the story almost impossible to sustain,based as it was on an implied analogy with the great Moses where Jesus in a certain sense was supposed to be following in the holy man's footsteps. In the second place Mark makes sure that Moses comes second,after Elijah,and it is unquestionably the latter figure which features more prominently in the scheme of the Markan Gospel and its Christological design[37].

If Mark's introduction of Elijah and Moses,then,is designed to play down the Moses-Sinai symbolism,just what exactly is Mark thinking about when he introduces these two prophets ? What is the theological symbol now at work in his mind ? From the third century onwards, after the allegorical exegesis of Origen has had a widespread effect,these two figures have stood in our minds for the Law and the Prophets, but this is clearly a Hellenistic allegorisation of the text that has no substantiation in first century biblical idiom.It is an idiom that with the utmost confidence we can say was not operating in the mind of the evangelist when he introduced these figures into his text.Their significance,for Mark, lies elsewhere, and I suggest our attention should be drawn to 2

Kings 1.1-12 which recounts the glorious ascent of Elijah,his personal metamorphosis,as it were,into an inhabitant of the heavenly court.

Elijah's ascent on the Merkabah comes as the prophet's glorification after he has faithfully fulfilled his earthly ministry. That ministry was so charismatically great that Judaic tradition afterwards hailed him as one of the very few immortalised men inhabiting the court of Yahweh,enjoying even now the vision of the divine light.The company of these immortals was very select. The father of Methuselah,Enoch,was his companion there;the selfsame who at the end of the Enoch literature is revealed as the heavenly Son of Man[38]. Does Moses fit into this schema ? for even a very cursory reading of Deuteronomy will tell us that at the end of his ministry he died and was mysteriously buried[39]. Nonetheless the tradition of his own ascent to the throne of Yahweh as an immortal alongside Elijah and Enoch is attested by Josephus in his **Antiquities**[40] and corroborated by the remnants of the book of **The Assumption of Moses** preserved in Clement of Alexandria[41]. Josephus,writing circa 94 AD is alluding to an older tradition which must have been at least contemporaneous with Mark,if not a great deal older. By means of rabbinic principles of exegesis it is easy to move from the one tradition of the death and burial of Moses to the other interpretation of an immortal ascent to heaven in the body (the latter haggadah keeping pace with Moses' constantly growing status in later Judaism). The first stage in the argument is that Moses wrote everything in the Pentateuch.It follows,therefore, that he himself wrote the words telling of his own death.If so, he cannot have been dead when he finished the book.Josephus concludes the argument for us by supplying the motive for the subterfuge : Moses was a man of such great humility that he wished to put people off the scent and cover the tracks of his ascent to heaven by telling everyone of his death.An ancient rabbinic saying preserved in the Mishnah,which cannot be dated precisely,shows the crystallisation of this tradition of the heavenly immortals : 'Three went up alive into the heavens;Enoch,Moses and Elijah.'[41] We might, then, deduce that Mark's own motive in replacing the Sinai-Moses symbolism of his source with this Elijah-Moses symbolism of his own redaction is comparable to that of Josephus,in that both were attempting to theologise about the post-ministerial Δοξα of their respective heroes. This would mean that Mark's redactive introduction of the prophets signals a notable change in theological emphasis, a moving away from a Mosaic type of Christology,that is a Christology of Paideia that would have looked to the Torah of Jesus as its mainspring,towards a Christology based on the glorification experience of Jesus after his martyrdom[43],a glory that Mark anticipates here in his Transfiguration narrative (though carefully setting it within the aegis of Jesus' sufferings by having it preceded by the first prophecy of the Passion,and followed by the logion on the death of the new Elijah,John[44].Such a motive is well substantiated by the general theological tenor of the Gospel of Mark which in its Christology is evidently more concerned with the deeds and person of Jesus than with the content of his teachings.

A further corroboration that Mark is concerned to move away from a Mosaic Christology is perhaps given to us in the other Markan redaction of the implied correction of Peter's mistake. Peter offers three tabernacles to the three prophets.There is a presupposition of equality of status here,even if Peter does wish to venerate his own master as first among that prophetic brotherhood. It is this implicit prophetic Christology, I believe, that Mark is concerned to reject,and for this end has transformed the voice from the cloud from its original significance as a Sinaitic motif to a new function as a specific revelation,like a Bath Qol in the rabbinic sense, which is designed to correct Peter's faulty theology by emphasising the unique and special status of Jesus as Beloved Son of God - a uniqueness that has replaced and outstripped all prophetic predecessors and hence the meaning of the phrase :'And looking round they saw no-one only Jesus.'[45] If we translate these concerns into modern idiom,then it would seem that the original Kephas homily of Sinai haggadah employed a Christology that worked by means of **analogia**

comparationis. No matter how much one puts Christ first in the line of comparative analogies by which the process works,it is still difficult in terms of the logic of the argument to substantiate a claim for Christological uniqueness. Put another way this argument makes for a Christological difference by degree,not by kind.By a subtle redaction which has amounted to removing the radiant face motif,transforming the two angels of covenant into Moses and Elijah, relocating the awe of the disciples away from the cloud theophany towards the appearance of the prophets,introducing the correction of Peter by means of a patronising excuse, and finally reintroducing the theophany words from God now as a Bath Qol to throw all our attention specifically onto Jesus alone - by means of such editorial reworkings,then,Mark has effectively removed the last lingering vestiges of prophetic Christology from the story and pointed us quite clearly in the Christological direction subsequently explicated by the patristic church. What I think Mark has arrived at is more a generic reflection on the uniqueness of Jesus' entrance into the Shekinah,or in other words Jesus' unique envelopment in the heart of God.

The patristic church,driven by similar concerns to ensure a Christology differentiated by kind rather than by degree[46], puts the Markan theology through a further stage of interpretative development (just as Mark himself treated Kephas) and so arrives at our traditionalist interpretation of the text with which we began namely that the story is a manifestation of the inherent divinity of Jesus. The patristic idiom of ontological statements moves more and more away from semitic idiom, and in fact comes to remember less and less about biblical modes of thinking.But in this instance it is clearly the case that the root motive of both Mark and the Fathers can be found to be the same - a ringing of the death knell for a prophetic Christology, and a proclamation of Jesus' wholly unique glory.

This brief and summary investigation into the prehistory of the Markan text is set here to serve as a generic introduction to the more detailed analyses that follow. The substance of this analysis will now be argued from a detailed redactive study of the Markan text, following through verse by verse, in the chapter which follows.

NOTES TO CHAPTER ONE

1. Clement of Alexandria,**Stromata** 6.16.140.3,ET ANCL 12,Ed. A.Roberts,Edinburgh,1869,p.387.

2. Origen,**Contra Celsum** 6.68,ET ANCL 23,pp.410-411.

3. Hilary,**De Trinitate** 10.23-24. PL 9.361-362.

4. Gregory Nazianzen,**Oratio** 40.6,**De Baptismo**,PG 36.363-366.

5. Leo The Great,**Homilia** 51,PL 54.308-313.

6. London 1952,p.882.

7. The Christological sentiment is quite clear even though the factual interpretation is not quite accurate since the epiphany at Caesarea was,technically speaking,more public than the secret epiphany on the mountain.

8. Ibid.p.919.

9. London 1968.

10. J.L.McKenzie,**JBC**,vol.2,p.93. Once again the logic of the commentator seems obscure for if the original experience is 'impossible to reconstruct' one wonders how he can apparently be so sure that the narrative 'must rest upon some mystical experience of the disciples.'

11. London,1913,pp.114-123.

12. cf. V.Taylor,**The Gospel According to S.Mark.** London,1957, pp.386-387.

13. J.Wellhausen,**Das Evangelium Marci,**Berlin 1909,pp.68-71,
14. A.Loisy,**Les Évangiles Synoptiques,**Paris 1907, vol.2.p.39.
15. R.Bultmann,**Die Geschichte der Synoptischen Tradition,**Gottingen 1931,pp.278-281. See also E.Lohmeyer,'Die Verklarung Jesu nach dem Markusevangelium',**ZNW** 21,1922,185-215.

16.   The list of scholars who have so far interpreted the Transfiguration as something to do with the Resurrection mystery of Jesus is given in the critical article by R.H.Stein :'Is the Transfiguration a misplaced Resurrection account ?' JBL,95,1976,pp.79-96.

17.   A thesis maintained especially by E.Lohmeyer (cf.fn 15) and G.H. Boobyer,**St. Mark and the Transfiguration Story,**Edinburgh,1942.

18.   An argument that will be more fully documented in its fuller substantiation in the course of the following chapter.

19.   J.Malley,**JBC,**vol.2,p.42.

20.   Codex Beza supports the Lukan reading also having the reference 'with whom I am well pleased', but on text-critical grounds it appears to be in this Manuscript merely as a scribe's unconscious Matthaean assimilation. There are almost incontrovertible authorities to show that the Lukan text concurred with Mark at this point to omit the phrase in question.cf relevant critical apparatus.

21.   cf. Mt.13.43,Phil.2.15.

22.   cf. R.Reitzenstein,**Hellenistic Mystery Religions,** ET J Steely, Pittsburgh 1978 (esp.chs.11-12).

23.   cf.Acts 7.30,53.

24.   A theme perhaps familiar to Luke from his knowledge of the **incubus** tradition in the cult of Aesculapius the god of healing. cf.TDNT 3.p.432; Daniel10.9.

25.   For an illustration of the Gethsemane parallels cf. A Kenny, 'The Transfiguration and the Agony in the Garden.' **CBQ,**19, 1957,pp.444-452, also TDNT 8,p.554.

26.   For a further study of this theme of Mark's bias against the disciples cf. 'The disciples in Mark:the function of a narrative role.' by R.C.Tannehill, in W.Telford (Ed) **The Interpretation of Mark,** London 1985.

27.   The cloud ,which takes its origin from the classic theophany account of Exodus 34,comes in the rabbinic period to be synonymous with the Shekinah - God's presence as revealed to men. cf. A.M. Ramsey,**The Glory of God and the Transfiguration of Christ,**London 1949.

28.   cf. Dan.10.5-9.

29 The details,when reconstructed and put together are obvious: the mountain,the cloud,the voice or Torah of God,the angelic presence,the radiant face of the one who received the Torah, the awe of the earthly witnesses.

30. I am indebted for the original insight to the study by B. Chilton,'The Transfiguration:Dominical assurance and apostolic vision.' **NTS** 27,1,1981,pp.115-124.

31. The Deuteronomic text is probably the original source of the additional phrase 'listen to him' which is appended to a citation of Psalm 2.7.

32. For a prophetic Christology operating in the primitive church and the apostolic kerygma cf. Acts 7.37,Lk.24.19,Jn.6.14, Jn.7.40. See also O Cullmann,**The Christology of the NT**, 2nd Edn. London 1977,pp.13-50.

33. Exodus 34.29-35.

34. For the role of Nadab and Abihu cf. Exodus 6.23,Lev.10.1, Exodus 24.1,9. See also Chilton (fn.30)p.124. The casting of the two Sons of Thunder in the roles of these two priests can hardly have been their own doing considering the wholly subordinate status they have in the Exodus narrative, and also the unfortunate end to which they came in Numbers 3.4f.

35. Chilton (fn. 30) pp.123-124.

36. Apart from the evangelical narrative in which the word occurs only for Mark, and Matthew following him, it is elsewhere found only in Paul,cf.Rom.12.2, 2Cor.3.18, and (partially) Phil.3.21.

37. The synoptic tradition of the miracles of Jesus is clearly based, at some stage,probably pre-Markan, on a literary collection that paralleled them with the miracles of the Elijah cycle.cf. Lk.7.11f and Elijah in 1Kings 17;Mk.6.34 and 1Kings 22.17;Mk.6.45-55 and 1Kings 19 together with 2Kings 2 where Elijah crosses over water;Mk.7.24f and 2Kings 4.8; and finally Mk.8.1-10 and 2Kings 4.42.

38. Cf. Gen.22.24, and Heb.11.5. The apocryphal Enoch literature can be found in R H Charles (Ed) **The Apocrypha and Pseud-epigrapha of the OT.** Oxford 1913,cf.vol.2 pp.180ff.

39. eg. Deut.32.48f,Dt.34.5-6.

40. 'A cloud suddenly stood over him and he was withdrawn from view into a valley.He himself wrote in the sacred

books that he had died,for fear that some should dare to maintain (because of his outstanding virtues) that he had risen to the godhead.' **Antiquities** 4.326. This text and the ideas of exaltation behind it are discussed more fully in the subsequent chapter.

41.   Clement of Alexandria,**Stromata** 6.15; cf. Charles **APOT vol.2,pp.407ff.**

42.   Midrash ha Gadol on Deut.34;cf. **TDNT** 4.p.855.

43.   The implied argument would be that Jesus,after his resurrection, is an immortal mediator in the court of Yahweh, superior even to the greatest immortals of the Judaic tradition.The Son of God Christology (cf.fn.45) as it appears in Mark's text calls an end to a certain prophetic manner of interpreting the life of Jesus. If higher than a prophet then what ? An alternative Christology of the early Palestinian community would appear to have been the use of a form of Χριστος Αγγελος position.Again the Son Christology can function to call an end to this approach too, as is clear in **Hebrews,**and present a case for a generic distinctness in the person of Jesus. The substance of this argument is that the Son of God concept in Mark is far closer to the Johannine usage of Μονογενες Θεου than has usually been credited. This Christological argument will again be further developed in the following chapter.

44.   cf. Mk.8.31-38, Mk.9.9,13.

45.   A similar Christological movement, where Son Christology is being used to advance on 'prophetic' statements about Jesus,can be discerned in Heb.1.1-13. The Son Christology of this passage,so 'high' in tone,is again based upon the notion of glorification rather than that of Torah or Paideia. It is worthy of note that **Hebrews** like the Markan text itself is apparently a theology emanating from an Italian context.

46.   As in the Nicene movement from Homoiousios to Homoousios, or the election of Cyrilline/Chalcedonian Hypostatic union rather than the Nestorian Prosopic union. The issue lives still today and will continue to be at the heart of every Christology debate.

CHAPTER TWO

AN EXEGETICAL ANALYSIS
OF THE MARKAN TEXT

1. **Amen I say to you that there are some of those now stand-ing here who shall not taste of death before they shall see the kingdom of God come in power. (Mk.9.1)**

Αμην λεγω υμιν οτι εισιν τινες ωδε των εστηκοτων οιτινες ου μη γευσωνται θανατου εως αν ιδωσιν την βασιλειαν του θεου εληλυθυιαν εν δυναμει.

Mark's phrase 'six days later' (9.2) with which he begins his Transfiguration narrative proper,refers back directly to this Logion. The events happen six days after this saying and the evangelist , by so drawing our attention to this , evidently wishes us to read the subsequent narrative in the light of it. It suggests that ,for Mark at least, some of those bystanders who received the promise of the vision of the Kingdom come in power, actually had that promise fulfilled in their own lifetimes. It is Mark's way of dealing with the difficult logia of Jesus which seemed to promise that the apocalyptic day of the Kingdom would be consummated for his followers even within their own lifetimes,thus leading to intense expectations of an imminent Parousia in the first generation of primitive Christianity. This tradition, preserved in the Gospels quite clearly, was a source of great problems for the early church,which by the time the first New Testament writings were beginning to be composed, witnessed its members already dying without seeming to have realised the material fulfilment of Jesus' promise that the Kingdom would have come 'in power'. Paul's letters to Thessalonika are classic examples of such a crisis in early Christian parousial expectation. Paul offers his own interpretation of what eschatological hope should mean for the Christian,but in their own ways so do all the subsequent four Gospels.The issue of parousial delay is still sufficiently alive in the era of the Johannine writings as to provide both a radical departure from classical futurist expectation in the thought of the fourth Gospel, and a return to it in the text of the Johannine letters.

Mark has his own way, a relatively simple one at that, of solving the immediate problem - that in the Roman church of the mid sixties of the first century the generation that might have followed Jesus were truly passing away, and many must have begun to whisper that Jesus' promise of the Day being fulfilled in their lifetime had evidently been disproved.If this logion of Jesus is understood in the sense of promising a general consummation of the Kingdom for all,within the lifetime of the first disciples, it would have amounted to a serious theological skandalon. Mark remains faithful to the difficulties of this logion tradition in so far as he preserved the sayings intact for us, but he also points to a solution in so far as he argues an actual fulfilment of the saying **in a restricted sense.** He suggests, in other words,that Jesus only promised a vision of the Kingdom in their lifetime **to some** of the first generation not all of them, and that his words were perfectly fulfilled when he did take up some of them (ie. Peter James and John) to demonstrate in secret what the glory of the Kingdom would be. The theological redaction is clearly Christological from beginning to end. The evangelist has reinterpreted the apocalyptic notion of 'The Day' and 'The Kingdom Come' as an event which somehow, however mysteriously,takes place and is made present in the person of Jesus of Nazareth. He has made a radical Christological interpretation of the logion, but as a parousial theology (a way of explaining the delay of the Parousia by suggesting Jesus' apparent promises of a quick consummation really meant a vision he gave to the apostolic pillars) it is not sufficiently deep in itself to provide a lasting answer to the needs of the church. This is one of the dissatisfactions Luke has with the theology of Mark,and which motivates him to compose a Gospel that presents a far more complex ecclesiology and offers a much more worked-through conception of the Parousia than Mark appears to him to offer. Luke's conception of why the Parousia is delayed is arguably one of the great themes of his Gospel's inner structure, as outlined,for example,in Conzelmann's classic redactive analysis of that Gospel[1].

Long before Mark's redaction of the phrase 'those who have not tasted death',however, the term can be found in the apocalyptic pseudepigraphon **4th Ezra** 6.26, in the context of a promise that those who survive the great tribulations of the end-times shall see 'the men who have been taken up,who have not tasted death from their birth.' This appears to mean the faithful martyrs,those saintly heroes who have already (as for example in 2 Maccabees) been raised up by God and translated as inhabitants of paradise as a reward for their exceptional fidelity on earth in the face of persecutions.

In the text of **4th Ezra** these saints in paradise are offered as an encouragement to the faithful still on earth who are currently undergoing the last apocalyptic trials before the appearance of the Day of the Lord,that final revelation of his Kingdom. Such a notion of encouragement in the face of apocalyptic persecution is a discernible theological tendency all through the Gospel of Mark[2], and even the immediately preceding verses Mk.8.34-38) have set this scene. The initial indication we receive, then, about the evangelist's mind as he begins his Transfiguration narrative is that it was perhaps concerned to offer an encouragement for his own church,at Rome,in the face of the Neronic persecution, and in order to do this set out the Transfiguration story as a paraenesis for them just as it was once an encouragement for the three chosen apostles (who by the time Mark was writing had all succumbed to the lot of their martyrdom) in the face of their approach to the Passion of their Lord.

This context of exhortation in difficult and dangerous times, then, is the motive that leads Mark redactively to change the import of the divine voice at the end of the story.As it now stands in the Markan text it is no longer an identification of Jesus as the Mosaic prophet (on the basis of Deut.18.15 used as proof text) but is now a specific and particular allusion to the teaching Jesus has given previously(and will again repeat immediately after the event) which is to do with standing firm in the great tribulation so that one may not be rejected by God from the joys of paradisial victory[3](cf.Mk.8.

36-38).The divine command 'Listen to Him' is,therefore, meant by the evangelist as a paraenesis on the necessity of adhering to the Master's teaching on forthcoming trials, most specifically,that is,his prophecies of suffering,death, and resurrection that encircle the Trans- figuration story as its textual 'setting'.In other words the voice saying 'Listen to Him' means 'Listen to what he has just been telling you in his first prophecy of the Passion'(Mk.8.22f). In Mark's conception of the end-times it is the sufferings of the Messiah that will definit- ively inaugurate the apocalyptic time of trials (probably understood as the trials presently afflicting his church).Peter in particular (Mk.8. 33)could not bring himself to accept Jesus' kerygma of the cross.The voice on the mountain,and therefore the Transfiguration narrative as a whole in some sense,is also designed by Mark to validate the economy of the cross. It underlines Peter's confession at 8.29, and also Jesus' own testimony, amplifying (and perhaps correcting) Peter's confession,at 8.31. Such an approach to the narrative,from this initial starting point of Mark's theology of the suffering Messiah,also gives us an explanation of the obvious parallelism between this event and the Baptismal theophany (Mk.1.9-11) which is provided mainly by the use of the same psalm (2.7) celebrating the enthronement of the Messiah.This suggests that the encouragement which Mark offers his church in their trials is the vision of the glory of Jesus - his glorious enthronement in the Kabod of Yahweh : a notion that stands behind , and at one and the same time embraces,the extrapolated Christian traditions of Resurrection,Exaltation,Ascension and Parousia.

Mark,then, has redacted the narrative in line with his frequent concern to demonstrate that the Messiah's glory is achieved only through a divinely appointed suffering, and that this will be a pattern for disciples to follow.In this he reproduces the Pauline theodicy. In this sense we define the narrative as being intimately bound up with articulating the nature of Christ's envelopment in the glory of God - that is the glory of his exaltation to the right hand of the throne of Yahweh after his sufferings and death.Briefly put, this means that the Transfiguration story is the evangelist's comment on the mystery of Christ's Resurrection status. To say this,however, is not to state that it is a Resurrection narrative **per se** ; rather that it emanates from,and in spite of many Markan redactions and Haggadah developments,still faintly evokes a much more primitive stage of Christian theological tradition when the notions and separate 'stages' of Resurrection,Ascension,and Exaltation (especially as these began to be understood as chronological episodes) had not yet been particularised and synthesised. It is because the narrative is thus concerned with the exaltation status of Jesus that it is also concerned with Parousial theology . The Resurrection of the dead is not only the greatest of the apocalyptic signs that the end-time has arrived, but Mark also uses the story as a whole - by means of his device of relating 9.1 to the epiphany - to comment on, and in part explain,the delay of the Parousia up to the present era of his own church. In this he appears to have a two-fold theological argument. In the first place he tries to argue the fulfilment of Jesus' difficult prophecies of the imminent arrival of the Kingdom as taking place within the generation of the apostles[4], but secondly, and more importantly,he shifts theological focus even as he does so onto the present and enduring state of glory enjoyed by the Risen Lord. This is in germinal form an understanding of the Resurrection of Christ in the Pauline manner of an abiding and ever present mystery that of itself can answer all the problems of the early church over the delay of the Parousia, and reaffirm their hope in the abiding Lordship of Jesus.

Many previous commentators have engaged with this narrative and greatly assisted in our understanding of its complexities, but it must also be admitted that some previous scholarship has added to our difficulties in understanding it by trying to force the text into Procrustean beds of their own devising : insisting that it is entirely a Resurrection narrative imaginatively displaced, or else wholly a Parousial story[5]. Such hard and fast distinctions did not operate as theological categories in the most primitive stages of the Christian tradition, and more often than not if we insist on applying them rigidly to the text in hand the result is eisegesis not exegesis proper.

The text of 9.1 represents one of the several Amen sayings in Mark[6]. This Aramaism gives a force of special solemnity to Jesus' word.The Amen sayings tend to gather together in Mark's Gospel towards the end of his narrative,particularly in the Book of the Passion. The present use is only the third occurrence in his text so far. It is paralleled with a similar usage at Mk.13.30 : 'Amen I say to you that this generation will not pass away until (Μεχρις) all these things take place.' This saying too is dealing with Jesus' difficult prophecies that the Kingdom of God would apparently be consummated in his own generation - difficult at least for the Markan church which seems to have laboured under quite diverse conceptions of the nature of apocalyptic idiom , as can be deduced from the several conflicting eschatologies preserved without assimilation in Mk.13, and which was now in the very process of 'outliving' all of Jesus' own generation. Many of the Amen sayings are concerned with the nature of the Kingdom,and are designed to invoke the special witness of God (or the heavenly court) to what Jesus has to say. This concern can be discerned quite clearly at 9.1 and suggests to us that the glorification of the Lord on the mountain is most intimately connected with all that Mark understands by 'the Kingdom come in power'. The appeal to the divine witness implicit in the Amen, is made explicit in the text at Mk.9.7. B.D.Chilton argues from the promise of 9.1 that the original state of the tradition made this appeal to heavenly witness even more explicit.Mark, it is argued,has changed the force of Jesus' words and made them refer more explicitly to the apostles who will come with him up the mountain.The original tradition , as Chilton reads it, set out Jesus' word as a solemn prophetic statement,sworn before the witness of the heavenly prophets (those who had not 'tasted death'),that the Kingdom of God would certainly come soon :

'Mark 9.1 does not promise immortality to the disciples, it swears, by immortal witnesses, the efficacy of the Kingdom in power. It is true that a 'not taste of death' complex did develop to make such a promise (Jn.8.52,Thomas Logia 1,18,19,85) but in this saying the disciples are told of an immortal group from which it is assumed they are distinct. Jesus refers to this group by way of asseveration (cf.Mk. 13.19 + par;14.25 + par; Jn.13.38;Acts 23.12,14,21) just as Moses does in the Jerusalem Targum to Deut.32.1 (swearing by witnesses which shall not taste death). Once the meaning of the Jesus saying is appreciated,the step to Moses and Elijah is a short one for these are pre-eminently οιτινες ου μη γευσωνται θανατου.'[7]

This insight is a most useful one for helping us to understand the process of tradition development.But as the promise of 9.1 stands in Mark's text it is clear, as Chilton appears to agree, that he wishes his reader to understand it in reference to Jesus' earthly audience, including the apostles. It is the evangelist's intention to preface the Transfiguration narrative with this promise of an imminent coming of the Kingdom from the lips of Jesus himself,precisely in order to show that it was perfectly fulfilled on the mountain.Some of those standing there when these words were spoken,that is the three 'pillars',did see the Kingdom come in power,in Galilee,even before they had died. Mark is trying to make a distinction for his church between Jesus' prophecy that the Kingdom of God would come in his own lifetime (a conception surely synonymous with the belief in an imminent or urgent advent),for which see also Mk.13.30, and between his words on the time of the Parousia or ultimate fulfilment of God's purposes which the Markan Jesus does not specify, for which see Mk.13.32.

Again, to have said this much,that Mark is offering his version of the Transfiguration narrative as part of an overall solution to the problem of a delayed Parousia,is by no means the same, however, as identifying with the position adopted by Boobyer that such a parousial theology sums up the entire meaning of the text.

Boobyer mistakenly defines Δοξα as a 'parousial' word on the basis of Mark's use of that term elsewhere to connote the glorious return of Jesus[8]. And yet, we must note that the word is not used by Mark at all in his Transfiguration account - even if the concept is admittedly evoked. It is only Luke who uses the word explicitly.More importantly,however, Riesenfeld[9] has clearly demonstrated that the word has a far wider significance than Boobyer's limited definition would admit. The risen Jesus,in the mind of the early Church,was in glory (εν δοξη) and enjoying the status of enthronement from the time of his resurrectional exaltation to the right hand of God. Δοξα is therefore just as much to do with Resurrectional theology as it is with the Parousia.The early Christians were in no doubt about this and in fact the tendency is that to the same degree that an expectation of an imminent Parousia wanes (a tendency observable in parts of the Markan narrative),then so does parousial glory come to be envisaged more and more in terms of Jesus' enduring state of enthronement glory as the Risen One. The high point of Stephen's speech at Acts 7.55,which he himself delivers as one who is transfigured εν δοξη [10],already shows a sense of the glory of God embracing Jesus as an established reality, if not a static one,in the heavenly court . This notion is reworked later in **Acta Philippi** 20 (in the light of the canonical versions of the Transfiguration)in terms of an even more thorough-going enthronement theology. By the time of this text the notion that Christ would return imminently in that glory to peform the eschatological function of judging the world has faded out drastically. The writer of the **Acta** wishes to draw all our attention to the present status of Christ :'The heavens opened and Jesus appeared in glory,his face seven times brighter than the sun, and his raiment whiter than snow.'[11]

M.E.Thrall supports the terms of such an analysis[12].She draws attention in this regard to the association of the Son of God title (solemnly given by the divine voice) with the understanding of the Resurrection as witnessed in Romans 1.4 and Acts 13.33. The **Akhmim Fragment** of the **Apocalypse of Peter** ,and the Ethiopic text of the same, although considerably later than Mark's text and most probably dependent on it[13], both present the Transfiguration in similar terms of Resurrection-enthronement rather than Parousia (all The Fathers' exegeses following the same trend). The texts in question are as follows :

Apocalypse of Peter. (Akhmim Fragment).[14]

'And the Lord added, and said : Let us go unto the mountain (and) pray. And going with him, we twelve disciples begged him to show us one of our righteous brethren that had departed from the world, so that we could see what manner of men they are as to their form, so that we might take courage and thus also encourage the men that should hear us (preach). And as we prayed suddenly there appeared two men standing before the Lord upon whom we were not able to look for there issued from their countenance a ray as of the sun, and their raiment was shining so as the eye of man never saw the like. And no mouth is able to declare and no heart conceive the glory in which they were clothed, and the beauty of their countenance. And when we saw them we were astonished for their bodies were whiter than any snow and redder than any rose. And the redness of them was mingled with the whiteness. In a word, I am not able to describe their beauty. Their hair was curling and blooming (lit. flowery) and fell gracefully about their countenance and their shoulders like a garland woven of nard (sic.) and various flowers, or like a rainbow in the air. Such was their beauty.

And when we saw this beauty we were filled with astonishment at their sudden appearance. And I drew near to the Lord and said : Who are these men ? And he told me : These are your righteous brethren whom you desired to see. So I said to him : And where then are all the righteous ? What kind of world is it in which they live in such glory ? And the Lord showed me a very great region outside this world of exceedingly bright radiance, and the air of the place was illumined with the beams of the sun,   and then the earth of its own accord flowered with blooms that never faded, and was full of spices and plants with beautiful incorruptible flowers that bore a blessed fruit. So great was the blossom that its perfume carried from that place even to us.

And the dwellers in that place were clad with raiment of shining angels, and their raiment was like their land. And angels ran about them there.And the glory of all who lived there was of the same degree; with one voice they praised the Lord God with all rejoicing in that place. Then the Lord said to us : This is the place of your leaders (High Priests), the righteous ones.'

Apocalypse of Peter.(Ethiopic Text).[15]

'And my Lord Jesus Christ,our King, said to me:Let us go to the holy mountain.And his disciples went with him,praying. And behold there were two men there and we could not look upon their faces for a light issued from them shining greater than the sun, and their raiment was also shining.It cannot be described, nothing in this world is a fitting comparison. And the sweetness of them....... that no mouth is able to speak of the beauty of their appearance, so astonishing and wonderful was that appearance. And the other one,great I say, shines in his appearance more than crystal.The appearance of the colour of his aspect and his body was like the flower of roses.....his head (their head) was a marvel.And upon his (their) shoulders ....and on their foreheads was a crown of nard woven out of fair flowers.Their hair was like the rainbow in the water;such was the beauty of their countenance adorned with all manner of ornament. And when we saw them so suddenly we were struck with wonder. And I drew close to the Lord (God) Jesus Christ and said to him : My Lord who are these men ? And he said to me : They are Moses and Elias. So I said to him : (Where then are) Abraham and Isaac and Jacob and the rest of the righteous fathers ? And then he showed us a great garden,spacious,full of fair trees and blessed fruits, and the odour of perfumes.Its fragrance was great , and reached even to where we were. And of that tree I saw much fruit. And my Lord and God Jesus Christ said to me : Have you seen the companies of the fathers ? The honour and glory of all that are persecuted for my righteousness' sake is like the repose that these enjoy. And I was filled with joy and I believed and understood that which is written in the book of my Lord Jesus Christ. And so I said to him : My Lord, do you want me to make three tabernacles ? One for you, one for Moses and one for Elijah ? But in anger he said to me : Satan is making war against you and has veiled your mind so that the allurements of the world prevail against you. Your eyes must be opened,your ears unblocked,so that you may see a tabernacle not made by human hands,which my heavenly Father has built for me and for the elect. And then we beheld it and were full of gladness.

Then suddenly there came a voice from heaven saying : This is my beloved Son in whom I am well pleased. He has kept my commandments. Then there came a great,brilliantly white cloud over our heads which carried off Our Lord and Moses and Elias. And I trembled and was afraid.And we looked up and the heavens opened and we saw men in the flesh, and they came to greet Our Lord and Moses and Elias, and went into another heaven. Then the word of scripture was fulfilled : 'This is the generation which seeks him, which seeks the face of the God of Jacob'. And great fear and commotion was then in heaven, and the angels pressed one upon another that the word of scripture might be fulfilled which says :'Open the gates you princes'.

After this the heavens were closed that had formerly been open.And we prayed and went down from the mountain glorifying our God who has written the names of the righteous in heaven, in the book of life.'

In the Ethiopic version we can clearly see that the Transfiguration has been remodelled as an Ascension narrative. The account preserved also in the Gnostic text **Pistis Sophia,** similarly depicts it as an Ascension story :

Pistis Sophia[16].

'Now it came to pass that the disciples were sitting together on the Mount of Olives,speaking these words and rejoicing greatly, and saying to one another :Blessed are we above all men on earth since the Saviour has revealed these things to us, and we have received the fulness and complete perfection. This they were saying to one another while Jesus sat a little way apart from them.

But it came to pass on the fifteenth of the moon in the month of Tybi,which is the day on which the moon becomes full,on that day now,when the sun was come out upon its path there came forth behind it a great power of light,gleaming very bright,and the light that was in it was beyond measure. For it came out of the Light of Lights, and it came out of the Last Mystery,which is the twenty-fourth mystery,from within outwards,those mysteries which are in the orders of the second space of the First Mystery.

But that power of light descended upon Jesus and surrounded him entirely,while he sat apart from his disciples, and he shone exceedingly, and the light that was upon him was beyond measure. And the disciples did not see Jesus because of the great light in which he was, or which was upon him, for their eyes were darkened because of the great light in which he was, but they saw only the light,which sent forth many beams of light. And the beams of light were not like unto one another, and the light was of different kinds, and it was of different form from below upwards,since one beam was more excellent than the other.........in a great and boundless splendour of light; it extended from beneath the earth as far as the heaven.And when the disciples saw that light they were in great fear and agitation.

This now came to pass on the fifteenth moon on the day on which it becomes full in the month of Tybi. And it came to pass when Jesus went up into heaven,after three hours, all the powers of heaven were troubled, and they all trembled together, they and all their Aeons and all their places and all their orders; and the whole earth was moved, and all that dwell upon it.And all men in the world were troubled, and the disciples also, and all thought :Perhaps the world will be rolled up ? And all the powers that are in heaven ceased not from their agitation,they and the whole world, and they were all moved one against the other from the third hour of the fifteenth of the moon Tybi until the ninth hour of the following day.And all the angels and their archangels and all the powers of the height all praised the Inmost of the Inmost,so that the whole world heard their voice without ceasing until the ninth hour of the following day. But the disciples sat together ,in fear, and they were exceedingly troubled; but they were afraid because of the great earthquake which took place, and wept with one another, saying : What then will happen ? Perhaps the Saviour will destroy all places ? While they now said this and wept to one another,then the heavens opened,about the ninth hour of the following day,and they saw Jesus descend,shining very bright,and the light in which he was was beyond measure.For he shone more than at the hour when he ascended up to the heavens,so that the men in the world could not describe the light that was upon him, and it sent forth many beams of light, and its beams were beyond number, and its light was not like one to the other,but it was of different kind and of different form, since some beams surpassed the others countless times; and the whole light was together,it was of three different kinds, and one surpassed the others countless times; the second,which was in the midst, was superior to the first,which was beneath; and the third,which was above them all,was superior to both those which were beneath; and the first beam which was beneath them all,was like the light which came upon Jesus before he ascended into the heavens, and was like only to itself in its light. And the three lights were of different kinds of light,and they were of different form, whereby some surpassed others countless times.

But it came to pass when the disciples saw this,they were exceedingly afraid, and were troubled.Jesus now,the merciful and kind-hearted,when he saw that his disciples were greatly troubled,spoke to them saying : Be of good cheer,It is I,be not afraid.(cf. Mt.28.10, Lk.24.38 - where the theme is found in the Resurrection narratives)

Now it came to pass when the disciples heard these words, they said : O Lord if it be thou,draw to thyself thy glorious light, that we may be able to stand,else are our eyes darkened and we are troubled, and also the whole world is troubled because of the great light that is in thee.

Then Jesus drew to himself the splendour of his light; and when this had come to pass all the disciples took courage,stood before Jesus,and all fell down together and worshipped him,rejoicing with great joy; they said to him : Rabbi whither didst thou go ? or what is thy ministry to which thou didst go ? or why rather were all these upheavals and earthquakes which have taken place ?

Then spoke Jesus,the merciful, to them : Rejoice and be glad from this hour on, for I went to the places out of which I came. From henceforth will I speak with you openly from the beginning of the truth unto its completion, and I will speak with you face to face without parable. I will not hide from you from this hour anything of the things of the height and of the things of the place of the truth. For to me is given by the Ineffable and by the First Mystery of all mysteries,the power to speak with you from the beginning to the fulfilment, and from within to without, and from without to within. Hear now,that I may tell you all things.'

We notice,however, that the Ascension of Jesus depicted here is a temporary one,for Jesus descends again 'on the ninth hour of the following day'. We may take the point of the parallels between the Transfiguration seen as a narrative dealing with glorious exaltation, and the extra-biblical texts which also support the same intent. There are,however,discrepancies that must be registered.

To date, the clearest argument against interpreting the Transfiguration as a misplaced Resurrection narrative (and thus ,implicitly,
interpreting it in a 'resurrectionist' light) has been set out in a series
of comprehensive summaries by R H Stein, who follows Boobyer
and Dodd[17] against Bultmann **et alia**,to argue that the differences
between the Transfiguration narrative and the resurrection accounts
in the other Gospels, and 1Cor.15, far outweigh the similarities of
the type that can be adduced by reference to the extra-biblical
sources such as the **Apocalypse of Peter,**[18] or the **Pistis Sophia,**for
example, which we have just read. Stein's article sets out to establish
that the Transfiguration narrative is not a Resurrection narrative,
and he does his task very well. But without wishing to trivialise
a serious study,it appears to me that he does not sufficiently address
the problem whether or not the evangelist had Resurrectional   Δοξα
in mind when he constructed his narrative form. To establish that
the Transfiguration account is not the same tradition-form as the
Resurrection narratives found elsewhere is to demonstrate what is
obviously admissible, and to this extent Stein's argument serves as
a proper criticism of Bultmann's speculative theses. The argument,
however,seems to me not to take proper cognisance of two very
important facts : firstly that the primitive tradition of Jesus'
glorification did not have such a rigidly classified view of the
different stages of the glorification. This is a fact which Boobyer,one
of Stein's major sources, himself admits[19] ,though arguably without
acknowledging its full import.Secondly it must be noted that if we
were to deal solely with the Resurrection narrative found in Mark
16, we would be unable to delineate anything like the Resurrection-
form supplied in the other Gospels and the Pauline letter,because
two central parts of that common 'form',that is the appearances
of the Risen Jesus and the theme of apostolic witness and confirmation, are wholly lacking from the text of Mark. Those who have
argued for the Transfiguration being proleptically associated in the
mind of the evangelist with the resurrection glory of the Lord have
usually pointed to these apparent and strange omissions being supplied

to the reader in chapter nine.

Another of the arguments advanced against the Transfiguration being understood as in some sense 'resurrectional', is the incongruity of Peter's role. On the mountain he displays serious miscomprehension (at least in Mark) and is reduced to silence, whereas in the Resurrection narratives is he not meant to stand as the pre-eminent witness ? M.E.Thrall has supplied a sufficiently weighty answer to such objections already[20],to which I would only add that the theme of Peter's misunderstanding carries on even in the more formalised resurrection narratives themselves[21]. Moreover, the resurrection account in Mk.16.7 by no means establishes the figure of Peter as the great witness par excellence, at that point, and it is questionable how far Mark wishes to do so in spite of the implicit rehabilitation implied in the angel's instructions to the women. If 16.7,then, is to be read more as a rehabilitation,in the light of Mk.14.66-72, it may thus be more comprehensible as a parallel to John 21. Peter's name in Mk.16.7 is offered **after** the other disciples, not before them as is usually the case. Mark depicts the first witnesses, regardless of what Paul has to say in 1Cor.15, as women; and they themselves are so struck with fear (cf. Mk.9.6, and 16.8) that they cannot give the correct proclamation,as Peter cannot on the mountain. Both parties are rendered dumb before a divine epiphany.

M.E.Thrall, who argues for a resurrectional interpretation of the Transfiguration story,draws attention to the great importance Mark's text attaches to the presence of Elijah and Moses. This she takes as her starting point for a thoroughgoing criticism of Boobyer's parousial thesis. She notes[22] that of the seven verses of the narrative as a whole (9.2-8) no less than three refer to these figures explicitly, and another two refer to them implicitly. She concludes:'This suggests that they are absolutely essential to Mark's presentation of the Transfiguration. They are not merely part of the symbolic background scenery. They do not simply reinforce the meaning the evangelist wishes us to attach to the revelation of Jesus in glory. In some sense they are figures upon whom the whole story turns.' This is a critically important observation, that has not been properly noted in previous exegetical studies. Why then should Elijah and Moses appear ? Why does Mark record their appearance in that peculiarly untraditional order ? What conclusions does he wish his readership to draw from their presence ?

Boobyer uses their appearance as one of the main pillars for his thesis that the text is meant to be read in a parousial light [23]. He regards the presence of the two prophets as one of the decisive proofs against the Transfiguration being read as a comment on resurrection theology : 'To the theory that the Transfiguration was at first a resurrection story, or that it prophesies the resurrection, this verse has been persistently awkward.'[24] But, in stark contrast, it is the presence of these two figures that provides us with one of the strongest indications of all that here we are dealing with the notion of the ἀναστασις of great heroes. Boobyer's argumentation at this point suffers from relying excessively on **argumentum e silentio** to try and make a case that there was, in Jesus' day, a lively sense of the expected return of both these OT heroes on the Day of the Lord, and therefore that when Mark presents them in his narrative it would be a clear sign to his Christian readers that he was speaking about the theology of the Parousia of Christ. The reasons why I find this approach misfocussed will be discussed in greater detail at the end of the subsequent section of comments on the assumption of Moses. It will suffice for the moment to note that the tradition of a return of Elijah (for which there is some hard evidence) is, as far as Mark is concerned, consistently and wholly subsumed in the Gospel to cover the themes of false Christological confessions that precede but must give way to a true confession that can only emanate from divinely given faith. It is a mark of his scheme, for example, that the crowds who often represent faithlessness (or at least neutrality of committment) in the early stages of the Gospel, are the ones who keep identifying the coming Messiah with Elijah[25]. In short, Mark does not attach much Christological weight to the tradition of Elijah's return, and is therefore unlikely to have made it a central concern of his Transfiguration narrative. He shows sufficiently that he wishes the theme of the returning Elijah to be wholly subsumed in his treatment of the witness of John the Baptist, and the verses immediately following the Transfiguration account emphasise this point most forcibly.As Christ descends the mountain he tells his disciples that Elijah has already come : αλλα λεγω υμιν οτι και Ηλιας εληλυθεν (Mk. 9.13) and this does not mean on the mountain of a few verses previously,but refers back to the passion of John the Baptist at 6.14-29. For Mark, then, the tradition of the **prophetus redivivus** is assigned only to the unbelieving crowds and he consistently corrects it by pointing to its real fulfilment in the person of John the Baptist. This makes it most unlikely that Mark would see Elijah's presence on the mountain in the sense that Boobyer suggests. In any case the tradition of the parousial return of Elijah and Moses **together,**which is central to the concerns of our text,is simply not around in Mark's own time. Boobyer appeals to evidence here, in support of their mutual association as eschatological agents,which by his own admission could be mediaeval, and which in general does not bear much weight[26].

I suggest that we are to find the real significance of the two OT figures given to us in Mark's reference to 'not tasting death'. As Chilton has suggested, these prophets are the heavenly witnesses that substantiate this promise to the disciples in so far as they were pre-eminently the OT figures (alongside Enoch) who had not tasted death.But they stand alongside Jesus primarily as the witnesses of the resurrection glory which will ultimately validate Jesus' kerygma of suffering and death, for their presence is a demonstration of Jesus' own **testimonium** of the efficacy of resurrection when, for example,he said in reference to the OT patriarchs : ουκ εστι θεος νεκρων αλλα ζωντων . (Mk. 12.27). Before considering the cases of Elijah and Moses in the light of the promise of 9.1 in greater detail, it is necessary to make a short excursus on the nature and significance of the idea of resurrection from the dead in apocalyptic idiom of the time of Jesus.

The Jewish apocalyptic tradition itself forces us to associate the conceptions of spiritual exaltation,metamorphosis,resurrection from the dead,and ascension to the throne of Yahweh,in a manner that recognises a profoundly intimate and substantial relationship between them all[27]. In the apocalyptic idiom each of these events can stand as the sign of the final establishment of the Kingdom of God. Later apocalypticism, and here we include the developing record of the NT writings themselves, extrapolates these signs into a more and more formalised scheme of stages.The Lukan scheme of the glorification of Jesus given at the end of his Gospel and the opening chapters of Acts,is a clear example of a formal attempt to give a systematic structure[28] to an expansively varied set of original traditions.Luke has canonised these varied approaches to the same mysterious experience of Jesus' glorification as separate and distinct happenings.But even within the canon of the NT the Johannine scheme of the glorification of Jesus (ie. his chronology of the death,exaltation, resurrection, ascension and bestowal of the Spirit) presents us with a radically different schema to that proposed by Luke. In the third Gospel the scheme of stages has a more historicised appearance,and in the course of the Christian centuries it is this schema which has been reinforced in our consciousness by the liturgical cycle of the church. But all the same, we must be wary of taking the Lukan redaction of the Resurrection and post-resurrectional events as the archetypal version - for it is most assuredly not.Even the different chronologies of John and Luke's accounts of the glorification of Jesus serve to underline their different authors' visions of the meaning of Jesus' glory. Behind them both,and behind all the NT narratives,lies the **Grundschrift** of apocalyptic;and in the apocalyptic idiom the metamorphosis of the Hero-Martyr may be depicted in terms of either Exaltation-Enthronement, or Resurrection-Enthronement. Let us consider more closely this concept of Resurrection-Enthronement.

The theology of Resurrection is an immense area. It has attracted,as is fitting,a body of literature of correspondingly great proportions (a synopsis bibliography on Resurrection is offered at the end of the book). The revived interest in the resurrection of Jesus as theological event is bringing the debate once more into the forefront of dogmatic reflection and exegesis, a position it has perhaps not commanded since the second and third century controversies on resurrection occasioned by the Christian gnostics. Many of the same issues are in fact resurfacing.

In the classical OT tradition, the idea of survival after death plays little part in religious consciousness. To be alive, in ancient Hebraic anthropology,was the result of the embodiment of the Ruah-spirit. If a man suffered bodily death, therefore, the principle of his human existence was substantially disrupted. There could be no disembodied life.Such a view is normative in Judaism until its later period exposed it to other ethnic belief systems - especially in the Exilic period. The OT knows of survival of the self (nephesh) after death,but this self which descends to Sheol[29] is utterly powerless. There will be no remembrance of God in Sheol, no continuance of the covenant relationship, no continuance of life in any meaningful sense[30]. The Rephaim who inhabit its regions are but shadows of sadness.Although the power of Yahweh extends even into this realm and the very heart of Sheol[31],it is God's fixed and certain law that no man is ever to be lifted from the place of death to which he has been sent. Elijah calling the son of the widow of Zarephath back to life is recalling a spirit that was thought not to have yet entered Sheol definitively[32]. Passages elsewhere in the OT which suggest 'raising up' from Sheol do not signify a resurrection from among the dead[33] but are simply using Sheol as a synonym for physical death and thus idiomatically refer to the individual's avoidance of death (for example after a serious illness) by the mercy of God[34]. Sheol is not a place of punishment, for the dead have passed out of memory and care. The notion of the places of punishment ,Sheol and Gehenna,only arises much later in apocalyptic Judaism[35] of the

last century BC and is antithetically dependent on the notion of
resurrection to new life as the glorious reward of the just. This
idea gains strength as the older OT idea,that the just and wicked
receive their respective deserts even in their own lifetimes,loses
ground before the individual and corporate experience of the Jewish
people in the post-exilic period. In the time of Jesus it is the
Sadducees who are characterised as the exponents of this ancient
tradition of Sheol[36].But even then they were preservers of an
archaism that was to be generally overtaken throughout Judaism.
The earliest example of the incipient change of attitude to the after-
life is the 'apocalypse' of Isaiah[37] which uses a resurrection motif
as an image of the post-exilic restoration of Israel[38].

The apocalyptic reinterpretation of the Kingdom of God
theology places the idea of God's judging power at the centre of
all its thought. Correspondingly,it proleptically envisages the judgement
of God (in a way that is reminiscent of earlier texts but which
advances on them[39]) as a force that penetrates beyond the grave.The
apocalyptists' unique vision of meta-history provides a particularly
favourable context for this development to take place. And so, in
several of the apocalyptic texts, part of Sheol is envisaged as the
place of punishment for the wicked,who shall be separated off from
the righteous dead. **Ethiopic Enoch** 22.8f is the first instance of
such a division of the underworld in Hebraic tradition[40]. Here the
places of punishment outnumber the places of rest by three to one.
Jesus' parable of Dives and Lazarus[41] shows awareness of this view
that the souls of the just are in the underworld, in regions beside
the wicked, even though a long way off (απο μακροθεν)[42] and radically
separated[43]. But the same Gospel that preserves the parable is also
aware of the newer conception of the souls of the righteous being
admitted to a world of paradisial bliss,there to await the final
judgement of God : that is the total establishment of the Kingdom
which will involve the general resurrection of all mankind[44]. If the
flourishing of evil upon earth is seen as the apocalyptic sign 'par
excellence' that the Last Age is coming, then so the routing of the

forces of evil and the resurrection of the dead are taken as the great signs that it has arrived. This is the root meaning of the NT accounts of the ministry of Jesus as a series of powerful signs (healings,exorcisms,and the forgiving of sins) which demonstrate God's victorious conquest of evil[45],and it is this which provides the substantial unity between his great signs on earth (The Kingdom is coming) and the great sign of his lifting up from the earth in resurrection glory (The Kingdom has in fact come). Both must find their correct interpretation in the apocalyptic idiom.

By the time of the high point of Inter-Testamental literature, we can distinguish no less than four distinct Jewish doctrines of resurrection. The rich complexity of resurrection traditions runs on even into the NT period and should warn us against too rigid a view of what does or does not constitute resurrectional thought in the NT. The four alternative approaches can be listed as follows :

(a)   All Israelites,but only Israelites will be raised from the dead; Dan.12.2; 1 Enoch.1-34,37-70,73-90; LXX Ps.65; 2 Macc.7.9; 2 Bar.50-51.

(b)   Only righteous Israelites will be raised; Is. 35.8; (Is.26.19) Ps.16.10;Ps.17.15;Ps.49.15;   Ps.73.24;   Job.14.13-15;Job.19.26-27; 1 Enoch. 91-104; Pss.Sol.3.16 , 13.9, 14.7 , 15.15; 2 Bar.30; Josephus,Ant. 18.1; Bell.Jud. 2.8,14; and thereafter in Talmudic orthodoxy. See also Lk.14.14.

(c)   All men would rise: 4th Ezra 7.32; Test.Ben. 10.6-8. Both these witnesses are very late pseudepigrapha.

(d)   The soul that is righteous shall enjoy an immortal life with God. The body ,or flesh, once cast off will not need to rise; Wis.Sol.3.1;4.7;5.16;8.20; Jubilees 23.30. This is a heavily Hellenised current of Jewish thought owing much to the Platonic notion of the spiritual immortality of the soul.The extreme form of Hellenistic 'immortality' remains alien to Jewish tradition but the influence this approach had was nonetheless extensive and may account for some of the arguments in and behind the text of Paul in 1 Cor.15,for example.

Through all this there abided in Jewish apocalyptic thought a special belief in the outstanding claim of the martyr, even for a particular and immediate resurrection. The claim of the martyr to resurrection is advanced so strongly in those texts written during severe persecution that it comes to embrace a belief that such as the martyrs will receive resurrection on an individual basis perhaps even before the general resurrection of the rest of Israel. To this extent the martyr's resurrection anticipates the Last Day. Such a belief is first set out in the Maccabean literature : 'It is the creator of the world who in his mercy will give you back your life (LXX:την ζωην υμιν παλιν αποδωσει) seeing that you now despise your own existence for the sake of his laws.'[46]   Or again: ' They who have died in grief shall arise (in joy) (and they who were poor for the Lord's sake shall be made rich [47]) and they who are put to death for the Lord's sake shall awake (to life).' [48]

This concept of the immediate resurrection of the martyrs is echoed in Jesus' promise to the thief from the cross,in the Lukan redaction: 'Amen I say to you, this very day you will be with me in paradise.' (Lk.23.43) This sets apart the martyr's glory as a 'special case',a fitting reward for his exceptional fidelity, and leads us to consider the notion of the exaltation of the righteous hero as indeed the possible archetype behind the general apocalyptic concept of resurrection from the dead. In this regard the notion of the hero of God should be understood as more ancient and widespread than the simple tradition of the martyr in the Maccabean literature and beyond. The heroes 'par excellence' are the suffering prophets of Yahweh who remain true to their proclamation despite the opposition of Israel (an opposition that comes more and more to be interpreted in folk-traditions of the martyrdoms of the prophets). This should,of course, remind us of the original starting point of our discussion since chief among these heroically enduring prophets in the OT tradition stand Elijah and Moses[49].

Nickelburg's important study of the intertestamental literature has led him to the conclusion that :' in intertestamental Jewish theology, the beliefs in resurrection, immortality, and eternal life, are carried mainly within the framework of three forms.'[50] The entire complex of the post-exilic tradition of resurrection, exaltation, and ascension, may thus be traced back to these parental literary archetypes[51]. The most significant of these forms is undoubtedly that of the righteous man who suffers unjustly.

The Servant theology of Deutero Isaiah and the homily in the Wisdom of Solomon that derives from it [52] are major archetypes for the apocalyptic texts dealing with the exaltation of the righteous hero to the throne of God[53]. Both of these OT sources are, of course, of primary significance for NT Christology because of their use as prime **testimonia** to the Passion of Jesus and his subsequent glorification. This notion of glorious exaltation, from its original connotation of the advancement of the courtier[54], comes in the intertestamental period to be envisaged more and more in terms of the image of resurrection-enthronement; and thus provides the early church with an intellectual model for conceptualising the glory of Jesus after his unjust execution.

From this general review of apocalyptic thought on the resurrection from the dead, which has of necessity been brief and selective, we can return to look more closely at the three figures who stand out most clearly as themselves being archetypes of 'those who have not tasted death', that is Enoch, Elijah and Moses. The two former figures represent narratives of translation-exaltation. Both are assumed to heavenly glory, and are thus deathless. In the case of Moses the tradition is less clear, though from Josephus and others we have already observed signs that a similar translation-belief had attached itself to him despite the explicit statements in Deuteronomy that he died on Mount Nebo.

The Deuteronomic tradition about the death of Moses is quite straightforward,[55] but under a two-fold stimulus (first of all that his immense standing in later Judaism is constantly being re-interpreted and heightened doxographically[56], and secondly that the original account of his last days was sufficiently mysterious to allow for legendary development[57]) the process of his 'glorification' is enabled to grow apace. By the time of the Hellenistic era, in both Palestinian and Diaspora Judaism,Moses is the supreme hero of Torah religion[58]. For Philo he is the Law personified and the supreme mediator for Israel[59]. He was Law-giver, Priest,Prophet and King[60]. In Palestinian Judaism he was the faithful servant of God[61],the one whom Yahweh knew face to face[62] and to whom he revealed his glory[63]. Hellenistic Judaism extolled him even beyond these bounds and came to depict him,as Jeremias puts it [64], almost as a θειος ανηρ who attracted all the usual legendary attributes of the genre.[64] Philo regards Moses as the archetype of man being exalted to the vision of God,and in this sense 'deified'[65]. It is in harmony with this position that he goes on to speak of Moses' metamorphosis after death as : εις νουν ηλιοειδεστατον [66]. It is only in a few late rabbinic midrashim on Deuteronomy 34 that we start finding clear reference to a belief in the bodily assumption of Moses into heaven. It is thus difficult to determine when such a tradition had first begun to circulate freely in Jewish piety. So,for example, we read :'Some say that Moses did not die but stands and discharges above the (priestly) ministry.'[67] And again :'Three went up alive into heaven: Enoch,Moses and Elijah.'[68]

Jeremias thinks that the origin of this idea is 'probably Hellenistic Judaism'[69] although he does not give any grounds for this supposition other than the fact that Josephus is the first [70] clearly datable text to make reference to the notion[71]: 'A cloud suddenly stood over him,and he was withdrawn from view into a valley.He wrote in the sacred books that he died,for fear lest some should dare to maintain,by reason of his outstanding virtues,that he ascended up to the Godhead.'[72] (προς τον θειον αυτον αναχωρησαι). It is equally likely,however,that the idea derives from apocalyptic Judaism,especially since the first of our cited rabbinisms seems to echo the closing parts of the **Assumption of Moses** fragments, where Moses, after his heavenly ascension and exaltation, is appointed as heavenly intercessor for Israel.[73] The present state of this particular text,which we now call the **Assumption** is the result of the fusion, sometime in the first century AD, of two distinct Mosaic works **The Testament of Moses,** and **The Assumption of Moses.** What is now extant largely represents the doctrine of the Testament, and there is hardly any trace preserved of the tradition of Moses' spiritual assumption to God[74]. It is ironic that the name of the **Assumption** survives while its particular concerns do not fare as well. **The** original version of the **Assumption** proper seems to have **elaborated** much more freely on the significance of Moses' post-**death** exaltation and metamorphosis as a heavenly power in the court of Yahweh.[75]

Josephus writes in Rome AD 94, but preserves an older tradition which he has not invented. It is reasonable to deduce , then, that it is a tradition at least contemporaneous with Mark, if not considerably older, and familiar to the Hellenistic Judaism that would still have comprised part of Mark's church in the mid sixties. It is undoubtedly this tradition of Metamorphosis to which Mark is alluding, and he thus parallels Elijah and Moses as examples of two immortals who have been lifted up , in times previous, to the divine glory. This αναληψις they have both experienced is the most probable reason why Mark wishes to use them to comment upon the glorious exaltation of Jesus. To try to find an alternative reason for the two prophets' association is an exercise that leads nowhere. Boobyer argues an eschatological motive on the part of the evangelist, and this springs from his desire to interpret the Transfiguration in wholly parousial terms. But there are hardly any references at all in Jewish literature to the return of Moses in an apocalyptic context[76]. What tradition there is, is an extremely late one[77], and again Boobyer's case appears to be founded upon arguments from silence[78]. His thesis on this point has been successfully countered by M E Thrall[79]. To whose arguments we could add the observation, yet again, that resurrectional concepts are a fundamental part of Jewish eschatological hopes, and to divorce them methodologically from one's conception of 'parousial', as Boobyer does, is to falsify the picture.

The tradition of Elijah returning as Messianic forerunner is more firmly established. It appears in Malachi and survives to the present day in Judaism - with the custom of keeping a special cup of wine for Elijah during the Passover Seder. The prophecy in Malachi had a long and lasting influence : 'Know that I am going to send you Elijah the prophet before my Day comes,that great and terrible Day.' (Mal.4.5) His role is to prepare for the heavenly King (Mal.3.1) by purifying the priesthood (Mal.3.2-4) and turning the hearts of the people (Mal.3.1.). In Sirach 48.10 he is endowed himself with some of the Messianic functions of the Servant,the Ebed Yahweh: '(You who were) designated in the prophecies of doom to allay God's wrath before the fury breaks.'[80] The verse that follows this is in a highly corrupt state, but of great interest for our present concerns. It reads in the LXX version : Μακαριοι οι ιδοντες σε και οι εν αγαπ- ησει κεκοσμημενοι και γαρ ημεις ζωη ζησομεθα. (Sir.48.11) Such a prophecy, whatever its original meaning, in the LXX text associates the vision of Elijah with the hope of immortal life and as such may have a primary bearing on the meaning of the promise of Jesus to the apostles at Mk.9.1, not least in the way that it shows how Elijah's apocalyptic role emanates from, and is subsidiary to, his role and significance as a deathless hero in the heavenly court: a living symbol of the hopes of immortality and resurrection as they began to grow in later Judaism.

Sirach seems to suggest that Elijah may even be the Messiah himself. This is a tradition which Mark knows, but as we have already noted, wishes firmly to discount by attributing solely as an opinion of the unenlightened masses[81]. But even though he retains the tradition from Malachi,of Elijah as Messianic forerunner,the way that Mark in practice wholly and consistently gives away this role to John the Baptist[82],who thus in a real sense displaces the Elijah mo- tif in Mark's text,should tell us that Elijah's appearance in the Transfiguration story is not likely to be meant by the evangelist to connote this aspect of his prophetic role,rather his role as a living witness to exaltation into divine glory; and in this stands as a symbol subordinate to Jesus.

Throughout his Gospel Mark has had two Elijah traditions

running concurrently : an open one in which he acknowledges the
Messianic traditions that have gathered round this great charismatic
figure of Judaism, and which he deals with by arguing their
fulfilment in the person of John the Baptist; but then he also has
a secret one, running behind his text which has not attracted sufficient
critical attention. This second Elijah tradition is not brought forward
in the narrative structure for one of two possible reasons. In the
first place Mark probably adopts it from the primitive Christian,
Palestinian tradition, especially a northern or Galilean tradition for
this area had always seen the charismatic prophet of the north as
the supreme holy man of Israel[83]. The Christian use of such an Elijah
tradition advanced upon this starting point, now to comment on the
superlative importance of Jesus by comparing him even more favour-
ably to Elijah. This kind of **analogia comparationis ab inferiore**,
however, will always be ambivalent in its approach to the heroic
figure it intends to use as a measure for its analysis of the Lord.
In the second place, since it has all the hallmarks of being an old
Palestinian tradition, one wonders to what extent Mark is personally
conscious of the precise degree of Elijah typology behind his account
of Jesus' ministry, that is - to what extent this tradition has already
shaped and determined the form of the material before he writes.
The fact that an Elijah cycle does stand as a foundational structure
of Jesus' miracle cycle in the kerygmatic preaching of the primitive
church is, however, beyond reasonable doubt. The Christological point
of such parallelism is again **analogia comparationis** lying behind the
form of the telling of Jesus' miracles. Although the ground covered
in the Elijah/Elisha cycles is traversed once more, in every case
Jesus is seen to excel the works of the earlier prophet, and calls
for a greater response to his own person from those who witness
his signs.

In the light of all these observations, then, the significance of Elijah in Mark's version of the Transfiguration narrative
becomes a little easier to deduce : His appearance is designed by
the evangelist to signal for us the heavenly glory that is enjoyed

by the greatest of God's heroes, those he has lifted up in a most special election into the very heart of the divine **Kabod.** This means primarily Elijah, but also Moses. The Christological motive of the evangelist is to tell the reader that their great glory is not in the same category as that heavenly glory enjoyed now by the Risen Son of God, Jesus [84]. The two prophets 'who have not tasted death',seem to be serving the purpose of analogues for Mark,to throw an enhanced light on the glorification of the Lord, though in this case he is most careful to offset the inherent weaknesses of the **analogia comparationis** model and clearly signal that the glory enjoyed by the analogues is of a different order.

The tradition of two heavenly witnesses at the Resurrection is already familiar to us in the Resurrection narratives proper[85] and it is also found in Luke's Ascension account : και ιδου ανδρες δυο παρειστηκεισαν αυτοις εν εσθησεσι λευκαις. (Acts 1.10) The notion of heavenly witnesses to the Messiah (even his attendants) was a notable theme of the frescoes of Dura - Europos , where the Christ was depicted on the synagogue wall as sitting enthroned in glory,flanked by two heavenly attendants[86]. All the other royal figures in the frescoes (Solomon, Ahasuerus,and Pharoah) likewise had two attendants at their thrones. The fact that Elijah and Moses were the two greatest charismatic heroes of popular Judaism , therefore, makes the Christological import of the narrative all the more telling for Christian readers when these same figures are introduced to stand alongside the Lord - almost as his Messianic attendants.We shall return to this idea later in commenting on the significance Mark attaches to the mistake of Peter who offers all three a tabernacle of honour (Mk.9.6). But for the moment it suffices to note (given that the tradition of Elijah as a heavenly immortal is much more biblically elaborated than the similar but later tradition of Moses) why it is that Mark quite clearly regards Elijah as the more important narrative character for his purposes[87]. He reverses the traditional order of their biblical cataloguing : Ηλιας συν Μωυσει, (Mk.9.4) and this is a sign that he himself is personally responsible for introducing these characters into a story that previously did not have them. The original Sinai Haggadah most likely contained reference only to the two Angels of the Covenant. But the fact that Mark instinctively cites Elijah first indicates that he has identified him as the more important 'type' for his own theological purposes.

The understanding of Elijah and Moses as representatives of the Law and the Prophets,which has come to be traditional in exegesis from the time of the Fathers, while it can be logically extrapolated from the above, is not the Evangelist's intent in the Transfiguration narrative. As to why Mark chooses Elijah and Moses as the pair of heavenly witnesses (as opposed to what might have seemed a more likely association of Elijah and Enoch) is open to question. Jeremias comments :'Outside the NT,and in passages not influenced by Mk.9.4f,and Rev.11.3f, the forerunners are almost always Enoch and Elijah,the link between them being that they were both translated alive according to the witness of the OT[88].If Mark 9.4f and independently[89] Rev.1.3f substitute Moses for Enoch,this is obviously because of a tradition which taught a translation of Moses similar to that of Enoch and Elijah.'[90]

The Enoch traditions had become so suspect to orthodox Judaism by AD 90 that they were excluded from the Hebrew canon. This fact alone may attest to their widespread circulation in Christian circles, but it may also give us a motive why ,decades earlier, Mark preferred to use more central figures of the biblical tradition to present his apologia for Christ's unique glory. If the Enoch literature was not accepted by the Jewish community in Rome as canonical in Mark's day, then all the apologetic force of his narrative would have been lost , an apology perhaps designed more for Jewish Christians within the church who upheld 'prophetic' Christologies.

We may,therefore, sum up this introductory section with the utmost brevity before passing on to comment on the rest of the Markan text. It is the reference to 'those who shall not taste death' which first of all leads us to see in the Transfiguration story a theology which fundamentally relates to the mystery of Christ's immortal glorification in the sense of his enthronement glory **as an enduring state.** This is at one and the same moment a Christological motif in which Elijah and Moses play no small role, as well as a Parousial motif. The Parousial motif,however, is subordinate to and dependent on the Christological because the **enduring** state of Christ's resurrection glory prefigured on the mountain is Mark's device for explaining why the glorious return of the Risen Lord has been delayed even up to his own day[91]. The Transfiguration narrative,then, also has a profound relationship to the Logion of Mk.8.38 on which it serves to comment.

2.   **And after six days Jesus takes Peter , James and John with him, and leads them up a high mountain, by themselves, alone. (Mk.9.2)**

και μετα ημερας εξ παραλαμβανει ο Ιησους τον Πετρον και τον Ιακωβον και τον Ιωαννην και αναφερει αυτους εις ορος υψηλον κατ ιδιαν μονους.

Several commentaries have read the detail of the six days as a reference to the six days the cloud of the divine presence **(Shekinah)** remained on Sinai in Ex.24.16. Although the Transfiguration narrative is certainly based on a Sinai Haggadah at some stage in its life, I believe the former Shekinah interpretation is 'overzealous'. It is a time reference which is no more than a redactional device to provide the linkage between the pericope 8.34 - 9.1 and the narrative here 9.2-8. Mark wishes us to read the one in the light of the other. Vincent Taylor interprets the 'six days later' as having a starting point at Peter's confession at 8.29. There is no justification in the text for doing this.It is clearly based on **a priori** theological motives, and indeed the most natural reading is the one proposed earlier. In other words, six days after giving the mysterious Logion of 9.1, Jesus points, even more mysteriously, to its fulfilment.

The mountain is deliberately left unspecified by Mark. Patristic exegesis later identified it with Thabor in the light of the Psalm text : 'Thabor and Hermon shall rejoice in your name.'[92] but the original tradition has left it unspecified since it is supposed to be associated with that archetypal mountain theophany at Horeb (the mountain where both Elijah and Moses had come into the presence of Yahweh)[93]. Elsewhere in Mark, mountain scenes have appeared as the setting for prayer,the election of the disciples, and apocalyptic teaching[94]. One other purpose of the mountain setting, then, could be to emphasise the motif of the special 'election' of the three disciples. The κατ ιδιαν μονους of 9.2 is a very strong emphasis on this election which parallels the other election stories of Mk.1.16-20 and 3.13,which again takes place in a similar setting : και αναβαινει εις το ορος και προσκαλειται ους ηθελεν αυτος. In this latter text we also see the special election of this inner group of three (cf. Mk.3.16-17). These are the three chosen to witness his greatest epiphanies : his raising of the dead (5.37),his transfiguration in glory (9.2), and his transfiguration in the sorrow of death (14.33f)[95]. This election theme serves to validate the special apostolic authority of these three 'pillars' for their testimony on the power of Jesus over life and death (Jairus narrative),on Jesus' sufferings (Gethsemane account),and his exaltation (The Transfiguration story). Attention has already been drawn to a similar theme of validating the authority of the successor, in the narrative of Elijah's metamorphosis in 2Kings. The presence of the three on the mountain of Transfiguration confirms them as witnesses of the glory of the Lord. In practice this means a confirmation of their role as witnesses of the Resurrection (cf.Mk. 9.9-10) as well as of the Christology they subsequently explicate in their preaching. This perhaps is why Mark omits this important theme of the apostolic witness to the Resurrection of Jesus from the ending of his own text of the Gospel in Ch.16, whereas the other evangelists all make it a critical element of the Resurrection 'form' proper.

The εμπροσθεν αυτων of 9.3 (in their presence) again displays the evangelist's concern to emphasise who are the audience of this epiphany (as at Mk.2.12) which further stresses the influential position the three, and particularly Peter, hold in this narrative[96]. We are dealing here, in some significant way, with the issue of apostolic authority.From what has emerged about the style and tenor of the Markan redactive changes to his inherited source it appears that he is introducing a certain qualification into the notion of apostolic authority,even while in general terms maintaining it. B.D.Chilton supports the inference that the Transfiguration narrative is in some way intimately bound up with establishing the authority of the apostles within early Christianity. He uses the thematic parallels of the text with the Sinai theophany,to expand on his views : 'We know from 2 Cor.3.7 -4.6 that at least one apostle could define his διακονια in respect of the M osaic revelation . Is it unlikely that his counterparts in Jerusalem would have articulated their authority with such a typology ? [97] By his own testimony,Paul came to Jerusalem ιστορησαι Κηφαν (Gal. 1.18) and returned to check his Gospel with the 'pillars' (Gal.2.2,9).Peter, James and John were the normative agents of the Jesus tradition.It is a reasonable inference from our analysis that these three claimed a place akin to that of Aaron,Nadab and Abihu in their account of the Transfiguration, and that Paul, who initially accepted their authority,later trumped their claim by comparing himself directly to Moses.'[98] We could add that Mark,by redactively introducing the implied criticism of Peter into his own version,somewhat checks this claim to unquestioned primacy of priestly authority,without necessarily rejecting out of hand the status of Peter as 'pillar' of the original tradition, or for that matter (at least by the time Mark was writing) as glorious martyr for the Lord.

The parallels between the Transfiguration and the Sinai theophany,then, originally had an 'apostolic' significance beyond the Christological.The central core of Sinai parallels - the radiant light and the cloud of God's presence,will be discussed later under their own headings.Some commentators have read the fearful amazement of the crowds who greet Jesus on his return from the mountain at Mk.9.15 : και ευθυς πας ο οχλος ιδοντες αυτον εξεθαμβηθησαν, as a deliberate parallel with the amazement of the Israelites who see the lingering vestiges of the theophany in the radiance of Moses' face,still glowing when he came down from the mountain : και ην δεδοξασμενη η οψις του χρωματος του προσωπου αυτου και εφοβηθησαν εγγισαι αυτω . (LXX.Ex.34.30) The response of both crowds is to gather eagerly round the teacher after they have overcome their initial astonishment : και προστρεχοντες ησπαζοντο αυτον (Mk. 9.15) : και επεστραφησαν προς αυτον Ααρον και παντες οι αρχοντες.......... και μετα ταυτα προσηλθον προς αυτον παντες οι υιοι Ισραηλ. (Ex.34.31-32) Two things in favour of such an interpretation of Mk.9.15 are first of all that the mountain is thus clearly designated as a Sinai parallel which, as we have seen, must have been the mainstay of the tradition which reached Mark: the crowds and the other disciples left behind are thus designated as the sons of Israel who were forbidden to set foot on the mountain in case they should see the glory of the Lord and die. If this is the case then the original tradition which reached Mark was indeed making spectacular claims for the authority of the three apostles in so far as they are introduced onto the mountain and into the very theophany. The second favourable aspect of such an interpretation is that it thereby affords a very good textual link between the narrative of 9.2-8 and that of 9.14f. Nonetheless, it is by no means assured that we should in fact read the amazement theme of 9.15 in this light. This is because Mark appears,in his redactive changes to the prior source,to be concerned with reducing the Mosaic theme rather than emphasising it.To suppose that the people's amazement was the result of Jesus' face still shining with radiance,forgets that Mark has carefully omitted any reference at all to the radiant face as found in Luke and Matthew.Moreover Mark strongly suggests an abrupt end to the epiphany as early as 9.8.

It is certainly possible that the strange allusion in 9.15 is a carry-over from the original source which Mark has assimilated badly,thus leaving a somewhat redundant outcrop.In other words he has personally removed the motif of the radiant face at 9.2 and then not consistently followed through the implications of this redactive excision at 9.15. There are several other times in his Gospel when other similar redactive inbreaks of the evangelist are followed through raggedly,either within the rest of the selfsame pericope or in the adjacent pericope. Examples may be found in the mention of 'other boats were with him' at Mk.4.36 which then play no part at all in the subsequent narrative,but which are a residual memory of the story's origination as a Haggadah on Psalm 107.23f (LXX). Or again in the premature announcement of the death of the Baptist at Mk. 6.16.

3. **And he was metamorphosised before them.** Mk.9.2b.

και μεταμορφωθη εμπροσθεν αυτων.

The word Metamorphosis (Latin : Transfiguratio) at the centre of the narrative, is rare in NT Greek[97] and Luke is careful,in his redaction,to omit it altogether[98]. He does this probably to distance himself from the popular myths of Hellenistic paganism (the Μορφαι θεων) but Mark,typically, has no such scruples about incidental Hellenisms of this type. While the tales of the Μορφαι θεων have had no apparent influence on his narrative,the same cannot be said of the quite distinct Hellenistic Mystery theme of the Μορφη Θεου. The latter is a synonym for the spiritual transfiguration of the intellect, and the theme may well have had some influence on the theological mind of Mark. Some investigation,then,of the philosophical concept of Metamorphosis is called for.

The Greek myths witness an abundance of instances where the gods change their Form (viz. Μεταμορφωσις) and turn into something else to accomplish their ends upon earth. Hellenistic literature abounds with the same notion.Ovid's **Metamorphoses** and Apuleius' **Metamorphoses of Lucius** (The Golden Ass) are but two of the more famous examples. In the age-old manner of the folk-myth, transformation stories are a winning combination of pure entertainment and symbolistic moral. Unfortunate mortals frequently end up as fish[99], frogs,or flowers, and even the simplest of these folk tales was capable of bearing a higher symbolism, in the context of Hellenistic mysteries which we often overlook today[100]. At the higher end of the mythic scale the 'transformation' may be used to connote a profound spiritual progress ,such as the transformation (metamorphosis) of a man from an ordinary mortal into an initiate who learns to 'see' the deity : ο μεταμορφουμενος εν ταις ορασεσιν Αιων Αιωνος.[101] It may signify the transition of the man of God into a prophet who speaks in divine ecstasy :[102] λεγων αμα ενεθουσια μεταμορφουμενος εις Προφητην. And Clement of Alexandria uses the term to connote the transition of the Christian from a hylic to a pneumatic, transfigured by Christ into the true man : και παντα αρα ταυτα τα αγριωτατα θηρια και τους τοιουτους λιθους η ουρανιος ωδε αυτη μετεμορφωσεν εις ανθρωπους ημ− ερους.[103]   Similarly Apuleius is transfigured from an Ass into a man when he sees the spiritual mysteries of Isis and becomes illuminated. His physical metamorphosis[104] is symbolic of his spiritual exaltation from the state of a man addicted to sensual pleasures,to that of a free initiate.

It is this latter understanding of metamorphosis,akin to exal-tation to a higher spiritual plane,that also predominates in the apocalyptic tradition : not so much the god coming down in an earthly guise to greet terrestrial creatures, but the lifting up of men to spiritual levels. It is in this area alone that some of the Hellenistic literature stands comparison with the apocalyptic, and consequently with the evangelical narratives. The Hellenistic mysteries regarded Transfiguration as synonymous with re-birth (Παλιγγενεσια)[105] or deification (θεωσις); two concepts so close in the Hellenistic wo-rld view that perhaps we should look again at Mark's manner of redactively linking the Transfiguration narrative with the Baptismal theophany by the recurring motif of Ps.2.7 :You are my Son, today I have given birth to you.' This coronation or enthronement psalm celebrates the rebirth of the prince who has been lifted up to become the Christ of Israel. It too, clearly associates the images of rebirth and exaltation. The new King is depicted as having been exalted to Messianic Δοξα by the act of God stooping down to vindic-ate him.Likewise in the Baptismal narrative we find this two-fold sense of ascent and descent : ευθεως **αναβαινων** εκ του υδατος   ειδε σχιζομενους τους ουρανους και το Πνευμα ως περιστεραν **καταβαινον** επ'αυτον (Mk.1.10). Interpreted in the manner of a narrative of Παλι-γγενεσια Πνευματικη , in which sense many of Mark's educated gentile congregation could have read it[106], we could reinterpret as follows: As Christ rises from the waters / the grave / the heavens open to his comprehension (cf. **Pistis Sophia**) and his life is clearly seen to be merged with the divine spirit. This would underline the affinities of the Baptismal αναβασις with that of the Transfiguration , and further explain the textual parallels Mark wishes to draw between the two narratives by means of quoting the Messianic psalm.

While Mark's theological redaction springs from a Judaic source (including the apocalyptic) it is equally clear that his Roman readers,Jewish as well as Gentile,will have recognised at least the terms of his discourse as the language of Mystery-Exaltation. The presupposition that Mark the evangelist was himself of Jewish lineage , the John-Mark mentioned in the Pauline literature, is entirely fanciful and the most natural reading of his Gospel reveals a gentile Hellenistic mind. In the higher forms of the Hellenistic Mysteries the initiation experience was itself seen as a transformation to a new spirit-life. The initiate, by means of charged symbolic forms (τα μυστηρια, sacramenta) enters , when his heart has been made ready , into the divine reality of his god. This transformation is the ultimate in religious experience (Το Μυστηριον [107]). Profound spiritual metamorphosis is involved , in sacramental form , in this kind of language. An immortal body is achieved, a rebirth of consciousness, a transcending of earthly limitations : ορων τιν εν εμοι απλαστον ιδεαν γεγενημενην εξ ελεου θεου και εμαυτον δι εξεληλυθα εις   αθανατον σωμα και ειμι νυν ουχ ο πριν αλλ αν εγεννηθην εν νω .[108]

Or again :   Πασων γαρ των σωματικων αισθησεων τε και κινησεων επιλαθομενος ατρεμει περιλαμψαν δε παντα τον νουν και την ολην ψυχην αναλαμβανει και ανελκει δια του σωματος και ολον αυτον εις ουσιαν μεταβαλλει. [109]

Both these texts speak of the transition from the sensible (Σωμα) to

the intelligible (Νους). This final example depicts the same   Transfig -
uration as a transcending of the body which is nothing short of a
holistic spiritualisation :εως αν εμαθον μετασωματουμενος πνευμα γενεσθ-
αι .[110]   Seneca , roughly contemporaneous with Mark, evokes the radical nature of ethical conversion,similarly describing it as a spiritual
metamorphosis, or a beginning to comprehend one's ways and motives.
He too identifies this transfiguration as a 'new birth' of consciousness:
Intellego ,Lucili, non emendari me tantum sed transfigurari.Nec hoc
promitto iam aut spero, nihil in me superesse,quod mutandum sit
.... et hoc ipsum argumentum est in melius translati animi, quod
vitia sua,quae adhuc ignorabat, videt ..... cuperem itaque tecum
communicare tam subitam mutationem mei.[111]   Such a metamorphosis
is comparable to a dying and rising to life[112]. This sense of spiritual
transformation is found in Paul's exhortation to the Romans, one
of the very rare texts in the NT which uses the word metamorphosis:
και μη συσχηματιζεσθε τω αιωνι τουτω αλλα μεταμορφουσθε τη ανακαιν-
ωσει του νοος   (Rom.12.2) This Metamorphosis experience of the spirit
may symbolically be extended to external matters such as the ritual
clothing of the initiates of the Mysteries[113]. The Christians,like
the Mystery initiates,would wear splendid garments to witness their
participation in the great mystery of rebirth.Such garments were
traditionally described in both Christian and Hellenistic literature
by reference to the splendour of the sun.Apuleius,for example, described his appearance after he had been admitted into the Isis cult,and
been clothed in the initiate's vestments, as one 'dressed like the
sun'[114]. Philo's description of the metamorphosis of Moses employs
the   analogy : εις νουν ηλιοειδεστατον .[115] The evangelical account
of the radiance of Christ's garments, then , while it should rightly
be read in an apocalyptic context (for this is its original source),
nonetheless would have evoked traditional motifs for a gentile audience
concerned with spiritual exaltation in the Mystery genre. To a gentile
congregation, and there must have been many of them in the Roman
church of that period, this part of the narrative would have come
across as doubly familiar. To argue, therefore, that the Transfig-

uration story in Mark : 'has nothing to do with Metamorphosis in the Hellenistic sense ....'[116] is only a part truth, and one that has resulted in a considerable amount of distortion in those exegetical studies which have followed the opinion blindly. It has resulted in most commentators completely ignoring the Hellenistic metamorphosis tradition in their scriptural analyses. The author of the statement, Behm , is correct only in so far as he suggests that we do not need to look so far as the Mystery Cults to furnish our apprehension of Mark's meaning ,for it can be deduced from the apocalyptic tradition of intertestamental Judaism. The statement is also true in that it tells us that Mark's Gospel cannot be classified in the genre of Hellenistic Mystery literature **per se** ,nor is it influenced by the popular folk-tales of the divine metamorphoses of heroes[117] (which is probably all that Behm meant to signify in the first place).But the statement is a distortion in that it fails to take cognisance of the fact that Mark's text shares many features in common with the Hellenistic notion of the mystery of spiritual transfiguration. In the wider term he not only shares the world of religious thought in which the Mysteries were the highest form of religious articulation around him,but he also has many points where his literary and theological intent comes very close to that of the Mystery writers. Mark too, for example , is concerned with leading men to become initiates through faith, passing into the great mystery of the Lord's life-giving death that is destined to transfigure their lives just as it transfigured the lives of the apostolic characters in his narrative. Although he is a redactor of Aramaic sources and traditions, the evangelist appears to be a gentile,a Roman encouraging his congregation to meet persecution willingly for the sake of their Lord.His theological bias is clearly as an apologist of a Christ for gentiles. The text of the Gospel frequently makes us doubt whether the evangelist had any real personal knowledge of Palestinian geography,even of common Jewish customs.If our resistance to the widespread myth[118] that he was the 'John Mark' cousin of the Levite Barnabas was brought forward more into our critical consciousness, surely the issue of his possible Romano-Hellenistic influences would gain more attention than it hitherto has attracted since the early (and often extravagant) forays into possible Hellenistic influences on Gospel tradition in the early decades of this century. The whole issue stands in need of fresh critical examination.But even work on the exorcism tradition,so central in the Gospels of Luke and especially Mark,can show that the Hellenistic religious milieu is just as important as the apocalyptic matrix, and has had just as great a modifying influence on the theological intentions of the evangelists in question.[119] At at least one instance Roman oratory has determined the form of a Jesus Logion in Mark[120]. Indeed Cicero's own words on the inner meaning of the Mysteries could stand as a synopsis of the Christian intent of his Gospel : Initiaque ,ut appellantur, ita revera principa vitae cognovimus neque solum cum laetitia vivendi rationem accepimus,sed etiam cum spe meliore moriendi.[121]

And so,the Hellenistic imagery of Metamorphosis, if stripped of a crude understanding of it as sympathetic magic, apotheoses of demi-gods, or such like, is nonetheless a profound medium for the first century man to speak of and envisage the notion of spiritual ascent to the deity. We should not be too eager wholly to excise this Hellenistic background from the mind and thought of Mark as if it were impossible for the evangelist to be influenced by it in any way at all simply because he is dealing with Aramaic source material. What his narrative of Metamorphosis deals with noetically is essentially allied to both Judaeo-apocalypticism and the higher Mysteries, but cannot be restricted to either , for it amounts to the notion of spiritual exaltation, one of the greatest and most fundamental of all religious concept-structures. In the central import of what they wish to express,then, the apocalyptic and Mystery texts are quite similar, and room for accomodation can be found between them. It is more in the manner of their expressions that they part company.

In considering Metamorphosis as exaltation,we must also consider the key term of Δοξα (glory : Latin **claritas,gloria**).The Term bears the closest relationship to Μορφη in denoting the advancement of status, a change of condition for the better , or in other words metamorphosis as a glorification experience. Δοξα is the LXX term used to evoke the glorious presence of Yahweh himself. In this it advances on the conceptions of the Hebrew bible by conflating more than one Hebrew term to produce a richer and more diverse understanding of the doctrine of 'The glory of God'. In particular it stands in place of two keywords in the biblical and Targumim accounts of theophany, the Hebrew **Kabod** [122] and the later rabbinic Aramaism **Shekinah**[123]. Luke's redaction of the Transfiguration expressly introduces the word Δοξα to describe the heavenly glory that embraces Moses and Elijah but is proper to Jesus alone[124] : οιτινες ησαν Μωσης και Ηλιας οι οφθεντες εν δοξη ελεγον την εξεδον αυτου ην εμελλε πληρουν εν Ιερουσαλημ ο δε Πετρος και οι συν αυτω ησαν βεβαρημενοι υπνω διαγρη - γορησαντες δε ειδον την δοξαν αυτου και τους δυο ανδρας τους συνεστωτας αυτω. (Lk.9.30-32) In two verses here the term is expressly introduced twice. In this, Luke is most probably influenced by the LXX account of the radiance (δοξα) on Moses' face when he came down from the Sinai theophany : LXX Ex.34.30. Mark does not use the word at all in his narrative, again the reason for this may be his concern to reduce an overt Sinaitic,or Moses - Jesus parallelism, on Christological grounds. But as Kittel recognises, the notion is clearly there even though the word is not[125].

Mark's description of Jesus' transfiguration clearly sets it within the terms of the entrance of Jesus into the glory of God; his being lifted up and enfolded in the radiance of the divine **shekinah.** In rabbinic literature Moses is the archetype of such participation in the divine[126],but the coming Messiah is also spoken of as destined for a share in the **Kabod,** and in one passage at least Elijah too is explicitly associated in this glory in so far as he also had been granted resurrection[127]. The notion of this glorious radiance becomes traditional in apocalyptic literature from the time of Daniel 12.3 onwards : και οι συνιεντες λαμψουσιν ως η λαμπροτης του στερεωματος και απο των δικαιων των πολλων ως οι αστερες εις τους αιωνας και ετι .[128] The NT theology of 'The Glory' ,therefore, bears out the word's role as a transfiguration term connoting glorious glorious exaltation by God , being touched by the divine δυναμις ,entering into the very **Kabod** of the Holy One. The resurrection of Jesus is depicted in this sense of glorification : θεον τον εγειραντα αυτον εκ νεκρων και δοξαν αυτω δοντα [129]; for the Resurrection comes about δια της δοξης του Πατρος [130]. Stephen[131] sees the risen Lord within this divine glory : ειδεν δοξαν θεου και Ιησουν εστωτα εκ δεξιων του θεου, just as the apostles on the mountain,in Luke, see Moses and Elijah εν δοξη ,that is to say not simply 'glorified',but properly speaking enveloped and contained within the glory of God. Throughout the NT[132] the use of the word is designed to make a comment on the glory of the risen Lord, or the glory of that exalted Lord when he comes again at the Parousia.[133] It is misguided to make too radical a distinction between the glorification of Jesus in terms of either a resurrection theology or a parousial theology,as if they were mutually exclusive categories,since the biblical concept of the glorious exaltation to the divine **Shekinah** at once embraces both notions.Moreover, the apocalyptic idiom of resurrection from the dead is in essence a parousial or eschatological event anyway.

The earliest of the Christian proclamations of the resurrection of Jesus show how the themes of αναστασις and αναληψις must be considered in parallel when they describe the Father's exaltation of the crucified one to Messianic Δοξα[134]. A similar understanding is observable in those kerygmatic interpretations of the passion and glorification of Jesus which work from the Isaian text of the lifting up of the suffering servant of Yahweh. This servant of God had suffered disfigurement/dishonour (αδοξησει) at the hands of men and was thereby judged worthy of transfiguration into glory by Yahweh. The LXX text of Isaiah uses the word Δοξα in two senses , as appears again in the Fourth Gospel ; in the common Hellenistic usage of 'good opinion', and in the more profound sense of divine glorification (that is the good opinion that Yahweh has of the individual despite the opinions of men) which is manifested in his election of that servant to be lifted up into the divine glory.In the Isaian text, as it follows, we can note the 'amazement theme' (θαυμασονται εθνη πολλα) that celebrates the glorification of the servant. This is to be properly understood as the typical response of onlookers to a divine epiphany,and therefore analogous to the amazement theme in the Sinai narrative, and throughout the whole of Mark's Gospel[135]. This is so because the glorification itself **is a theophany** by virtue of the fact that it has emanated directly from the divine **Kabod** : ιδου συνησει ο παις μου και υψωθησεται και δοξασθησεται σφοδρα.ον τροπον εκστησονται επι σε πολλοι ουτως αδοξησει απο των ανθρωπων το ειδος σου και η δοξα σου απο υιων ανθρωπων. ουτως θαυμασονται εθνη πολλα επ αυτω και συνεξουσι βασιλεις το στομα αυτων • οτι οις ουκ ανηγγελη περι αυτου οψονται και οι ουκ ακηκοασι συνησουσι.(Is.52.13-15,LXX) It is clear that here the glorification is held to be synonymous with 'lifting up' (υψωθησεται). And this again should remind us of the danger of separating too radically our notions of the resurrection,exaltation, ascension, or enthronement of Jesus, since they were originally a holistic tradition before they were so categorised.They all celebrate one and the same mystery from different perspectives. In the apocalyptic idiom the notion of 'lifting up' extends quite specifically to embrace the concepts of resurrection from the dead and exaltation to glory. Moreover, considering the immense importance the Isaian servant theology has for the early church's attempts to understand the meaning of the Lord's abasement and sufferings (his αδοξα) we perhaps would not be far off the mark if we were to take this Isaian sense of the glorification as one of the master keys for our correct understanding of the notion of Christ's Δοξα in the NT. This mystery of the servant's glory as both a suffering as well as an enthronement can be seen in the theology of 'Glory' in the Fourth Gospel, but it may also lie behind what is an evident parallelism in Mark between the glorious epiphany of the Metamorphosis and the sorrowful epiph-any of the Agony in Gethsemane[136].

4. **And his garments became exceedingly brilliantly white such as no fuller upon the earth is able to whiten them. (Mk.9.3)**

και τα ιματια αυτου εγενετο στιλβοντα λευκα λιαν οια γναφ-
ευς επι της γης ου δυναται ουτως λευκαναι.

The traditional description of the saints as those enveloped in the radiant **Shekinah** of God lies behind the evangelist's description of the unearthly radiance of Jesus' garments. The awkwardness of that description, with its double superlative 'exceedingly brilliantly white' and the somewhat lame comparison to a bleacher, has all the hall-marks of the evangelist's peculiar style. It is undoubtedly a personal redaction. Parallel texts have already been adduced from apocalyptic, as well as Hellenistic tradition, in which the analogy of radiant garments features as a description of the spiritual exaltation of the soul. Mark , unlike Matthew and Luke [137], makes no mention at this point of Jesus face. This is why he has emphasised the descript-ion of the garments. Streeter conjectured that the original text of Mark did have such a reference to the shining face, and Taylor followed him in this arguing further that the original manuscript archetype might have read : και εγενετο στιλβον το προσωπον και τα ιματια αυτου λευκα λιαν [138]. Both were being extremely hypothetical, of course. They were led to this inference because of the strange fact that Matthew and Luke seemed to disagree against Mark. Indeed they are undoubtedly right in their first deduction that the **original tradition** , as it reached Mark, did mention the radiant face of Jesus [139], but Taylor misses the point when he postulates that such a reference has fallen accidentally out of the text of Mark in the process of manuscript transmission, because such an excision was deliberate, and it was the personal work of the evangelist when he came to redact his original source. By removing reference to the shining face Mark economically removes the Mosaic Christological typology from the narrative. It is his concern to obviate this type of prophetic Christology in the Transfiguration story, and although he retains

a Sinai archetype as a structural form, he does not retain the
original theological point of using such an archetype in the first
place.When Paul uses the Sinai archetype,for his own theological
purposes,[140] he shows a very similar concern as that witnessed in
Mark's redactive procedure. Paul first establishes the inherent infer-
iority of the Mosaic experience of The Glory, and only then does
he go on to speak of : φωτισμον της γνωσεως της δοξης του θεου εν
προσωπω Ιησου Χριστου.(2 Cor.4.6) If the original tradition of the
Metamorphosis narrative can be traced back to Peter,then we might
be justified in concluding that Mark has been led to correct it in
a Pauline manner (as Chilton also suggested in a different context).
The two great apostolic figures,when preaching in the final years
of their lives in Rome,have found a mutual synthesis in the work
of the theologian who listened to them both before composing his
own written version of the Haggadah.

Boobyer's comment on the radiance of Jesus rightly associates it with the Δοξα Θεου, but then he goes on : 'It has been argued
that Mark here did not see Jesus in his resurrection body.(argued
ie.by Boobyer earlier in his text) What he did see, we now suggest,
was Jesus revealed in his parousia body.'[141] This distinction between
a 'parousia body' and a 'resurrection body' is an idiosyncratic invent-
ion however.It has already been sufficiently argued that Boobyer's
severe distinction of 'resurrectional' and 'parousial' does not operate
in the biblical idiom in the way that he puts it to service. But
besides all this, what is really at stake in the narrative at this point
is not so much the description of a body at all,but the intimation
that the person of Jesus was exalted in the divine glory. The Δοξα that
Jesus received at his resurrection and enthronement was the Δοξα of
none other than Yahweh himself. In NT theology there is no difference at all between this glory and that with which he shall return
at the Parousia to judge the world. There is only one glory in the
creation , as there is only one God,and one judgement.

The description of the garments which Mark offers finds
an echo in the Matthaean account of the resurrection angel : ην δε η

ιδεα αυτου ως αστραπη και το ενδυμα αυτου λευκον ωσει χιων (Mt.28.3)
The vision of this heavenly glory similarly inspires the response of
fear in the face of a divine epiphany : απο δε του φοβου αυτου εσεισθ-
ησαν οι τηρουντες και εγενετο ωσει νεκροι (Mt.28.4).

Mark's idea of what the risen glory of Jesus will be like is announced for us when Jesus speaks of the Resurrection state in Mk.12 :
εισιν ως αγγελοι εν τοις ουρανοις (12.25). The radiance of the angels
such as the one depicted in our previous Matthaean text, derives
from their proximity to the divine **Kabod** in the heavenly courts.It
is properly the radiance of Yahweh communicated to them.

The phrase ως χιων (like snow; as in Mt.28.3) has tended at
times to creep into the manuscript tradition of Mark 9.3.[142] The
reason for this is perhaps the textual archetype of Dan.7.9 (Theod-
otion) which had a great influence on the traditional description of
heavenly apparitions within Christian tradition, or even unconscious
Matthaean assimilation on the part of scribal copyists in the later
centuries.

All the descriptions of the radiance of the garments,therefore,
are traditional Δοξα manifestations that follow fixed forms. One may
cite as an incidental analogy the western folk-tales' descriptions
of 'the princess' which similarly follow fixed and traditional forms
such as : 'skin as white as snow,hair as black as a raven, and lips
as red as ruby.' There are remarkably similar passages in apocalyptic
literature that use this form. The chosen infant in **1 Enoch** is said
to have a body as white as snow and as red as a rose, and hair
as white as linen[143]. But in all biblical descriptions of this type,the
heart of the matter is always an evocation of the radiance of the
divine **Shekinah.**

Riesenfeld parallels the description of the radiant garments
of Jesus with the concept of the High Priestly robe[144],a sacred
symbol in Judaism, frequently alluded to[145]. Mark, however, unlike
John[146] makes no symbolic capital from Jesus' robe in his Passion
narrative[147] where he would be most likely to use the notion if it
was in his mind at all, and his personal conception of Jesus' priesthood[148] does not seem to use the vestment symbolism in any way

at all. It is most unlikely ,therefore , that any form of priestly symbolism was part of Mark's intention in the Transfiguration story. The points of coincidence which Riesenfeld notes can all be explained by the fact that the glory of the sacred robe which caused awesome reverence in the hearts of the beholders[149] did so precisely because it was recognised as a 'holy thing',and as such touched by the holiness of the divine **Kabod.** The **Kabod** is explicitly described as a sacred robe in Ps.104.1-2 :'Yahweh my God, how great you are,clothed in majesty and glory (LXX ευπρεπιαν) wrapped in light   as in a robe.' [150] It is,then, the fundamental concept of **the Shekinah** that stands behind Mark's description of the radiance on the mountain and one does not need to look further than this. It is this selfsame notion which accounts for Riesenfeld's supposed discovery of priestly symbolism in the narrative. That he is mistaken in this detail, in no way diminishes the profundity of his great work on the text, a study full of brilliant insights and scholarly illuminations.

Any hypothetical parallelism with the eschatological image of the 'fuller' and his bleach in Mal.3.2 is also to be discounted as an influence on Mark's text. There is no verbal connection at all between Mark's Greek and the LXX version which would surely have been the case if Mark was deliberately alluding to that biblical passage.

5.   **And there appeared to them Elijah,with Moses, and they were speaking together with Jesus. (Mk.9.4)**

και ωφθη αυτοις Ηλιας συν Μωυσει και ησαν συλλαλουντες τω Ιησου.

The heavenly visitors, although important in the narrative as a whole, are introduced in a noticeably secondary fashion. That is, their arrival on the scene occurs only when the radiant Metamorphosis of Jesus has already taken place. The strength of the phrase is almost : And

then after that there appeared.....and so forth. I take it that this means that the phrase in question is Mark's device for emphasising that the appearance of the two prophets is a commentary on the Transfiguration of Jesus, not the cause of it. It is therefore a redactional device distinguishing Jesus' experience of the divine Glory from that of any other 'glorified' prophet, even those called as witnesses. In this way Mk.9.4 stands as a direct parallel with 9.8 : και εξαπινα περιβλεψαμενοι ουκετι ουδενα ειδον ει μη τον Ιησουν μονον μεθ ε- αυτων. In 9.8 the great emphasis Mark puts on the sudden disappearance of Elijah and Moses, doubly stressed by the 'saw no one any more' and the 'but Jesus alone',argues that for him the prophets have served their purpose, and so the stage is now cleared once again so that full attention may be given to reflecting on the status of Jesus who **alone** has received the title Son of God from the voice of Yahweh. His unique heralding as the divinely validated Messiah radically marks him off from any other prophet. As M E Thrall puts it :'The divine proclamation does not simply distinguish Jesus from ordinary men in general, it distinguishes him quite specifically from Elijah and Moses,the two figures whom the disciples were still expecting to see as they looked about them.' [151]

Two of the most famous holy ones who 'did not taste death' are therefore brought alongside Jesus to demonstrate that his post-death exaltation is of a higher order than theirs. This is in line with the constant proclamation of the early church that Jesus' resurrection has of itself inaugurated the end-time and definitively proved that his life and ministry did indeed usher in the Kingdom of God. It is this distinct uniqueness of Christ's role,and Christ's glory,that Mark wishes to preserve even while using the analogies of other immortal figures [152].

The detail that the two prophets were engaged in conversation with Jesus is an enigmatic touch which has provoked Luke to amplify the text and give us the content of their discourse : 'They spoke of his death which he would accomplish in Jerusalem' (Lk.9.31). The final phrase here gives us the reason why Luke makes this redactional change - he has interpreted the figures of the two prophets in line with his consistent theology of the prophetic destiny that Christ must fulfil,**in Jerusalem**[153]. The whole redaction-structure of the third Gospel turns on the idea of the Messiah's prophetic journey to his death in the capital city. This explains why Luke amends the Markan text. But what was Mark's own intention when he made mention of the conversation ? We have no evidence to suggest that we should look for a similar prophetic theme in Mark as we find in Luke ; quite the contrary. Mark's phrase 'they were speaking together with Jesus' suggests,in distinction to Luke's serious interpretation, quite an informal exchange of greetings. Thrall again sums it up : 'In the preceding verses......we have been given the impression that Elijah and Moses are the equals of Jesus. All three appear as heavenly beings, and they converse together. Elijah and Moses are not represented as venerating Jesus or as respectfully listening to him. There is a suggestion of equality.'[154] It is this sugestion of 'equality' which I believe Mark is trying to convey by introducing the phrase συλλαλουντες, and he introduces it solely in order to correct it. It is a specific introduction into the tradition by the evangelist himself to heighten his subsequent treatment of Peter's suggestion. The whole Transfiguration narrative is Christologically motivated, and the consistent message is that Jesus is by no means an equal to Elijah and Moses, but of a wholly different order of importance. This explains the involved exchange that now follows immediately after in the text - Peter's mistake. His mistake,at least according to Mark, is precisely that he assumes, and takes for granted,that all three 'prophetic' figures are equals. It is a mistake which Mark considers so important that it stands in need of correction from the very heart of the **Kabod** itself.

6.   And Peter in answer said to Jesus : 'Rabbi it is good for us to be here.We shall make three tabernacles; one for you,one

for Moses, and one for Elijah.' For he did not know what answer to make, because they were all frightened out of their wits. (Mk.9.5-6)

και αποκριθεις ο Πετρος λεγει τω Ιησου Ραββι καλον εστιν ημας ωδε ειναι και ποιησωμεν τρεις σκηνας σοι μιαν και Μωυσει μιαν και Ηλια μιαν ου γαρ ηδει τι αποκριθη εκφοβοι γαρ εγενοντο.

Peter's exclamation is characterised by Mark as being somewhat foolish and misplaced. He excuses the statement by reference to the fact that the apostles were 'frightened out of their wits' (εκφοβος) in the face of an awesome epiphany[155] and thus talked nonsense. It is a very strong implicit rebuke to Peter nonetheless. This theological nonsense of Peter's is presented by the evangelist to his readers for a didactic purpose. We are supposed to reflect on why the statement was wrong , particularly so in the light of the divine teaching given by the voice of God at 9.7.

The first part of the statement he makes carries the title with which he addresses Jesus -'Rabbi'. This is paralleled at 11.21 where Peter again addresses Christ as 'Rabbi' on behalf of the other disciples. This title is Christologically very low-key in such a context; especially considering his previous profession at Mk.8.30, and the testimony the voice will soon give at 9.7 , but it is doubtful that this as such is the point on which Mark wishes to correct him, considering the instance of 11.21 which caused the evangelist no problems. It is noticeable,however, that both Matthew (Κυριε) and Luke (επιστατα) do wish to correct him on this point; and they personally amend the text of Mark in order to do so. [156]

The phrase : καλον εστιν ημας ωδε ειναι of 9.5. seems to look back to :εισι τινες ωδε των εστηκοτων at 9.1. And this would support the contention that the whole narrative of Transfiguration stands in some sense as the fulfilment of that promise to see the Kingdom in power. Moreover, as Chilton observes there is a significant verbal parallelism going on here : 'What is καλον about discipleship is explicated in 9.43,45,47.'[157] These latter texts all evoke the need for true disciples to pay the necessary price of suffering before arriving at the Glory of the Kingdom. As such they are theological as well as hermeneutical parallels to the Transfiguration. Part of Peter's mistake may therefore be interpreted in the light of Mk.8.32 and 14.28-30, as being the fact that he still has not got a proper perspective on what is truly 'good' about discipleship,that he still has a vision that cannot come to terms with the scandal of the cross. As Lagrange put it many years ago :'Il n'a toujours pas compris la leçon de la croix'[158].

The major part of his error in Mark's redaction, however, would seem to be the offer to build three tabernacles. Peter's exclam-ation about why it is good for the three disciples to be there could then be paraphrastically interpreted as saying : 'It is fortunate that we ordinary mortals are present today to be able to do the works of cultic service for you.' And this, for Mark, would underline his failure to understand what was happening around him.

Riesenfeld attaches great importance to this mention of tabernacles, and attempts to set the Transfiguration event within the theological context of the Feast of Tabernacles[159]. Such a contextualisation certainly provides a rich fund of associations ; for example the theme of the Tabernacle of God in the wilderness (directly related to the concepts of the **Kabod,**the cloud of Presence, the building of shelters) and the theme of the theology of light (so central to the celebration of the feast of Tabernacles)[160]. His attempt to set the narrative within the terms of such a festival of Messianic enthronement is an attractive one, especially when we consider the **testimonium** used (Ps.2.7) is the classic enthronement motif of the Judaistic cult of the Messiah, the very psalm in fact that had been sung at the ancient enthronement of the Kings. Riesenfeld's argument presents sufficient indication that the notion of Messianic enthronement had already made the transition from

the cultic sphere to that of apocalypticism[162], but a crucial problem
which he does not answer so eloquently is whether the notion was
in any way at all operative in the mind of our theologian,Mark.
Unless this can be established the whole structure of associations
must remain highly speculative. Mark's lack of concern elsewhere
in his Gospel (excepting the Passion narrative) for any of the theological connotations of the feasts of Judaism would argue against
Riesenfeld's thesis that the associations of Tabernacles are important
here. I believe that it is much more likely that the evangelist understood the Σκηναι in the much more common and generalised meaning :
that of the dwelling-tents of the holy ones in paradise [163]: ενθα εισιν
αι σκηναι των δικαιων και μοναι των αγιων μου Ισαακ και Ιακωβ   εν
τω κολπω αυτου. [164]   Paradisial union with God is envisaged in terms of
the Golden Age of the Jewish people,when God himself dwelt in a
tent in their midst,the whole range of their history up to the reign
of David. In later Judaism frequent appeal is made to this image
in connection with the theme of the 'Day of Salvation'.[165]   It is
an image that is preserved in Christianity[166].

Boobyer uses the reference to the tabernacles to support
a thesis that Mark was invoking the notion of the 'parousial' 'Great
Day of the Lord' when his tent would be re-established on earth.
In this,I believe, he has been sufficiently corrected by M E Thrall
who rightly draws our attention to the fact that the text of Mark
as it stands really does not put much emphasis on the idea of the
tabernacles as such (they are never built for instance) but rather
emphasises the notion of erecting **three** of them,which by implication
gives all three figures a similar status. If any one assumes such
a prophetic Christology - that is that Jesus is one alongside Elijah
and Moses as being an earthly prophet now rewarded by an immortal
exaltation - then Mark makes sure that the divine voice from the
cloud will soon dispel such a belief. The voice,when it comes, bears
specific witness to Jesus' unique status as Son.

All this would point to the correct interpretation of the
booths in the generic sense of tabernacle-shrines appropriate for

heavenly visitors. By virtue of his glorification, Jesus has passed into the heavenly world and this is why Peter wishes to build a tabernacle for him in the company of the saints rather than presuming he would ever return now back down the mountain to live again among mortal men. This is a further indication of the intimate connection between this narrative and the theology of the resurrection/ascension of Christ. The idea that association with God, and a visitation by the glory of God, such as that seen in the life of a charismatic prophet, radically marks off a man from earthly society is seen not only in the tradition of prophetic celibacy as it developed but also in the literature of apocalyptic exaltation.The narrative of the ascension of Enoch,as the heavenly Son of Man, is a clear example of this approach. One touched by the Glory no longer has a place on earth from the time of his visitation onwards.His home henceforth is in the heart of the **Kabod** with God[167].

7.   **And there came a cloud which overshadowed them, and there came a voice from out of the cloud : This is my beloved Son. Listen to him. And suddenly,looking all around, they saw no-one any longer, except Jesus alone with them. (Mk.9.7-8)**

και εγενετο νεφελη επισκιαζουσα αυτοις και εγενετο φωνη εκ της νεφελης,Ουτος εστιν ο υιος μου ο αγαπητος , ακουετε αυτου. και εξαπινα περιβλεψαμενοι ουκετι ουδενα ειδον αλλα τον Ιησουν μονον μεθ εαυτων.

The cloud is associated by Boobyer with the manner of the Son of Man's return at the Parousia 'riding on the clouds of heaven'[168] but he has failed in this hypothesis to note that Mark's apocalyptic mention of the Son of Man's return (immediately prior to the Transfiguration story)makes no mention whatsoever of parousial clouds. One must also note that the return is 'on the clouds' - always in the plural form. At 8.38 Mark only speaks of the glorious Son of Man's association with heavenly beings : οταν ελθη εν τη δοξη του Πατρος αυτου μετα των αγγελων των αγιων. In short, Boobyer has failed to distinguish between two quite different and distinct traditions here, as has already been noted both by Riesenfeld and Thrall : 'The mountain is connected with the enthronement of the Messiah before the Parousia [169];in dealing with the clouds Boobyer has confused two distinct motifs, the coming of the Messiah on the clouds,which belongs to the Parousia tradition, and the cloud which indicates the presence of God and covers the Messiah and the elect, and which is associated with the enthronement motif[170],which is what we have here[171].' The cloud (singular) of the Transfiguration narrative,then, is quite clearly meant by Mark to signify the presence of God[172]. It represents the **Kabod** or Glory of Yahweh itself[173]. Evidently this understanding of the glory of God's presence within the cloud[174] goes back to the literary archetype once again of the Sinai theophany where it says : και εκαλυψεν αυτο η νεφελη .[175]

Mark's use of the verb επισκιαζειν to describe the cloud's action equally connotes this overshadowing presence of the deity. It is the verb used by Luke to evoke the power of the Most High that 'overshadows' Mary and brings the Messiah to birth.[176] There may be an intention to contrast this with the offer Peter has made to Jesus of an honorific tabernacle. The contrast would be that between the glory the church is able to offer Christ and that glory which comes to him from God. The tabernacle offered by Peter would have set him as one among other heavenly heroes. The tabernacle of the **Kabod,** on the contrary, while it overshadows them all[177], radically distinguishes Jesus from all others first of all by removing the heavenly witnesses altogether, and secondly by bestowing on Jesus alone, without any fear of misunderstanding now, the supreme witness of the voice which declares him to be the Son of God. The ideas of 'shelters' and the overshadowing cloud are in some sense related in the process of what Riesenfeld calls the gradual 'democratisation' of the idea of the divine cloud in Jewish theology : 'Aussi rencontrons-nous les deux types de la nuée eschatol-ogique transposés dans des formes democratisées. Dieu étendra la nuée sur Israel dans le monde à venir; les justes seront transportés par une nuée jusqu'au trône de gloire; où bien ils seront revêtus au paradis d'une nuée de gloire.'[178] Chilton regards the voice from heaven at this point in our story as a redactive borrowing from the tradition of the Baptismal account at Mk.1.11, although he does not offer much redactive substantiation of his observation[179]. In marked contrast M Goulder regards the Transfiguration story as the primary account which is then read back into the Baptismal narrative[180]. This latter view, I believe, cannot be the case, for it does not allow for the redactive evolution of the respective stories from their textual archetypes in the OT. The Markan baptismal story evidently incorporates an early Christian haggadah on Isaiah 63-64 (O that you would rend the heavens and come down) and within that section of the Isaian source the notion of Israel's true 'sonship' is an integral and constant theme. The Transfiguration narrative, on the other hand, is based on a literary archetype ultimately traceable to the Sinai story in Exodus 34, and the proclamation of sonship is not part of that narrative form. We may deduce ,then, that Chilton's observation of the relative priority of the divine quotation 'This is my beloved Son', is the correct one. It is Mark who has brought in, at this critical juncture, as his own redactive device, and in line with the previous epiphany in the Jordan, the proclamation of Jesus' sonship. The Christological motive is the determining factor.Apart from the general notions of the idiom of theophany, the only thing that really makes the two narratives stand in any kind of **textual** relationship is the repeated use of Ps.2.7.

In the previous discussion of the Hellenistic notion of Meta-morphosis it was suggested that the idea of spiritual rebirth (Παλιγ – γενεσια) might lie as a root concept behind both accounts, and partly account for the manner in which Mark redactively parallels them. The Psalm envisages the enthronement of the Messiah, or his exalt-ation, in terms (like Ps.110) of an intimate association with the

divine glory. Such an exaltation is like a new birth : εγω σημερον γεγ-
εννηκα σε (Ps.2.7) But alongside this we should also consider that the
overriding theological symbolism of the opening of Mark's Gospel
is that of **Baptism** , by which term he primarily signifies not washing
in water but precisely - suffering and death[181]. A similar concern
with the theology of suffering can be traced in the Transfiguration
narrative in so far as both epiphanies are the prelude in some sense
to rejection and suffering. As Braithwaite put it : 'If the Baptism
is the prelude to the ministry, the Transfiguration is surely the
prelude to the Passion and Resurrection.'[182] The fact is that both
the Baptismal narrative and that of the Transfiguration are concerned
with teaching that Christ's glory is inextricably bound up with the
mystery of his sufferings and death. This, I believe, is the real reason
Mark wishes us to remember the Baptismal story at the point of
9.7.

The voice itself is yet again a Jewish tradition that has
developed from the original archetype of the Sinai story, where
Yahweh thundered out on the mountain top. In Judaic tradition this
was why thunderclaps were envisaged as the sound of God's voice[183].
In the more primitive of the Sinai accounts, preserved at Ex.19.16-
20, and 20.18-21, the thunder and lightning and the blasts of the
ram's horn stand as signs of the approaching presence of deity,
concealed from mortal eye in the cloud of the **Kabod.**[184] In rabbinic
Judaism from the period after the NT this tradition of the divine
voice (Bath Qol) suffered a certain diminishment. It was regarded
as a secondary phenomenon, always subject to revelation already
received in the Torah. The idea of a closed canon was the governing
factor in this conservative development[185], but in Mark's time the
tradition of the heavenly voice still had its more elevated role as
an authentic and specific revelation given by God[186], and the
evangelist's manner of alluding to that voice shows that he regarded
it as no less than the voice of Yahweh himself speaking from the
very heart of the **Kabod** to underline (for Peter's benefit and that
of the Markan church) what a correct Christological perspective

should be. The use of Psalm 2 (and its own implied prologue: Κυριος ειπε προς με...) further underlines the essential correctness of this approach. The voice, therefore, gives a witness to Jesus beyond all other witness. It is a testimony to the truth of his Sonship that cannot be gainsaid for the evangelist, and it thus consummates the witness that has already been given to Jesus' true identity by spirits of the underworld[187], men of earth[188], and most recently by heavenly immortals.

In this manner of singling out Jesus alone for the divine validation as Son (the manner in which Mark has signalled the removal of the prophets from the scene so that the apostles must know that it is Jesus **alone** who is meant) Mark appears to be arguing for an understanding of the important title Υιος του Θεου that is especially Hellenistic-Christian. It is a usage of the title that has already passed beyond the purely 'functional' connotation it possesses in the OT appearances of the term, and seems already to be connoting **generic distinctness** for Mark. It can thus be said, even at this early date, to be approaching the Johannine sense of the Μονογενες του Θεου. It is a Christological point of the utmost importance and significance.

After the voice has proclaimed Ps.2.7, we find the **addendum** 'Listen to him.' This is a reminiscence of the original Sinai Haggadah where the Moses - Jesus parallel was of central import[189] and thus Jesus was designated at this point, originally, as the 'prophet like Moses' (according to Deut.18.15) to whom the people are commanded to listen : Προφητην εκ του αδελφων σου ως εμε αναστησει σοι Κυριος ο Θεος σου ,αυτου ακουσεσθε. If this has been the original proof text in the primitive version of the story which reached Mark, then the evangelist's addition to it of the Psalm text taken from the Baptism story signals a theological motive on the part of the redactor to announce the transference of authority away from Moses to Jesus. The Lord continues to stand under the divine cloud and receive validation from God himself, while Moses withdraws after his prophetic εξουσια has been transferred. In so far as Mark has made these redactive changes - then his root motive is yet again manifested as a desire to remove the Moses-Jesus parallels from a Sinai Haggadah, which when it reached him, must have been full of them. In this case the 'Listen to him' must take on another association for the evangelist, no longer having reference to Deut. 18.15. And what it means now for him is, I think, fairly easy to deduce from the flow of the narrative. It means listen to what he has just said before the Transfiguration event took place. This is what he will repeat just after the event is finished - that is Jesus' prophetic statements that the Messiah's glory must include suffering and death before the final vindication of the Resurrection : 'And he began to teach them that the Son of Man was destined to suffer many things....... to be put to death, and after three days to rise again.(Mk. 8.31-33; see also Mk.9.12;9.30-32;10.33)

At first Peter was characterised by the evangelist as unable to listen to what Jesus had to say about suffering, and even here in the Transfiguration narrative he shows that he has still not understood the message of suffering preceding glory, because he wishes to offer his master the honour of a shrine in the company of the prophets without making allowance for the prophetic fate that must overtake his master before there can be any talk of honours, the fate of rejection and death. Mark brings in the divine voice in order to correct Peter, for didactic reasons, and in order to confirm and underline Jesus' prophecies that the Messiah will only enter his glory through the abasement of his Passion.

This, then , is the meaning of the phrase αυτου ακουετε. It also explains why immediately after the phrase all the wonder and glory of the Transfiguration events is so suddenly withdrawn (Mk.9.8) and why the two following pericopai on rising from the dead (before which the Transfiguration kerygma cannot be given Mk.9.9-10) and the sufferings of the new Elijah (Mk.9.11-13) are both concerned with elucidating this mystery of suffering so soon after such a glorious epiphany. The sudden disappearance of all the radiant signs of glory is itself the Father's confirmation of what he has just spoken

From this point onwards in Mark's text, the prophecies of the Passion
will accelerate our progress into the Passion narrative itself[190].
A similar tradition of a heavenly voice confirming the Messiah's
passion is found at Jn.12.23-30. And further corroboration that we
should thus interpret the Metamorphosis in terms of such a theology
of glory that is manifested only through the cross, is provided by
the redactive parallels drawn between this episode and the narrative
form of the Gethsemane story.[191]

Conclusion.

In so far as this exegetical analysis, following Mark's text,
has returned often to the same ideas from slightly different perspectives, then it would be otiose to present a lengthy summary here.
It will suffice, then, to make a set of statements which seem to me
to sum up the most important points of the Markan redaction of
the Transfiguration, and this can also stand as our synopsis of the
biblical aspect of our present study.

In the first place we find in this narrative the evangelist's
treatment of the most profound and lofty concerns. It is a narrative
of supreme importance - not only to the text of Mark itself where
it occupies a central and pivotal structural position - but for
Christian theology in general, for it deals with the mystery of
Christ's true glory, and the nature of the church's cult. Jesus'
entrance into the divine glory is presented to us in such a way that
the evangelist's concern to make a statement about the **unique**
position of Christ within the **Kabod** is clearly discernible. This Christological motive in his redaction of the narrative is the guiding force
of all his theological amendments. It has been described here as
a transition from prophetic-Christological categories rooted in Jewish
faith and piety, to a Son of God Christology which lays emphatic
and specific stress on the unique status of Jesus as the chosen and
beloved Son , and which appears to be approaching the notion of
generic distinctness that we similarly find in the Johannine theology

of the 'Only Begotten'. It is therefore a Christological movement which eventually flowers, albeit in the soil of a different idiom and in a different age, in that kind of Christological wonder so notable in the patristic homilies   on the narrative that we shall soon have the opportunity to examine.[192]

Secondly, this Transfiguration tradition, not only in its primitive form as a Sinai haggadah, but even more clearly in the manner of its Markan redaction, is intimately concerned with the mystery of Christ's Resurrection[193] when this is correctly understood in the primitive Christian sense as a mystery of God's glorification of his Son Jesus. Such a tradition represents a Christian vision that pre-dates the Lukan aspect of compartmentalising , in chronological order, the single Paschal Mystery of the glory of the Lord in order to re-present it in the various stages of Resurrection, Ascension, Enthronement, and ultimately Parousia. The varied primitive traditions of Jesus' glorification used these separate strands to comment on what they knew at heart was one Christ-mystery. The sense of this holistic aproach can be discovered, for example, in the Resurrection narrative of John 20, where Resurrection, visionary appearances, Ascension and the gift of the Holy Spirit, all occur within the space of the same day. In an analogous sense the understanding of the Transfiguration narrative is critical for Christian reflection on the meaning of the Resurrection status of Jesus, and it presents us with a particularly fruitful source of tradition that is of value not least for the way in which it elevates the Resurrection debate from the channels set by the other evangelical Resurrection narratives, and forces us to consider the mystery above and beyond the narrow perameters that mark so much of the contemporary debate on the subject. These remarks are not meant to suggest that our text is, as it now stands, a misplaced Resurrection account, as some comment-ators have previously maintained - especially if one understands the term ' Resurrection account' by reference to the other Gospels and the Pauline Letter. It is not a Resurrection narrative in this sense. But in so far as it theologises about the glory of Jesus which is sensed now but will be perfected and proclaimed after his death (Mk.9.9-10) then it does have an intimate and substantial relationship with the mystery of Christ's exaltation - that is his Resurrection from the dead, and his heavenly enthronement.

Thirdly, Mark's redaction makes us appreciate yet again the pivotal role the sufferings of the Messiah had for the evangelist and of course for the faith of the early church. The Transfiguration glory is a vindication of the Messiah who was dishonoured by men. This vision of the glory of God's justice in an unjust world had a deep relevance for the early Christians of Mark's church, for it gave them hope in the midst of their dangers and sufferings under Nero. It continues to have relevance as the ultimate Christian answer to the mystery of the justice of God in a world of continuing injustice and pain. It has pressing relevance for the faith of the individual in so far as it brings the modern reader up against Mark's fundamental challenge (the doorway to his very description of Christ on the mountain), that challenge of faith which as a catechist or presbyter in Rome he had built his Gospel text around : Ὑμεις δε τινα με λεγετε ειναι ;   Who do **you** say that I am ?   (Mk.8.29).

NOTES TO CHAPTER TWO

1.   H Conzelmann. **The Theology of St. Luke.** ET London 1960

2.   cf. Mk.4.17, and possibly 4.35f;8.34f, which immediately precedes the Transfiguration; also 10.28-30;10.40 and 13.9f. All these instances mount up to a consistent theme in Mark. Thus the text parallels Mk.9.42-50. The parallelism is further strengthened by the recurring motif of what is really good (Καλον) about discipleship.See the subsequent remarks on the text of Mk.9.5.

3.   Mk.8.33.

4.   The evangelist suggests a literal fulfilment of 9.1 . 'Some of those standing by' refers to Peter, James and John.

5.　　　G H Boobyer,**St. Mark and the Transfiguration Story,** Edin-
　　　　burgh,1942 represents the leading Parousial interpretation.
　　　　For the list of the Resurrectionists cf R H Stein,**Is the
　　　　Transfiguration a misplaced Resurrection account ?** JBL
　　　　95,1976,79-86 (esp.p.79).

6.　　　cf. Mk.3.28; 8.21; 9.1; 10.15; 10.29; 11.23; 12.43; 13.30;
　　　　(which last is an important parallel with 9.1) 14.17; 14.30;
　　　　and 14.25.

7.　　　B D Chilton, **The Transfiguration: Dominical assurance
　　　　and Apostolic vision.** NTS 27,1,1981,115-124. (se p.123 and
　　　　fns. 19-20 thereon).

8.　　　Mk.8.38.; 10.37; 13.26.

9.　　　H Riesenfeld, **Jesus Transfiguré.L'arrière** plan du récit
　　　　évangelique de la Transfiguration de nôtre seigneur. Acta
　　　　Seminarii Neotestamentici Upsaliensis, No.16, Copenhagen
　　　　1947 (p.295). See also 1 Peter 1.11,21; Heb.2.9; 1 Tim.3.16.

10.　　Acts.6.15.

11.　　**Acta Philippi 20.** M R James, **The Apocryphal New Test-
　　　　ament.** Oxford 1926,p.441.

12.　　M E Thrall, **Elijah and Moses in Mark's account of the
　　　　Transfiguration.** NTS 16,1969-70,305-317, (cf.p.310).

13.　　For dating opinions see Stein (1976) p.87; also E Hennecke,
　　　　New Testament Apocrypha , vol.2, London 1975, pp.663f.

14.　　James (1926) p.508 (with stylistic amendments).

15.　　James (1926) pp.518-519 (with stylistic amendments).

16.　　**Pistis Sophia** cc.2-6,E Hennecke,**New Testament Apocrypha**
　　　　vol.1, London 1973,pp.253-256.

17.　　C H Dodd, **The Appearances of the Risen Christ,** in **Studies
　　　　in the Gospels,** Oxford 1955,p.25.

18.　　Stein (1976) p.87f.

19.　　Boobyer (1942) p.14.

20.　　Thrall (1969-70) p.305. see fn.4.

21.　　Jn.20.2-10.

22.　　Thrall (1969-70) p.305.

23.   Boobyer (1942) pp.69-76.

24.   Boobyer(1942) pp.69-70.

25.   Mk.6.15; 8.28.

26.   Boobyer (1942) p.70.

27.   Boobyer's point (p.14) that we should not equate the ideas
           of Resurrection and Ascension, he bases on the argument
           that the NT texts themselves do not do so : 'To speak
           of it as a resurrection story and ascension story as if
           they were one and the same thing is a mistake which
           obscures a significant point. In the earliest thought of
           the church resurrection and ascension were ,no doubt, one
           and the same event; but well before the close of the NT
           period a distinction had been drawn between them, which
           put the ascension after a period of renewed association
           of Jesus with his disciples.In Luke's Gospel the change appears.'
           His argument,however,works against itself for by his own
           admission such a separating out of previously synonymous
           traditions of exaltation he attributes to Luke and then
           on through the rest of the NT texts; but our purpose in
           hand is to analyse the first of all the Gospel records -
           the text of Mark. We make a fatal error if we presume
           Mark will have the same theological ideas as Luke on
           this matter. Boobyer is right in his insistence that there
           is some differentiation to be observed in the various trad-
           itions of exaltation, but we should conclude that they are
           different nuances of approach to one and the same reality.
           The Ascension (Anabasis) theology of Acts 2.22-36,for
           example, is clearly a resurrection (Anastasis) kerygma,
           and is based on the resurrectional proof-text taken from
           LXX Ps.118.16 (see also Acts 4.11; 1 Peter 2.7; Mt.21.9
           and parallels; Mt.21.42 and parallels; Mt.23.39 ; Lk.13.35;
           Jn.12.13; Heb.13.6). There is,then, no strict division between
           these ideas even in the later NT texts. Boobyer has over-
           stated his thesis. Resurrection in the NT is essentially
           about 'lifting up' to enjoy enthronement glory (cf. the
           subsequent use of Ps.110 as a **testimonium** at Acts 2.35).
           This important passage in Acts finishes its argument at
           2.36 by stating that in his resurrection Jesus is constituted
           the Lord (of Ps.110) and the Christ (of Ps.16). Resurrection
           is thus a metamorphosis to heavenly glory.

28.   Note the καθεξης of Lk.1.3.

29.   cf J.Jeremias,**TDNT** 1,146-149.

30.   Is.38.18; Ps.6.6; Ps.88.5-13; Is.14.9-11.

31.   Deut.32.22; Ps.139.8; Amos 9.2; Prov.15.11; Job 26.6; Is.7.11.

32.　A similar concern can be seen in the Lazarus narrative when the Fourth Gospel insists he has been dead for **four** days to accentuate Jesus' power over death (on the fourth day the soul was thought definitively to set off for Sheol); cf.Jn.11.39.　CK　Barrett,**The　Gospel　acording　to　John.** 2nd Edn. London 1978,p.401.

33.　The εκ νεκρων formula of the NT.

34.　Eg. a sick man recovering his health has been 'rescued from Sheol' or 'lifted out of the pit of death'. cf. 1 Sam. 2.6; Pss.16.10; 30.4; 49.16; 86.13; 116.3f; Jonah 2.3f.

35.　The idea of after-life punishment in apocalyptic literature, so influential on the Christian consciousness, owes much to Persian and Hellenistic ideas of the after-life.

36.　cf. Mk.12.18-27 where Jesus and the Sadducees clash over the issue of Resurrection. Mark presents rabbinic apologetics in action here : over and against the Sadducean objection that the Word of God (eternally valid) suggests in Deut.25.5 that there shall be no individual resurrection, Jesus sets the more fundamental theophany text of Ex.3.6, basing his theological point on the present tense implicit in the name Yahweh, a present tense which embraces all over whom he is God. Thus, Abraham,Isaac and Jacob live in God's present and presence.

37.　One of the later parts of the Isaian text.

38.　Is.26.19 is the hopeful antithesis to the lament in Isaiah's apocalypse stated at 26.14. The reference to resurrection here 'probably refers to national existence' (Ringgren, cf **TDNT** 4.341). See parallels in Ezek.37f; Hos.13.14. The notion of the collective restoration of Israel was possibly the original significance attached to the mysterious exaltation of the Servant in Is.52.13; 53.10-12. The LXX keywords at Is.26.19 are αναστησονται and εγερθησονται & at Is.52.13 they are : υψωθησεται and δοξασθησεται.

39.　cf. Ps.139.8

40.　R H Charles. **The Apocrypha and Pseudepigrapha of the Old Testament.** Oxford 1913, vol.2. Henceforth **APOT,** p.203. Here four places are set apart for men's spirits: one with a bright spring of water for the righteous; one for sinners who escaped judgement on earth; one for sinners who are 'still making suit'; and one for sinners who are seemingly destined to be abandoned in the pit - neither slain nor raised again. Josephus attributes this view of the separation of the spirits to the Pharisees, cf. Ant.18.14

41.   Lk.16.23f.

42.   Ibid.

43.   cf. Lk. 16.26 : μεταξυ ημων και υμων χασμα μεγα εστηρικται

44.   Lk.16.9; 23.43;   Josephus ,as a Pharisee, held to the view
       that the souls of the righteous lived in the heavenly world
       and there awaited the resurrection, but he too retains
       the older tradition alongside this, that the souls of the
       righteous dwelt alongside the wicked in Hades. cf. Ant.18.4,
       Bell.Jud.2.163.

45.   cf. Mk.3.27. The Messiah's function par excellence is to
       give the sign of the Kingdom of God by breaking the power
       of evil. Such is the significance Mark attaches to Jesus'
       ministry of exorcisms summed up in this strong-man (Geber)
       pericope.

46.   cf. 2 Macc.7.23; 2 Macc.7.11,14; 14.46.

47.   The bracketed clauses are probable Christian interpolations.

48.   Test. Judah 25.4

49.   cf. Thrall (1969-70) p.306. A R C Leaney has identified
       them as suffering figures in his study :**The Christ, of the
       Synoptic Gospels,** suppl. to the New Zealand Theological
       Review, Selwyn Lectures 1966,pp.22-25.   The NT speaks
       of both as suffering figures, cf. Mk.9.11-13; Acts 7.17-
       44; Heb.11.23-29; Rev.11.3-10.

50.   G W E Nickelsburg, **Resurrection Immortality and Eternal
       Life in Intertestamental Judaism.** London 1972, cf. p.170.
       These forms are listed as : (a) the vindication of the right-
       eous man, (b) the judgement scene proper,(c) 'two-way'
       theology viz. texts speaking of right and wrong with their
       respective rewards and punishments outlined.

51.   Nickelsburg (1972) pp.170-180.

52.   cf. Jeremias, **TDNT** 5.684, and also his article : **Wisdom
       of Solomon 2.10 - 5. A homily based on the 4th Servant
       Song.** in JBL 76,1957,26-33.

53.   Is.13-14;52-53; and WS.2.10f; Dan.12; **Assumption of Moses**
       10; **Enoch** 104;   Nickelsburg (1972) p.171, and p.58f where
       he lists the parallelism of the forms.

54.   Nickelsburg (1972) p.170.

55.   Deut.34.5-8;   Deut.31.14,27,29;   Deut.33.1,50;   Deut.34.7;
        Jos.1.1-2.

56.   For the final Deuteronomic doxology cf. Deut. 34.10-12.

57.   Deut.34.7. In later legend his grave is mysteriously connect-
        ed with the cave of Macpelah. cf. TDNT 4.853-854.

58.   It is arguable that in popular piety, especially in the
        charismatic/apocalyptic circles of Judaism, Elijah was
        regarded as the more significant figure. See G Vermes,
        Jesus the Jew, London 1973, pp.58-82.

59.   Philo, **Vita Moysi** 1.162. αυτος εγενετο νομος εμψυχος τε
        και λογικος.

60.   Philo, **Vita Moysi,** 2.292; cf TDNT 4.851.

61.   Ex.14.31; Num.12.7,8; Deut.34.5 etc; Josephus Ant.5.39
        who calls him 'servant of God'; also Baruch 1.20;2.28,
        where the LXX version also attributes the title child/
        servant to him.

62.   Deut.34.11.

63.   Sir.45.1-6. Sir.45.2 in the Hebrew text reads :'He magnified
        him as a god.' The LXX translation softens this to 'as
        one of the saints'.

64.   cf. Jeremias, **TDNT** 4.850-851, referring to the texts of
        Eupolemus,Artapanus, Pseudo-Aristobulus, and Josephus.

65.   Ex.24. cf. Quaest. in Ex.2.29: transmutatur in divinum,ita
        ut fiat Deo cognatus vereque divinus.

66.   Philo, **Vita Moysi** 2.288f.

67.   Bar.in S.Deut.357 on Deut.34.5; cf.**TDNT 4.855 fn.97.**

68.   Midrash ha Gadol on Deuteronomy; cf. **TDNT** 4.855.

69.   **TDNT** 4.854.

70.   Excepting, of course, our text in consideration viz. Mk.9.4
        which may allude to such a tradition. cf. Chilton (1981)
        p.123.

71.   Ant.4.326.

72.   cf **TDNT 2.939.**

73.   Charles **APOT** 2.424.**Assumption of Moses** 12.5-6: 'All things which are to be in this earth (note future tense depicting the role which Moses will assume after his death) the Lord hath foreseen and lo ! they are brought forward (into the light)......the Lord hath on their behalf appointed me to (pray)for their sins and (make intercession) for them.

74.   Apart from the above cf. the ancient editorial amendment to the Manuscript at **Assumption of Moses** 10.13, APOT 2.422,fn.12; and ibid. n.2° p.408.

75.   The text is preserved in Clement of Alexandria, **Strom.** 6.15. See Charles **APOT** 2.407-409.

76.   Boobyer(1942) p.70f.

77.   Boobyer uses as one of his sources, the supposed oracle of Johanan ben Zakkai (If I send the prophet Elijah, ye (Moses) must both come together) which he himself acknowledges could be as late as 900 AD.

78.   Eg. on p.78 Boobyer explains away Moses' non appearance in most of the relevant texts he has examined to substantiate his thesis of an apocalyptic return of a Mosaic figure in the following terms : 'Is it not simply fortuitous that the names of Moses and Elias are not appended to the list on the last quotation?' He would have been better advised to conclude, as the lack of texts itself indicates, that there is not a solid apocalyptic tradition of a returning Moses, although there is a tradition of Moses' heavenly translation, and thus modified his exegesis of the Transfiguration narrative accordingly. Moreover his appeal to the Sibylline Oracle 5.256-259 (cf.APOT2.402) is highly dubious. If it is not a wholesale Christian interpretation as Lanchester notes in his edition, then it is a likely reference to the crucified figure we meet in the **Ascension of Isaiah,** although this is another text highly interpolated by Christians.

79.   Thrall (1969-70) pp.305-6.

80.   cf. Is.49.6; Jeremias **TDNT** 2.931.

81.   Mk. 6.15; 8.28.

82.   Mk.1.6 where the description of John's dress evokes that of Elijah in 2 Kings 1.8; se also Mk.6.14-15 where the name of John is associated with Elijah, and Mk.6.17f where the death of John is narrated with some implied parallels to the conflict of Ahaz and Jezebel with the prophet Elijah.The explicit identification of John with Elijah is

given to us at Mk.9.13.

83.   cf G.Vermes, **Jesus the Jew,** London 1973, passim.

84.   This is probably the irony lying behind Mark's represent-
ation of Jesus quoting Ps.22 from the cross at Mk.15.34-
35. The faithless crowd misinterpret this as a suppliant's
appeal to Elijah in his role as patron of the needy and
the dying. The evangelist wishes to highlight a truer faith-
response in terms of the Son of God title coming from
the lips of the centurion. His reaction takes the reader's
interest away from Elijah and serves to present Jesus in
his own glory as Son of God, in no way dependent on the
assistance of Elijah.

85.   cf. Lk.24.4; Jn.20.12; see also the heavenly witnesses of
Zech.3.4,7; Dan.7.16; 2 Macc.3.26. See Riesenfeld (1947)p.254

86.   Fresco 6; see Grabar, Revue de l'histoire des religions,vol.
123,1941,pp.161f; ibid. vol.124,1941,pp.14f.

87.   cf. B D Chilton (1981) pp.117-118 for the exegetical
argument. Mark regards the Elijah - Jesus association as
having some value (a) in depicting Jesus' charismatic
ministry, and (b) in providing some kind of parallel to
his Anastasis.

88.   For Enoch see Gen.5.24; Sir.44.16; 49.14; Jubilees 4.23;
Ethiopic Enoch 70.1f; Slav. Enoch 36.2; WS.4.10; Heb.11.5;
Josephus Ant. 9.28. For Elijah see 2 Kings 2.11; Sir.48. 9,12;
Eth.Enoch 89.52;93.8; Josephus Ant.9.28.

89.   So Jeremias, although I am not so sure that the latter
really is independent of Mk.9.4 in this regard.

90.   Jeremias, **TDNT** 2.939.

91.   Thrall (1969-70) pp.315-316. This theological concern of
his to explain the parousial problem is again evident in
his materials throughout ch.13 of the Gospel, where he
seems to be arguing against the belief that the fall of
Israel will usher in the end-time: cf. H Conzelmann, **Geschichte und eschaton nach Mc.13.** ZNTW 50,1959,210-221.

92.   Ps.89.12.

93.   For Sinai parallels in the Transfiguration narrative see
Chilton (1981) pp.120-121.

94.   Mk.3.13; 6.46; 13.3.

95. For the textual parallels between Mark's Transfiguration story and that of Gethsemane, cf. A. Kenny, **The Transfiguration and the Agony in the Garden.** CBQ 19,1957,444-452. If the Transfiguration is an epiphany of a metamorphosis to glory, then the agony is the other side of the coin, a metamorphosis to suffering. The two-fold metamorphosis symbolism of the Isaian servant theology (discussed subsequently) in Is.52.14-15 may be at the root of this parallelism.

96. Chilton (1981) pp.123-124.

97. Rom.12.2; 2 Cor.3.18; Mt. 17.2 following Mark; 1Peter 1.16.

98. Lk.9.29 : και εγενετο.......το ειδος του προσωπου αυτου ετερον. This type of metamorphosis description is clearly heightening the Moses parallelism by emphasising the radiant face motif; yet it is also reminiscent of the : εν ετερα μορφη of the Resurrection body at Mk. 16.12.

99. Την Νεμεσιν ποιει διωκομενην υπο Διος και εις ιχθυν μεταμορφουμενην. Athen.8.10; cf Behm,**TDNT** 4.756.

100. If we take the instance of the myth of Narcissus' metamorphosis we can see a deeper meaning attached to the story if we reinterpret it in the mystagogic manner - as symbolically figuring the destiny of the soul which becomes trapped in matter : 'The soul looks down from heaven and sees its own image mirrored in the deceptive surface of matter. Entranced by the sight it rushes to embrace the image and finds itself tumbling headlong into a watery grave. When it comes to, it is rooted in the cold earth, beautiful but unconscious.' J Godwin,**Mystery Religions in the Ancient World.** London 1981,p.53.

101. Mithraic lord of Time and deliverance from death. (Preisendanz,Magical papyri 13.581f) cf. Behm,**TDNT** 4.756.

102. Philo, **Vita Moysi** 1.57.

103. **Protreptikos** 1.4.3.

104. He is released from a donkey's body by the grace of the goddess Isis.

105. For the affinity of Μεταμορφωσις and Παλιγγενεσια see R Reitzenstein, (ET) **Hellenistic Mystery Religions**, Pittsburgh 1978,pp.39-40.

106. Viz. the rebirth to a different level of spiritual relationship

with Yahweh, as witnessed in the psalm text : For this day I have begotten you (Ps.2.7). That this motif may be operating in Mark's mind does not deny, of course, that the original tradition of the baptismal narrative was clearly based in its archetypal form on a haggadah of Is.63-64.

107.   cf. Reitzenstein,(1978) chapters 11-12.

108.   **Corpus Hermeticum,13.3 TDNT 4.757.**

109.   **Corpus Hermeticum,10.6.TDNT.4.757.**

110.   Words of the alchemist Zosimos. cf. Reitzenstein (1978) p.334. **Corpus Hermeticum** 4.11

111.   Seneca,Ep.6.1f. See also Ibid. Ep.94.48 : qui didicit et facienda ac vitanda percepit,nondum sapiens est,nisi in ea quae didicit animus eius transfiguratus est.

112.   Such is the import of the description in Apuleius' **Metamorphoses of Lucius** (The Golden Ass) c.18.

113.   cf. Reitzenstein (1978) pp.334-6.

114.   Apuleius, **Metamorphoses.c.18.**

115.   Philo, **Vita Moysi.** 2.28f.

116.   So Behm in his conclusion to his article in **TDNT** 4.758.

117.   This is not to deny that Mark is influenced by a similar vein of 'Hellenisms' ; such an influence can be discerned in his personal style of telling the miracle stories . (see fn.119).

118.   It is wholly indefensible to transform the John Mark of Acts and the Pauline (and pseudo-Pauline) literature into the 'Mark' of the Petrine pseudepigrapha and then on the basis of such a leaking argument transform him into our evangelist.cf. J. McGuckin. **Thoughts on the John Mark assumption. Zoe** vol.1,1982,pp.17-23. Journal of the Theological Faculty, LSU College, Southampton.

119.   See ,for example, the study by J M Hull, **Hellenistic Magic and the Synoptic Tradition.** London 1974.

120.   Mk.9.40 (cf. the Matthaean redaction of the same saying at 12.30 which I take to be the more authentic rendering. Mark seems to reverse the basic sense.) Caesar was reputed to have made such a remark about his chances in gathering

supporters for his bid for power on returning to Roman political life. At other instances Roman catchwords have influenced Mark's redaction. The list of 'Kalon' sayings at Mk.9.43, especially the recommendation that it is better to lose one's hand than to submit (to persecuting interrogators ?) is so obviously an allusion to the Roman hero Mucius Scaevola that Mark must have known his readers would have recognised the image.

121.   Cicero, **De Lege.** 2.14.

122.   **Kabod** (Glory) cf. Ps.29.3-5; Ps.97.2-6; Is.6.1-4. See also I Abrahams,**The Glory of God.** London 1925; Kittel/Von Rad in **TDNT** 2.237f; A M Ramsey, **The Glory of God and the Transfiguration of Christ.** London 1949.

123.   viz. the 'dwelling' of God. It is an attempt to go beyond crude anthropomorphisms and speak of God's presence in a transcendental way, eg. Lev.26.12 'I will walk among you', becomes in the Targum to the same text - 'I will cause my Shekinah to dwell among you.' cf Ramsey (1949) pp.18-20, **TDNT** 2.245-247. Shekinah may be rendered in Gk. by Σκηνη (tent or tabernacle) and thus we see points of contact made between the notions of God's Glory, and the 'tents' that may symbolise it.

124.   The redaction opens by stating that Moses and Elijah were seen 'in glory' but the following verse strongly suggests that the glory in which they became visible was not common or amorphous since we have a distinction made between : ειδον την δοξαν αυτου (Jesus alone) and και τους δυο ανδρας ; which I would read as follows : 'They saw his glory, and (they saw) the two men with him.' Luke's redaction goes further in appropriating all the 'glory' to Jesus.

125.   **TDNT** 2.249. 'Only the word and not the matter is peculiar to Luke.'

126.   Targum JI, cf. **TDNT** 2.246 : 'There shone the radiance of his features which had come to him from the light of the glory of the Shekinah of Yahweh.'

127.   'To Elijah too he imparted glory, and he thus gave life to one who was dead.......God will give the Messiah a share in his Kabod, and will invest him with his own raiment.' (Nu.r.15, on 10.2) also Pesikt.r.37.163a 'God will spread over the Messiah the radiance of his own glory.' See **TDNT** 2.246-247.

128.   cf. **4 Ezra** 7.97 :'Their face is destined to shine like the sun and they are to be made like the light of the stars

......for they are hastening to behold the face of him whom in life they served, and from whom they are destined to receive their reward in glory.' Charles **APOT** 2.589. See also 2 Bar.51.3,10; 1 Enoch 39.7; 1 Enoch 51.5; 104.2; 4 Ezra 7.125; Test. Levi 18.1-14; Mtt.13.43.

129.   1 Peter 1.21; 1 Tim.3.16.

130.   Rom.6.4.

131.   Acts.7.55

132.   Whose usage   of the word , as Kittel says, 'takes a decisive step by using in relation to Christ a word which was used in relation to God.' **TDNT** 2.248

133.   cf. Mark's eschatological use of the word 'Glory' at 8.38 and 10.37, and also the classic statement at 13.26.

134.   cf. Acts 1.22; 2.24; 2.31f; 4.33; 10.41; 13.33; 17.3,31; Rom.1.4; 1 Cor.15.1f; **TDNT** 1.370 fns. 11-12. In Heb.7.11,15 ανιστασθαι is used to signify elevation to the High Priesthood - an enthronement glory motif. For a general discussion of the interrelatedness of the concepts see W Kasper. **Jesus the Christ** London 1976 pp.146f.

135.   The 'amazement' of the onlookers of a glory-epiphany is, of course,clearly visible in the Transfiguration narrative but is not restricted to that : cf. Mk.1.22,27; 2.12; 4.41; 5.15; 5.42; 6.52; 9.6,15; 16.6.

136.   cf. A Kenny (1957) pp.444-452.

137.   Mt.17.2; Lk.9.29.

138.   V Taylor. **The Gospel According to St. Mark.** London 1957, p.389. Streeter, **The Four Gospels.** London 1924,pp.315f.

139.   See Chilton (1981) p.123f. The implication of the argument here is that the Sinai archetype that stands behind the Transfiguration narrative would have originally supported a Moses-Jesus typology where the radiant face would have been in order. Mark's redactive concern, as will be argued later, is to remove the Moses typology altogether, for Christological reasons; this necessitates in the process, the removal of the radiant face motif.

140.   cf. 2 Cor.3.7-18.

141.   Boobyer (1942) p.67.

142.   cf. Taylor (1957) p.389.

143.   1 Enoch 106.2,10; cf. Riesenfeld (1947) p.123 fn.44. See also the description of the saints in the **Akhmim Fragment** of the **Apocalypse of Peter** cited earlier.

144.   cf. Riesenfeld (1947) c.8 'La Robe Sacrée' pp.115-129.

145.   cf. Ex.28.4f; Ex.39.1f; Sir.45.6f; Sir.50.1f; Test.Levi 8.2; Philo Vita Moysi 2.109-135.

146.   The seamless robe of Jn.18.23 parallels Josephus Ant.3.7.4 (Lev.21.10).

147.   Mk.15.24.

148.   Which is most clearly brought out in the third of his mockeries : (a) as a prophet 14.65   (b) as a King 15.16-20   (c) as a Priest 15.29-30.

149.   Pseudo Aristobulus 99. cf. Riesenfeld (1947) fn.35 p.121.

150.   cf Matthew's redaction at 17.2 : τα δε ιματια αυτου εγενετο λευκα ως το φως .

151.   Thrall (1969-70) p.305.

152.   Thrall (1969-70) p.316 : 'I suggest that this was the kind of situation (viz. explaining the delay of the Parousia) Mark had in view when he wrote his account of the Trans-figuration......Jesus is raised from the dead, rather than translated to heaven, and consequently he is God's Messiah. In his own person he is the beginning of the eschaton and so the guarantor of its eventual consummation.'

153.   Lk.9.53; 13.33

154.   Thrall (1969-70) p.308.

155.   The word εκφοβος only occurs in the NT here and at Heb. 12.21. 'Where it refers to Moses in the face of το φανταζ-ομενον on the mountain of Exodus 19.' Chilton (1981)p.119.

156.   The rebuke Jesus gives to Peter in the Ethiopic **Apocalypse of Peter** for his 'foolishness' is done on Christological grounds : Christ will not suffer a tent built by the hands of men.

157.   Chilton (1981) p.118.

158.   **Évangile Selon S.Marc.** Paris. 1929, p.230.

159. Riesenfeld (1947) c.16. pp.265-280.

160. Ibid.p.233.

161. Ibid. p.234; cf. **Psalms of Solomon.**17.

162. Riesenfeld (1947) c.13.pp.223-235; also Goodenough,JBL 48,1929, 186- 97.

163. Riesenfeld (1947) pp.146-205.

164. Test.Abraham 20; cf the μοναι of Jn.14.2

165. cf. LXX Ezek.37.27; 43.7-9; Joel 3.21; Zech.2.10f; 8.3,8.

166. cf. Lk. 16.9 'into the everlasting tents'. Rev.13.6; 15.5; 21.3 - God dwelling in the tent with his saints; see also 1 Cor.5.1-4.

167. cf. Charles **APOT** 2.p.463 **The Secrets of Enoch.**

168. Dan.7.13; 4 Ezra 13.3 and NT parallels such as Mk.14.62.

169. Riesenfeld (1947) pp.293,295.

170. Ibid.p.269.

171. Thrall (1969-70) p.310 cf. fn.2.

172. For a fuller account see Riesenfeld (1947) pp.130-45.

173. cf. 1 Kings 8.10; 2 Chron.5.13; Ezek.10.3-5.

174. Or the 'smoke' of the Temple as depicted in Isaiah's vision (Is.6.1-13.)

175. Ex.24.16-17; Ex.13.22; 19.16.

176. Lk.1.35; cf. Riesenfeld (1947) p.139 who follows A.Allgeier, **Episkiazein:Lk.1.35,** in Bibl. Zeitschrift, 14,1916-17,338-343.

177. Thus I read the textual context of the αυτοις since the previous third person plural (εκφοβοι γαρ εγενοντο) referred to the three disciples. The αυτοις of the following verse seems to embrace these three alongside Jesus and the two prophets. Others would restrict the αυτοις to the latter three.

178. Riesenfeld (1947) p.135.

179. Chilton (1981) p.119.

180.   M.Goulder,**The Evangelist's Calendar,** London 1978,pp.279-280.

181.   This is seen not only by his account of the Baptist's own baptism of suffering (Mk.6.17f) but also by his identification of the term 'baptism' with martyrdom at Mk.10.39.

182.   W C Braithwaite, **The Teaching of the Transfiguration,** Expository Times,17,1905-1906,p.372.

183.   Amos 1.2; Is.29.6; 30.30f; Jer.25.30; Joel 2.11; 2 Sam.22.14; Ps.18.13; see also the response of the onlookers at Jn.12.29.

184.   **TDNT** 9.282-284 (Betz).

185.   **TDNT** 9.288-90.

186.   'Whereas in rabbinic literature these voices are looked upon as a sort of inferior substitute for prophecy, the NT commonly represents them as the directly heard voice of God.....' C K Barrett, **The Gospel according to St. John.** 2nd Edn. London 1978,p.425.

187.   Mk.1.24; 1.34; 3.11; 5.7.

188.   As in Mk.8.30.

189.   cf Chilton (1981) pp.123-124.

190.   Mk.9.30-32; 10.32-34.

191.   cf. Kenny (1957) p.444f.

192.   This is not to suggest that the patristic exegeses and the Markan theology are synonymous, which would be wholly anachronistic, but it does suggest some interesting lines of connection between the biblical and patristic ways of re-telling the Kerygma.

193.   The list of those who have read the narrative as a resurrection story is summarised by Stein(1976) fn.2 p.79.

194.   The chronological ordering of an apocalyptic tradition,while understandable as a search for narrative historical clarity, is ultimately self-contradictory.The apocalyptic tradition cannot be reduced to chronological schemata since the heart of the idiom lies in its being meta-historical in essence.

CHAPTER THREE
THE PATRISTIC INTERPRETATION OF THE TRANSFIGURATION

The Patristic interpretation of the Transfiguration of Jesus gives us the Fathers at their very best. We find here a study of more than a thousand years' tradition of highly symbolistic exegesis and mystical speculation. In the course of such a long Tradition-History, as would be expected, complex structures of theological inter-pretation evolved, and eventually came to be fixed by the repetition of later theologians. This present chapter is offered here as a summary prologue to part two of the study which offers the texts themselves in translation - texts that comprehensively represent the church's response to the biblical narrative of the Metamorphosis. The themes and doctrines of more than a millenium may, then, become more approachable if presented in a systematic form. Such a systematic reduction is of course alien to the expansive homiletic style of the Fathers themselves but may have value for the reader, especially one who is unfamiliar with Patristic writing, as a guide through the complex subtleties of the homilies.

The Patristic exegetes, needless to say, are far from being Redaction Critics in the modern sense of biblical criticism. Only a few had any critical awareness of Hebraic idiom and those that had this, had little of it. None of them could share the historical sense of the modern church. The kind of exegesis the Patristic church offers, then, is of a wholly different order. It works on different premises and by different methods. To take the Patristic exegesis as somehow opposed to the findings of modern criticism, and to prefer Patristics to modern commentary is a misunderstanding of the worst type. Theologians who strive to denigrate modern criticism because it is not patristic,[1] or those who regard the whole course of Patristic exegesis as 'antiquated nonsense' are suffering from the common ecclesiastical disease of reductionism. The

100

Patristic commentaries give us results, on their own premisses, that are often not only of the highest literary order and poetic merit, but even full of the most profound religious spirit and mystical vision. It is this that ensures their abiding place within the church's tradition of reflection on the biblical accounts of Jesus, not necessarily the interpretative details of their exegesis, many of which do not survive the insights of modern research into Primitive Christianity of the first two generations. It is an aspect, and always has been an aspect , of the true spirit of catholicism in the church that our understanding of Jesus evolves in the mutual interpenetration of scripture and tradition. Let us not have, then, Bible without Fathers, or Fathers without Bible but on the contrary read the whole Tradition of Christianity together for the wisdom and grace it has to offer us.

Even though the Patristic commentary on the Transfiguration is represented by so many of the major Fathers of both Eastern and Western churches, and stretches out over a millenium, it nonetheless becomes apparent on analysing the literature that this tradition of theological interpretation can be reduced to three main areas which summarise almost all of their more particular statements. These are: The Transfiguration considered as Theophany; The Transfiguration as soteriological event; and the Transfiguration as epiphany of the New Age. The Fathers thus analyse the event in the three modes of Theology, Soteriology, and Ecclesiological Eschatology. Let us begin our analysis with the primary category of Theophany. The Patristic writings will be referred to, but texts cited with the utmost economy since the full versions are given in part two of the book and can be stduied more comprehensively in their distinct contexts.

3.1. The Transfiguration as Theophany.

3.1.1. Divine Incognoscibility.

From the earliest writings on the subject we find the Fathers stressing the Transfiguration as proclaiming the hiddenness of God

as much as being a revelation. There is a strong homiletic theme:
Vere deus absconditus es (Is.45.15). Irenaeus in his **Adversus Haereses,**
who begins this theme in Transfiguration literature, comments on
the central paradox of the Transfiguration as being the impossible
made true - a revelation of the invisible deity that is authentically
accurate. It is an aspect of his Logos Theology; the basic premiss
of the Logos school being the mediating function   of the divine
Word who was considered as the Divine Power in its relations
ad   extra, especially creation and revelation. Irenaeus posits a
solution to the paradox he finds in the notion of a revelation of
an unseen God (with the help of Colossians 1.15) by means of his
theology of the Incarnation. Such a revelation is made authentic
and possible by a new economy: **Deus in carne absconditus.** 'He
truly revealed God to men, but also presented man to God, all the
while preserving the invisibility of the Father.'[2] Irenaeus demonstrates
the promise of God (The Word) to Moses - that he should look upon
the face of the Lord - as something that could not possibly be
fulfilled in the lifetime of Moses,but one that was fulfilled when
Moses was brought back from the dead to see the face of God-in-
the-flesh on the mountain of Transfiguration. By an ingenious
exegesis he notes that Moses saw God 'in the cleft of a rock'[3]
and this 'cleft' he interprets as the flesh of the Logos incarnate,
the final medium of revelation. Clement of Alexandria also
highlights the revelatory paradox to which the narrative testifies:
'He was numbered as a man, indeed, but was concealed as to who
he was.'[4] The selfsame concept is taken up in Gregory Nazianzen's
comments where he depicts the radiant light on the mountain as
the symbolic revelation of Christ's deity and yet stresses that its
effect was only partly revelatory since its power blinded the eyes
of the beholders: 'Light was that godhead which was shown to the
disciples on the mountain - a little too strong for their eyes.'[5]
Chrysostom defines the event as more a divine   ' condescension '
(Συγκαταβασις)   than a real revelation of God's glory,[6] and throughout

all his exegeses there runs this notion that the Transfiguration glory is but a poor symbol, radiantly beautiful though it may be, of the greater manifestation of glory that is to come when the saints see God as he really is, no longer in the limitations imposed by his bodily economy as the humble and suffering Lord. Chrysostom's 21st Homily does much to denigrate the sun as a fitting analogy for Christ's splendour. He takes the evangelist to task. The point he wishes to make is that any true revelation of the invisible deity must of its essence be an apophatic one that is rooted in the rational soul of the believer, wherein he finds his image and relationship with the Logos. Thus, Chrysostom rhetorically has the poor evangelist justify himself to God saying: 'Be merciful Lord for I did not say these things in foolishness but because of the poor limitation of our nature and speech. Nonetheless I do not remain standing in the poverty of these expressions but rise up on the wings of understanding.'[7]

Perhaps the greatest of the Patristic defenders of the divine incognoscibiity was Pseudo Dionysius the Areopagite, and it is, then, no surprise to find his exegesis of the Transfiguration narrative maintaining the same point. In the **Divine Names** he gives an elaborate theological demonstration that the radiance on the mountain is a harbinger of that true spiritual illumination of the New Age which will utterly transcend all our mental faculties. Pseudo Athanasius, writing a little earlier than Dionysius, puts it more simply and directly 'He will come again openly, in his own godhead, radiating an ineffable glory from that holy body of his which he took from Mary, just as he revealed it in part on the mountain.'[8] Maximus brings the theme to a classical resolution in his **Ambiguorum Liber** where he distinguishes between the incomprehensible essence of God and his revelatory operations: 'They learned mystically that the brilliance of his face which flashed with truly blessed radiance, overcoming the power of all eyes, was a symbol of his godhead which is beyond all mind or sense or essence or knowledge.' He depicts the revelatory medium of the event, in a memorable and esoteric phrase, as: 'an apophatic theological gnosis that sings of him as wholly uncontained.' His final word on the Transfiguration, later in the same book, returns again to stress the event as a sacrament of incognoscibility: 'For just as here the flashing of the light that came upon them overcame the power of their eyes, remaining incomprehensible to them, just so does God transcend all the power and working of the mind, leaving no trace upon the mind of any man who àttempts to think about him.' This theme of the divine incognoscibility, so strong among the Greeks, is largely restricted to Tertullian among the Latins, who is probably following Irenaeus when he notes[9] that the Father is wholly and continually invisible. It is the Son alone who can be seen, which is true for all the theophanies of the Old Testament since they are epiphanies of the Logos. Novatian repeats his sentiment.[10] Thereafter in the whole course of the Latin exegesis of the text it will only arise once more in the homily of Pseudo Leo who, in a manner again redolent of Irenaeus and undoubtedly dependent upon him, interprets the 'nether parts of God' which Moses saw[11] as the humanity of the Logos, and describes the Transfiguration in the Irenaean manner as the final fulfilment of God's promise to Moses that he should truly see the face of God. We could conclude, therefore, that this major theme of incognoscibility in the Transfiguration narrative, is an exegetical tradition proper to the Greeks and barely exists among the Latin Fathers except in texts that ultimately depend on the work of Irenaeus.

3.1.2.   The Charism of Spiritual Vision.

One possible consequence of the patristic stress on the invisibility and incognoscibility of God might well have been to devalue the revelatory nature of the event. This consequence the Fathers do not wish to invoke and so we find alongside, and as a mirror image of the previous theme, as it were, a consistent doctrine from the early Alexandrians to the high Middle Ages, of the special grace of spiritual vision that was afforded to the disciples on the mountain to make them receptive to things outside their grasp. The radiant light of deity was, then, truly invisible, ineffable and incognoscible if approached or viewed as a material phenomenon. The wonder was nonetheless a true revelation on the spiritual plane, and so it was that the disciples were given to see in a unique and special way. Clement is the first to articulate the doctrine: 'The disciples had not looked upon the light with fleshly eyes, for there is no affinity or intimacy between the light and the flesh except in so far as the Saviour's own power and will empowers the flesh to behold.'[12] But it is Origen who extrapolates it most fully and sets the pattern for subsequent generations of mystical doctrine. The concern is in a direct line of mystical tradition from the rabbinic theologians in the Targums who had portrayed the Kabod glory of the unapproachable God whose vision was fatal to the beholder in the new medium of the radiant Shekinah - that comprehensible light of the incomprehensible light. Like Clement before him, Origen emphasises the special election involved in the Transfiguration, an election symbolised in the chosen three disciples, and then offers us his own opinion, based upon this, that Jesus always appeared differently to each individual he met throughout his life, a difference that was dependent on the spiritual capacity of the beholder. This was why, he tells us, Judas had to kiss Jesus in the Garden of Gethsemani in order definitively to identify him to the guard.[13] Those who saw Jesus as a mean and abject figure (such as Celsus, Origen's pagan antagonist) were not seeing him, but were in fact looking at their own spiritual reflection in him. Likewise those who saw him solely as a sensible (or sensual) reality reflected their own limited spiritual capacities. Those alone who were of great and magnanimous spirit were capable of being graced with the vision of his truer self in a radiant Transfiguration. Origen's **Homily on Genesis** demonstrates the point succinctly, as does his **Commentary on Matthew.**[14] Maximus Confessor elaborates the notion with almost equal force in the seventh century, by which time it has been fed from the twin channels of Origenism and Pseudo Dionysian mystical speculation and has passed from being primarily a Christological statement (as it is in Clement and Origen) to become a doctrine of the mystical enlightenment of the Christian: 'So it was that the disciples passed over from the flesh to the spirit, even before they had ended their life in the flesh, by a change in the sensible operations which the Spirit effected in them, lifting the veils of the passions from their intellectual powers. Then, being purified in the senses of both body and soul, they were taught the spiritual meanings of the mysteries that were revealed to them.'[15] John of Damascus poetically expresses the paradox of the revelation of an invisible reality in his **Akrostich Hymn** when he says: 'The apostles see things that cannot be seen; the godhead shining out from the smallness of the flesh on Thabor.' In the **Festal Homily** he emphasises the mystical light as the revelatory medium: 'In this image he shows forth his own beauty for his face shines like the sun because it is made one, hypostatically, with immaterial light and so becomes the Sun of Righteousness.' By now we have all the basic materials for the later Hesychast approach to the Transfiguration: the doctrine of the revelatory energies of God as distinct from his essence, the mystical and purificatory effect of these energies in the faithful soul, and its ultimate readiness for the vision of God in uncreated light. The Hesychast approach is represented in our present texts only by Gregory Palamas.[16] Here the themes of the divine energies, and the uncreated light are very much to the fore, as could be expected in a work that was partly designed as an apologia. But the substance of his doctrine on the special manner of the revelation as an ineffable spiritual grace clearly locates him in the theological school of both Origen and Maximus.

This theme of a special faculty of spiritual vision being afforded to the disciples, is by no means as prevalent in Latin exegesis. It is found, as could be expected, in Tertullian and

Pseudo Leo, both of whom had spoken of the divine incognoscibility. Tertullian's approach to the issue in his **Adversus Marcionem** is already coloured by his Montanist sympathies: 'When a man is rapt in the Spirit, especially when he beholds the glory of God, or when God speaks through him, he necessarily loses his sensation because he is overshadowed by the power of God: a point concerning which there is a controversy between us and the carnally minded. It is quite easy to demonstrate that Peter was in ecstasy for how else could he have recognised Moses and Elijah except in the Spirit since no-one had their images or statues.'[17] Pseudo Leo asks himself exactly the same question about the problem of spiritual cognition in ecstatic revelation, again showing signs of being a close imitator of Tertullian, though he suggests an answer by quoting the exquisite hymn of Sedulius:

> 'O wondrous merit of these three
> who in the world
> saw things beyond the world's belief.
> Though their eyes knew it not
> by heart's light they saw Elijah
> And Moses bright with virtue.'[18]

Leo the Great, however, in a memorable passage, returns more directly to the Irenaean position when he discusses the epiphany as effective through the incarnate economy, and attributes the radiance, therefore, to the humanity of Jesus rather than his deity: 'This is that kingly radiance which pertains especially to the nature of the assumed manhood. He wanted this to be manifested to the three disciples for while they were still encompassed in mortal flesh it would be wholly impossible for them to gaze at or look upon the ineffable and unapproachable vision of the godhead itself.'[19]

3.1.3. The Ascent through Ascesis to the Vision of God

Closely related to the Patristic doctrine of the divine incomprehensibility is the manner in which man, a being of composite and corruptible nature, can approach to One who is non-composite and incorruptibly simple. The descent of the immaterial Logos into a fleshly epiphany is seen by the Fathers as itself the central validation of the possibility of man's approach to God. This scheme of the descending Logos is the revelatory movement considered from God's side to that of man. Yet in so far as God's revelatory out-reach is a soteriological act - done for man's sake not God's, and done to bring about an ontological rescue for a degenerating essence - then of its very nature it evokes and inspires a similar outreach to God from the side of Man. This is man's search for God. The fullness of revelation takes place when the divine condescension meets the highest human aspirations for the good and the beautiful. The Patristic exegesis of the Transfiguration gives over much space to the development of the notion which we may perhaps describe as the doctrine of the soul's transition by prayer and virtue to an ever deepening spiritual Katharsis, an ever increasing capacity of spiritual energy that at one and the same moment is a sacrament of the future in so far as it is a transcendent indicator within human experience that the vision of God is the ultimate destiny of man, and a sacrament of the present in so far as it brings about, in the course of its purifications, the very presence of the one the soul desires even within the limitations of the soul's condition. To approach to the contemplation of Him who is simple demands on the part of a composited subject some form of re-integration of being. The Patristic ascetical theology is quite clear on this and teaches that man's duty is to strive by prayer and virtue to re-establish the spiritual principles as the Hegemonikon of the whole human life. The soul which is consistently guided by its spiritual impulses rather than those of its fleshly nature is, in Patristic understanding, the closest to knowing what it is to be simple, or god-like, and it is to such a soul that God will bestow the heavenly visions of the life of simplicity.

Origen is the first to identify the mountain as the symbol

of the contemplative life[20] and the apostles' ascent as being
one of prayer and virtue that prepares the manifestation of God's
glory in the hearts of his faithful disciples. In the **Contra Celsum**[21]
he offers us an interesting symbolic exegesis on how Jesus gave
parabolic teachings to souls who dwelt on the plains, but for those
capable of climbing spiritual heights he gave a truer theophany.
This he takes as an enduring law of the spiritual life. Cyril of
Alexandria follows his great compatriot in his own exegesis of Luke
with some particularly beautiful comments on spiritual stillness
(Hesychia): 'He went up the mountain ... to show that an earthbound
mind would never be suitable for contemplation, only a mind which
has spurned earthly things and gone beyond all bodily matters to
stand alone in stillness beyond all the cares of this life.' Such a
mind, he goes on to say, will then be 'transformed into a certain
elect and godly radiance,'[22] like that possessed by its master on
Thabor. The theme of the soul's spiritual ascent to a radiant
metamorphosis in Christ forms the major substance of the
Festal Homily of Andrew of Crete. It is also the reason Maximus
posits as the cause of the special election of the three apostles:
'and so, some of the disciples of Christ, because of their diligence
in virtue, went up with him and ascended the mountain of his manifestation.'[23] The same ascetical doctrine is found in John of
Damascus in his **Festal Homily,** particularly section 10 of the same
which interprets the phenomenon as an ascetical symbol: 'It is necessary to leave earthly things behind on earth, to transcend this body
of lowliness and to stretch out towards that sublime and divine
mirror of love so as to see the things that cannot be seen.' The
whole section is devoted to the description of mystical ascent and
in the course of his doctrine he gives the memorable apothegm:
'Such a man will then pray of himself, for stillness (hesychia) is
the mother of prayer, and prayer is the revelation of the divine
glory.' In **Homily 35** Gregory Palamas draws an analogy between
the spiritual closeness of Christ and the soul, and the closeness of
Christ and his garments which are in a sense drawn within his

personal glory. Among the Latin Fathers the theme is only a minor one, represented by Jerome, Bede and Ambrose Autpertus. Jerome, in an exegesis of **2 Corinthians** attributes the daily transfiguration of the soul to the spirit of holiness. The Venerable Bede has the theme of moral ascent in a way reminiscent of Origen: 'In order to show his glory to his disciples he led them up a high mountain. This was to teach all of us who desire to see his glory, not to lie in the lowest pleasures or to serve carnal allurements, or to cling to earthly desires, but always to be lifted up to heavenly things, in love with what is eternal.'[24] Autpertus, a generation later than Bede, also turns his exegesis round this point: 'We should notice, however, that prayer precedes this glorification of the Redeemer. And Luke tells us that he climbed the mountain for this very reason, that he might pray. By this he evidently demonstrates how ceaseless prayer is essential for all who would strive to behold his glory; and not only praying in the depths, but always on the mountain. Only they can do this ceaselessly who do not succumb to earthly desires or the pleasures of vices, but rather bound fast in celestial love, look only to the things of heaven.'[25] He extends his treatment through the rest of his chapter as an exhortation to his monks to stay awake during the night offices of prayer. But in general the ascetical theme is nowhere developed among the Latins to the extent it is among the Greeks, which is unexpected given the profound moral cast of much of Latin homiletic, and explicable probably on the grounds that the approach emanates from Origen and is maintained by his Patristic sympathisers, whereas in the Latin West Origen had considerably less influence and a much smaller readership. Jerome and Bede were among the few Latins who were conversant with his works and it is apparent in their preservation of his tradition at this instance. Ambrose Autpertus picks it up in all probability from his reading of Bede.

3.1.4. The Epiphany of Christ's Deity.

Undoubtedly the major tenet of the Patristic exegesis of the Transfiguration is the interpretation of the epiphany as a manifestation by Jesus to the disciples of his own divine status. The theological stress, therefore, is subtly and deliberately placed. It is not a question, any longer, of God bestowing a status of glorification on Jesus since such a glorification would not be properly applicable until after the Resurrection and thus Thabor may only be tentatively evoked at best as a sign of what is to come. In the Patristic scheme such an attributed honour would be an **economic glorification,** part of the soteriological plan and limited to the bounds of the human condition within which God's act of salvation in Jesus was destined to be played out. What the Fathers, Greek and Latin, all concur in finding here, on the contrary, is an **essential glorification** - or the glory of his very being as the eternal Logos. Such a glory, being eternal, is unaffected by the unfolding stages of the economy and proper to him alone. This is the Christological vision that stands behind nearly every single Patristic commentator who treats the text. The wonderful epiphany of Jesus radiant on the mountain is seen not as a glory flowing to Jesus from without, but as a glory streaming from within. The whole tenor of all the Patristic exegesis, therefore, is properly speaking Christocentric rather than Theocentric as in biblical idiom. The entire Patristic vision is built firmly on the foundation of Pre-existent Logos theology.

One of Clement's main concerns in the **Excerpts from Theodotus** c.4, is to use the Transfiguration to symbolise the fact that the Logos cannot be considered as having been 'reduced' because of his incarnation. For Clement it was an economic not an essential Kenosis that he embraced as the 'power of the Father himself': 'He is the light from on high and he is that light revealed in the flesh. What became visible here was not secondary to the light on high, nor was it separated from on high when it was among us.' It is a theme that Athanasius is to develop at length in his **De Incarnatione.** Origen treats the same issue by relating the Metamorphosis concept of radiance on the mountain to the Kenotic metamorphosis hymn in Philippians 2.6f,[26] where the form of God is laid aside for the assumption of the form of a slave before a definitive resolution, at the end of the hymn, in a glorious exaltation. Origen, by means of a subtle exegesis, relates the idea to his doctrine that Christ appeared in different 'forms' according to the spiritual state of the beholder. For the chosen three, however, he is clear that the epiphany constituted a revelation **in forma dei:** 'Those who remain on the plains see Jesus according to the flesh, in the form of a slave, but on the mountain he is known in his divinity and seen in the form of God according to their knowledge.'[27] Gregory Nazianzen depicts the Transfiguration as the highest form of Theophany: 'Light was that godhead which was shown to the disciples on the mountain.'[28] And in the **De Moderatione in Disputando** he posits Christ's desire to give such a revelation as the sole motive behind the event. At about the same time the theme surfaces in Latin exegesis from Ambrose onwards and thereafter becomes the dominant theological note in the West as well as the East. Ambrose of Milan in his **De Fide** and again in his **Expos. in Lucam** spends much time commenting on the appearance of Moses and Elijah in order to differentiate their ontological and functional status from that of Christ: they are as slaves before their Lord, a theme also taken up by Augustine.[29] Christological doctrine is the dominant concern also in the **Tractatus** of Pseudo Augustine who applies his entire exegesis as a biblical refutation of subordinationist Christology in the Arian mode. The Christocentric interpretation of the narrative keeps pace, as we could expect, with the developing tradition of Christology within the church. By the time of John of Damascus, for example, the Christology has become more and more articulated to the point that the homilist can deduce the detailed format of Neo-Chalcedonian orthodoxy from the events on the mountain.

The clearest Latin exposition of the Christological mean-ing of the narrative can be found in Leo, one of the great Patristic architects of classic Christological orthodoxy. He has a developed section at the beginning of his **5lst Homily** on the theme that the teachings of Jesus are, in themselves, a parable of his humanity, his miracles on the other hand demonstrate his deity. The approach is found epitomised in that most familiar sentence of his Tome: **Una coruscat miraculis una succumbit injuriis.** In his Transfiguration exegesis he notes that as Peter had by faith confessed Christ as the Son of God on the basis of the 'human' sign of his teachings, so here he is granted the confirmation of the same faith by the epiphany of Christ's deity in glory. At the end of the same homily, commenting on the Father's voice, he interprets this as a demonstration of the mystery of distinctness and unity within the person of Christ and between the Son and the Father: 'The Father was indeed present in the Son and the essence of the begetter was in no way separated from the only begotten in that glory of the Lord, even though allowance was made for the limited vision of the disciples. The voice came for the commendation of the proper nature of each person.[30] And so in the vision the splendour of the body signified the Son, and in what they heard, the voice from the cloud announced the Father ... They trembled not only at the Father's majesty but also at the Son's for in a higher sense they understood the one deity of each person.' Among the Greeks the Christocentric interpretation is especially notable in the work of Chrysostom whose exegesis on the Transfiguration had much influence on Cyril and many later Fathers. He begins his exposition in **Homily 21** with the notice:'What does 'transfigured' mean? It means that he opened out a little of the godhead and showed them the indwelling deity.' The radiant illumination of Christ on the mountain was, then, his own divine nature mediated through the flesh which he himself allowed to beam out by an act of personal power (his 'eighteenth miracle' as Gregory Nazianzen says in the **Carmina**) as a private revelation to his chosen disciples. This theological approach is distinctive and proper to Patristic exegesis. Apart from those instances already observed it can be clearly discerned in Hilary,

Jerome, Proclos of Constantinople, Pseudo Athanasius, Anastasius of Sinai, Maximus, and Gregory Palamas. It forms the very backbone of John of Damascus' **Festal Homily** who, as a Patristic synthesist by profession, may rightly be taken as a single accurate indicator of how central this Christological theme is to all the Patristic exegeses of the narrative. It is to Palamas, however, the latest of the writers included in this present study, that we shall give the last word on the subject: 'According to the theologians, Christ was transfigured not by receiving something he did not have before, nor by being changed into something he previously was not, but as manifesting to his disciples what he really was, opening their eyes and from blind men making them see again.'[31]

3.1.5.   The Revelation of the Inner Life of God

Trinitarian speculation forms the last subject of the exegetical writings that consider the Transfiguration as a Theophany. It is not a major theme but it is a notable one in a few of the Greek Fathers. The Latins share with the Greeks the preliminary observation that the voice of God on the mountain not ony validates and confirms Jesus' claim to be the Son of God, but also confirms the distinctness of the divine persons themselves for the sake of the Church. The extrapolation of this insight into a full-scale meditation on the Trinity is, however, something that is not found in Latin exegesis at all, and even among the Greeks is restricted to Origen and Andrew of Crete. The former interpretation of the voice of God as a validation of Jesus' claims can be summed up in the words of Eusebius: 'The Father's voice comes through the cloud for this is the way God appears, and bears witness to the sonship of the Christ.[32] It was not fitting that it should be only from Peter that we should know that he was the Christ,the Son of the Living God, or that our understanding of him as coming from the heavenly Father should have come solely from Peter's testimony; and so the

Father's own voice sets the seal of truth upon this confession and witnesses that he is the Son of God.'[33] Or again in the words of Leo, for the Latins: 'This was a profound and far reaching testimony that was heard more in the force of the words than in the sound of the voice, for when the Father said: 'This is my beloved Son in whom I am well pleased', they heard quite plainly: 'This is my Son who is from me and with me, and who is eternally ... This is my beloved Son whom godhead does not separate from me, power does not divide and eternity does not distinguish. This is my beloved Son, not an adopted Son but a true son. He is not created by another but begotten from me; not made like me from a different nature, but from my own essence born equal to me.'[34]

This theme of the Father's validation of the Son[35] is a standard part of most patristic comment on the voice from the cloud. It is the appearance of the cloud itself, however, that becomes in Origen's treatment a symbol of the Trinitarian life of God revealed, an allegorical meditation that did not command sufficient Patristic support to become a normative exegetical **typos,** probably because within the same exegesis of Matthew, Origen offered the alternative exegesis that perhaps the bright cloud was a symbol of the Resurrection. He offered his trinitarianism, therefore, as a distinctly speculative possibility ; and even then it occurs within the ambit of what is for us a mutilated text: 'The bright cloud of the Father, Son, and Holy Spirit , overshadows the genuine disciples of Jesus.' Andrew of Crete[36] appears to be a solitary disciple in this regard. The identification of the cloud as the Spirit of God is a distinct and different notion and may be discovered in Hilary and John of Damascus. The former says: 'But while he was still speaking, white clouds overshadowed them and they were surrounded by the Spirit of divine power.'[37] It is not possible to relate this theme in Hilary to the trinitarianism suggested by Origen, however, as the former is much affected by primitive Christian binitarianism and his pneumatology is nowhere as prominent as that of Origen. A similar pneumatic interpretation survives in John of Damascus: 'The voice

of the Father came from the cloud of the Spirit: This is my beloved
Son. This is He who is.'[38] But nowhere in the text of John is
a trinitarian exegesis attempted, for him it is a purely Christocentric
epiphany.

3.2. The Transfiguration as soteriological event

The Fathers consider the Transfiguration event within the
wider terms of God's salvific economy in Jesus. Such an economy
is the whole reason for the appearance of the Logos in human form,
and a salvific motive therefore underlies the epiphany from the very
start. For the earlier Fathers, and in this case that means everything prior to the seventh century, the soteriological aspect of the
Transfiguration is treated under two aspects only; the preparation
of the Church for the Lord's Passion, and then the public ratification
of the New Covenant in the face of the Old. The Later Fathers
introduce a new treatment into the consideration, that of the deification of the flesh affected in the wonderful events. It is a
theological approach that is very ancient in Patristics, but which
does not form part of this exegetical tradition until after the
seventh century.

3.2.1. The Transfiguration as a Prelude to the Passion.

The first of the themes can be found in Cyril who interprets the
radiant epiphany as a kind of strengthening sacrament for the
apostles who were approaching the trials of the Passion. In his
9th Homily he says: 'In order to refashion them as men of courage
he inspired within them the desire of his glory for he said: I tell
you there are some of you standing here who will not taste death

until they see the Kingdom of God.' Following Luke's text Cyril draws his readers' attention to the fact that within such radiant glory the Lord's chosen subject of conversation with his prophets was 'the mystery of the economy in the flesh and the saving Passion which was to be upon his honourable cross.' Anastasius of Sinai, similarly following Luke's text about the prophetic conversation, comes to the same point as Cyril: 'According to Luke they talked with Jesus about his death which was to be fulfilled at Jerusalem. So it was that the disciples heard from them what they had not understood when Jesus had spoken to them, when Peter, thinking the things of man, rebuked Jesus for saying that he would be killed by men.'[39] Among the Latins the theme is eloquenty presented by Jerome and Leo. The former notes the trauma of the Cross as something the disciples could not hope to bear without the Lord's support. And so, like Cyril, he interprets the Logion of Mark 9:1 as an encouragement before trial: 'He wanted the apostles' dread to be healed by the hope of these promises.' And he adds: 'That knower of secrets who foresaw their objections, compensated their immediate fear with an immediate reward.'[40] Leo comments on the salvific purpose of the events as follows: 'The Transfiguration chiefly occurred for this end that the scandal of the cross should be taken away from the hearts of the disciples; and so that since they had been given the revelation of his secret majesty, the abasement of the Passion might not confound their faith.'[41]

3.2.2.   The Harmonisation of the Two Covenants

Speculation on the two covenants runs apace throughout almost all the Patristic exegesis on the narrative, both Greek and Latin. This is largely because of the appearance of Moses and Elijah alongside Christ. Irenaeus and Tertullian take their appearance as evidence that the God of the Old Testament and the New, are one and the same, thus refuting Marcion. But the main line of approach is that the two prophets symbolise the whole of Judaism under the titles of Torah and Prophecy, and how they harmoniously announce the coming of the Lord. Asking why they were present on the Mount of Transfiguration, Cyril answers for us: 'It was in order to show that the Law and the Prophets were the attendants of Our Lord Jesus Christ whom they foreshadowed to be the Lord both of the Law and the Prophets.'[42] As Proclos put it[43]: 'A high mountain on which The Law and the Prophets conversed with Grace.'[44] The same notion runs through all the Latins from Tertullian to Ambrose Autpertus, and as such is a regular **typos** of the exegesis.

Both these approaches to the soteriological value of the Transfiguration, however, are in a sense peripheral and secondary. Neither of them comes near the profundity of the third aspect of the soteriological interpretation (one that is notable not least for the way it emerges so late in this tradition) and that is the Patristic doctrine of salvific deification effected in the radiant epiphany.

3.2.3. Transfiguration and the Deification of the Flesh.

The notion of the deification of the flesh as a primary and salvific effect of the Incarnation of the Logos had been systematically set out as long ago as the early Alexandrian Fathers but it is not until the time of Andrew of Crete that we find any allusion to the idea in the course of the Transfiguration commentaries. Subsequently it is found in John of Damascus and Gregory Palamas. It is a theme wholly absent from Latin exegesis of the text as far as I can discern. As a soteriological interpretation of the epiphany it has far greater capacity than the earlier traditions and it is certainly strange that the theme (already well established in Christological thought) should have taken so long to be adopted in this area.

Andrew of Crete opens his **Festal Homily** with the words: 'Today we celebrate this feast, the deification of our nature, its transformation to a better condition, its rapture and ascent from natural realities to those which are above nature.' For him this deification is clearly an ecclesial mystery 'the deification of **our** nature' that flows directly from the greater mystery of the indwelling of the Logos in human flesh. He is following the line of thought set out by Athanasius in the **De Incarnatione** that the primary and greatest salvific act of God is the very Incarnation of the Logos, his epiphany as man, which thereby transforms human nature to a new and better ontological condition.

John of Damascus comes to a similar point by means of the Christological terminology of the hypostatic union. His Christic starting point means that for him the deification of the flesh is not proposed as an ecclesial sacrament as it is in Andrew, but interpreted (at least in this instance here) as something proper to the Man-God: 'Now are things seen that are beyond the eyes of man - an earthly body radiating the divine splendour, a mortal body pouring forth the glory of the godhead. For the Word is made flesh and flesh is made Word; though neither departs from its wonderful nature. O wonder exceeding all thought. Glory did not come to this body from without but from within, by the Word of God uniting it hypostatically to his own supreme deity in a manner past all telling ... This act of union happens hypostatically so that the things that are united are one, and form but one hypostasis in a distinction without division and with the unconfused union of the conjunction of hypostases safeguarded,[45] and the duality of natures preserved through the immutable incarnation of the Word and the incomprehensible and unchanging deification of the mortal flesh.'[46] The technicalities of the language, evidently designed to invoke the authority and terms of the 4th and 5th General Councils have almost lost for us the symbol of deification here, but it is apparent on a second reading of his final sentence above, that John too equates deification of the flesh with the salvific act of the Logos' own incarnation. This again is evidently in the Athanasian manner: 'He became what we are in order that we might become what he is.'[47] And although the exegesis of John remains wholly Christocentric at this point we need not thereby rule out of place the notion that the deification of the Second Adam's flesh was a gift won also for his Church.

Palamas witnesses to this theme, and it is an approach that may be particularly associated with the Hesychast school for whom the Transfiguration became so central and so profound a symbol, and who formed the present Transfiguration theology characteristic of the Greek Church today. He is referring to the concept we have met previously of the disciples being spiritually capacitated for a supra-sensible vision, but he goes on explicitly to relate this as a particular symbol of the deification effected in our nature by the incarnation of the Logos. When he talks in this passage of 'those who see the light' he is thinking not only of the three apostles but of the hesychast monks whom he was defending for their claim to be able to see the uncreated light of God in prayer, and beyond the monks even, of the possibility given to all Christians of the vision of God's light in Christ: 'So evidently that light is not sensory and it is clear that those who see it do not do so with sensory eyes only as transformed by the power of the Spirit. And so, they themselves were changed, and were therefore able to see this change taking place . This was not something new that happened, for it derived from his assumption of our condition which was thereby deified by this union with the Word of God.'[48] The Metamorphosis of Jesus, in the hands of this masterful theologian, becomes a radiant sacrament of the ontic and moral transformation of the believer living the Christ-life. This is the soteriological exegesis of the narrative at its highest flowering. His **35th Homily,** in the extracts provided in the present study, shows his continued development of the moral implications of this divine metamorphosis.

3.3. The Transfiguration as epiphany of the New Age.

The third and final aspect of the Patristic exegesis of the Transfiguration is its interpretation as a demonstration of an aspect of the New Age. Several of the Fathers treat the phenomenon as being related to the mystery of the Kingdom of God, the Parousia, or the 'Future Age', but almost without exception these concepts are regarded as synonymous, or at least readily interchangeable. The major interpretative school for both Greeks and Latins, however, is without question the correlation of the Epiphany on the mountain with the mystery of the Resurrection glory of the Lord. The other concepts such as the New Age or the Parousia can be regarded as synonyms in Patristic writing for they are no longer being used in their originally distinct biblical connotations. They are seen by the Fathers through the resolving mirror of Pauline and Lukan soteriology and have been reduced as subthemes to the now dominant notion of the Resurrection of Jesus. This too, has been refashioned in Patristic theology by being now wholly interpreted by means of Logos theology and it is seen not as a mystery gained for his own sake but as something brought about for the sake of his Church. The Resurrection of Jesus thus signifies for the Fathers what Paul intimated by his theology of the 'First-fruits', and the glory of the Lord is a paradigm of the glory that he will bestow upon all his faithful. This is why the Resurrection of Jesus is seen by the Fathers as being **per se** that New Age of fulfilled union with God, and why all the other notions such as Kingdom, or Parousia are rightly speaking no longer separate theological ideas from the Resurrection approach.

3.3.1. The Kingdom and the Parousia foreshadowed.

A few of the Fathers interpret the epiphany as a mysterious revelation of what Jesus meant by the 'Kingdom of God'. Such an interpretation is found in Cyril, Andrew, Anastasius, John of

Damascus and Gregory Palamas, among the Greeks, and in Hilary and Jerome among the Latins. It is surprising in a sense that it was not a more widespread view given that the biblical logion immediately preceding the Transfiguration narrative (Mk.9.1) explicitly introduces a promise that the disciples should see the 'Kingdom come in power'. Origen had probably discouraged such an interpretative school by offering his own opinion that such a view was an 'unspiritual exegesis'. Gregory Palamas is the only one who seems to have explicitly seized on the coincidence of the biblical text when he says: 'See how he identifies the Father's glory and his own Kingdom with the light of his own Transfiguration.'[49] Hilary was the first to develop the theme. He does so in the context of an exegesis of I Cor.15.26, and explains what the 'presently reigning body of Christ' is by reference to the epiphany on the mountain: 'And he was transfigured before them and his face shone like the Sun ... Here the glory of the body of Christ coming into his Kingdom was shown to the apostles. In this manner of the glorious transfiguration, the Lord stood revealed in the splendour of his reigning body.'[50] In the following chapter of the same text he interprets the selfsame 'manner' as the glory of the Parousia - again demonstrating that for the Fathers there is no great conceptual difference in the terms. Jerome interprets the ascent of the mountain as 'part of the Kingdom' mystically fulfilling that text: 'Many are called but few are chosen'[51], but he sees the Transfiguration itself in Parousial terms: 'There appeared to the apostles what the future would be like in the time of Judgement.'[52] Basil sees the event as the disciples catching a glimpse of the beginnings of the Parousia[53]; and in a fine passage Cyril of Alexandria interprets the epiphany as both a Parousial mystery and the inner meaning of the term 'Kingdom of God': 'The Kingdom he spoke of was the vision of his glory in which he will be seen in that time when he will shine out upon all men on earth.'[54] Andrew of Crete in another piece of fine Christological poetry describes the radiance as 'the unapproachable glory of that Kingdom' and identifies the

essence of what the Kingdom really is as the person of Christ himself 'shining brighter than the Sun for our sake and the sake of all
that is ours.'[55] Anastasius describes the whole event as a partial
and enigmatic demonstration of the Kingdom, and this treatment
thereafter becomes established exegetical tradition in the Greek
Fathers. John of Damascus in his **Akrostich Hymn** calls the
Transfiguration a revelation of the Second Coming: 'The Most High
God was seen by the apostles standing in the midst of the gods[56],
standing in ineffable radiance on Thabor with Moses and Elijah so
that the mystery of the Second Coming might clearly be revealed.'
The interpretation remains basically a Greek one not common in
the Latins.

3.3.2.   The Transfiguration as Resurrection Glory.

By far the greatest concurrence of texts suggests that the majority
of the Latins as well as the Greeks agree in seeing the epiphany
as essentially something to do with the Resurrection glory of the
Lord. There is hardly a Father who does not have something to
say on this issue, and it can be rightly taken alongside the
Christological exegesis (the manifestation of Christ's essential deity)
as the second great **typos** of all Patristic exegesis on the subject.

Some of the Fathers engage in number speculation based
on the symbol of the 8th day - which was the transcendence of
the Hexaemeron Creation symbolism, the cipher of the Age of New
Creation, or Paradisial life. Such 8th day speculation is found in
Clement and Origen and then falls out of favour until the late
period when it resurfaces in Andrew of Crete, John of Damascus,
and Gregory Palamas. Among the Latins it is a minor theme found
only in Hilary, Ambrose, and Bede.

Three of the Greek Fathers (Cyril, Andrew and John of
Damascus) interpret the appearance of the two prophets as a sign
of Resurrection - Christ the Risen Lord raising by his word of

command one figure from heaven and the other from Hades. In Latin exegesis only Jerome represents the idea[57]. Almost all the Greeks and Latins concur, however, in seeing the epiphany as a revelation of what the Resurrection will be like for both Christ (it is thus considered as an anticipation in his ministry of his Paschal victory) and for his church in the age to come. Clement's text is, perhaps deliberately, ambivalent in that it can be referred either to Christ or the church. Either way it clearly indicates a theology of Resurrection: 'He gave the revelation for the sake of his church that it could learn about its/his advancement after it/he passed from the flesh.'[58]

Origen has a lot to say on the matter. For him the Resurrection is a key to the whole mystery of the Transfiguration. He thus accounts for Jesus commanding the apostles to remain silent: 'Since his glorification in the Resurrection is akin to his Transfiguration and that vision of his face like the sun, this is why he wished the apostles to speak of these things after he rose from the dead.'[59] In his **Commentary on Ps.l**, he uses the epiphany as a symbolic demonstration that in the Kingdom of God we shall have spiritual bodies adapted to our new environment; a view that was to cause great controversy after him, but one that recurs time and time again in his work. Cyril of Alexandria partly follows him in also seeing the Transfiguration as a symbolic demonstration of what risen bodies shall be like, and a confirmation of the Church's hope that it shall rise alongside its Master: 'Since they had heard that our flesh had to rise again but did not know in what form it would be, he changed his own flesh in order to give an example of the transformation and to confirm our hope.'[60]

For Methodius, Theodoret and Antipater, their whole exegeses are carried out within the context of a Resurrection apologia. Antipater and Methodius in particular are concerned to counter the growing tide in favour of Origen's spiritual approach to the Resurrection. Among the Latins the Resurrection interpretation is equally strong and runs consistently through all the great commentators from Tertullian to the High Middle Ages; including Hilary, Ambrose, Jerome, Augustine, Gregory, Bede and Autpertus. The only two Fathers who do not represent the approach are Cyprian (who does not address the Transfiguration narrative directly in any case) and Leo (who has designed all his narrative as a dogmatic meditation on the person of Christ).

Tertullian uses the Transfiguration in the course of a philosophical argument that metamorphosis is distinct from annihilation of substance, and the transfiguration of Jesus therefore demonstrates a symbolic continuity of personal identity from one state of existence to the next. In the **De Resurrectione Carnis** it is an important part of his argument for a bodily resurrection. Augustine interprets the Lord's gesture of raising up the fallen disciples (in the text of Matthew) as a mystical allusion to the Resurrection, just as he interprets their falling down to the ground as a symbol of man's destined fall into the grave.[61] Jerome follows Tertullian, therefore opposing Origen , to teach that the epiphany demonstrates the substantiality of the risen body. And the anonymous Pseudo Jerome in his **Commentary on Mark,** in a manner reminiscent of Leo's homily, again reads the event as an anticipation of the glory of Easter to prepare the disciples for the trial of the Passion: 'He was transfigured in the presence of the disciples so that they who had seen with their own eyes the glory of the future resurrection, should not be afraid of the shame of the cross.'[62] Gregory offers the same interpretation in his **Moralium in Job** as if it were by now an evident and established exegetical tradition: 'In this Transfiguration what else is announced other than the glory of the final resurrection.' For Bede it is a theme to which he returns often like his mentor Origen, whom he evidently admired but followed with typical English reserve and caution. In his words: 'When the Lord was transfigured before the disciples he revealed to them the glory of his own body which was to be manifested through the Resurrection. He shows how great will be the splendour of the future bodies of the elect after the Resurrection. On this matter he says elsewhere: Then shall the just shine like the Sun in the Kingdom of their Father[63], and here as a sign of his own future splendour his face is as radiant as the Sun.'[64] This can stand for us as the perfect symbol of how the theme of the Risen Glory of Christ is used in all the Fathers as not so much a glory that advances the status of Jesus himself, but a glory that advances the status of his church, a salvific power that rescues his faithful from the powers of death and transfigures them 'like the sun' in the Kingdom of the Father.

3.4.1.   Conclusions

This brief synthesis represents the Patristic doctrine of Transfiguration as outlined in the exegeses of the biblical narrative from the second to the fourteenth centuries. The Fathers evidently pursue three concerns; the wonder of the event as a theophany, the power of the event as a salvific act of God, and the promise of the event as a paradigm of the Resurrection of Christ's saints. Within the whole tenor of the Patristic analyses two great themes emerge and they are firstly the vision of Christ's radiance as a manifestation of his own essential deity, a glory that did not come on him from without but rather proceeded out to his disciples from within; and secondly that the power which shone out from Jesus on the nucleus of his church should be interpreted as his promise of Easter transfiguration for that church universally. These are great and lofty themes and best read from the texts themselves to absorb all the original nuances. Before coming to the trans-lations, however, there is one final excursus that remains to be done, and it can stand in a sense as a concluding summary to the whole first part of this study: it is to look at the Transfiguration of Jesus as a spiritual symbol in the liturgy and hymns of the church; or how it has formed a spiritual tradition around itself. It shall be a brief review, and therefore a very short chapter but for a complete treatment of the Transfiguration it would be unthinkable to omit it.

NOTES TO CHAPTER THREE

1. As for example in the somewhat disappointing book of G. Habra: **La Transfiguration Selon Les Pères Grecs.** Paris 1973. which justifies its wholesale omission of any biblical perspective by attempting to argue that the entire findings of modern exegesis are misguided.

2. **Adv. Haer. 4.20.7.** The Patristic references in this chapter are primarily designed to refer to the translated texts in part two of the study. Complete references to the Patristic writings will be given there next to the relevant translations.

3. **Adv. Haer. 4.20.9.**

4. **Strom. 6.**

5. **Orat.40. De Baptismo.**

6. **Ad Theodorum Lapsum.**

7. **Hom. 21.**

8. **Ep. De Incarnatione.** c.4.

9. **Adv. Praxean.** 15.

10. **De Trinitate.** 18.1.

11. Ex. 33.23.

12. **Excerpts from Theodotus.** c.5.

13. **Contra Celsum.** 2.64. cf. J. McGuckin. **The Changing Forms of Jesus according to Origen.** Origeniana Quarta. Innsbrucker Theol. Studien, Bd. 17. 1986

14. **In Matthaeum.** 12.37.

15. **Ambiguorum Liber.** 1st excerpt presented in translation.

16. Hom. 34, and 35 passim. For further reading on the subject see my own version of **Symeon the New Theologian: Practical and Gnostic Chapters,** Cistercian Studies No.41; with relevant bibliography and preliminary introduction. Kalamazoo 1982.

17. **Adversus Marcionem.** 4.22.

18.   Ps. Leo. **Homily 20;** Sedulius, **Carmina** 50.3. vv.284f.

19.   **Hom.** 51.2.

20.   **In Matt.** 12.

21.   **Con. Celsum.** 2.64.

22.   **In Lucam.** 9

23.   **Ambiguorum Liber.** Excerpt 1.

24.   **Hom. 28.**

25.   **Orat. De Transfiguratione.** c.5.

26.   The only Father expressly to use the Philippians text apart from him is, I believe, Anastasius of Sinai, **Festal Homily** c.4.

27.   **In Matthaeum** 12.37.

28.   **Orat. 40, De Baptismo.**

29.   **Hom.** 28

30.   In which he means not the distinct ousia/natura of each person but the natural distinctness of persons.

31.   **Hom.** 34.

32.   Mt. 16.17.

33.   **Expos. in Lucam.**

34.   **Hom.** 51.6.

35.   Which Origen (and Jerome following him) interpret as the fulfilment of Jesus' prophecies in Jn.5.37, and 8.18. cf. PG.97.953.

37.   **In Matt.** 17.

38.   **De Transfiguratione.** c.16.

39.   **Festal Hom.** c.5.

40.   **In Matt.** 3.17.

41.   **Hom.** 51.3.

42. **Hom.** 9

43. Probably thinking of Jn.1.17.

44. **Orat.** 8.1.

45. John can talk of two hypostases in Christ united uncon-
     fusedly in one hypostasis because he follows Leontius of
     Byzantium's interpretation of Chalcedon in which he
     offered the Christological model of the Enhypostatisation
     of the human person within the divine in a theoretically
     real yet wholly dependent relationship.

46. **Festal Hom.** c.2.

47. **De Incarnatione** 54.

48. **Hom.** 34.

49. **Hom. 34**

50. **De Trinitate.** 11.37.

51. Mt. 22.14.

52. **In Matt.** 3.17.2.

53. **Hom In Ps.44.**

54. **Hom. 9.**

55. **Orat. 7.2.**

56. cf Ps.82.1f.

57. **In Ep.2 Ad Cor.**

58. **Excerpts from Theodotus.** 4.

59. **In Matt.** 12.43.

60. **Comm. In Lucam.** 9.

61. **Hom. 28.**

62. **In Marcum.** 9

63. Mt. 13.43.

64. **Hom. 28.**

CHAPTER FOUR

THE TRANSFIGURATION IN THE PRAYER
AND FAITH OF THE CHURCH

4.1.   The Liturgical celebration of the event.

The development of the feast of Transfiguration was at first a slow affair but it eventually established itself as a major 'dominical feast' in both Eastern and Western churches. The story of that development has been told several times before[1] and will not be repeated, for the intent of the present chapter is to investigate an aspect of the theological tradition: **Lex orandi, lex credendi.** What then does Christian cult have to say about the Transfiguration as both event and theological symbol?

All in all the liturgical texts present us with a rich ascetical and mystical theology. A brief look at some of the salient offices and prayers of the day is perhaps in order here, even though they are all readily available. In the Roman Office for the 6th of August the intercessory prayers of first and second Vespers offer a fine ascetical interpretation of the epiphany:

'On this day we pray to the Son of God, who revealed himself to his friends in the fulness of his glory, and we say: (Responsorial) Lord, that we may see.

Bless the church ever more with your risen life - so that the world may see in her the integrity of your mission.   R.

You appeared with Elijah and Moses, accepting their homage - may the world accept your word, and live by your law of love.   R

Even before your Passion your disciples saw your risen glory - give us the vision to accept both suffering and joy. R.

Emptied of glory, you preached the kingdom of God, and your own people did not accept you - help us to find you in the poor and deprived, and to love them in your name.   R.

You showed to your friends the splendour of the Living God - take to yourself those who have died and make them glorious.   R.[2]

The concluding prayer of First Vespers, which is the General Collect for the Feast, in tune with the previous Scripture reading of Phil. 3.20-21, interprets the Transfiguration in the Pauline manner as the confirmation of our faith in the glory of Sonship :

'Father, at the Transfiguration in glory of your Only-Begotten Son,
You confirmed the mysteries of faith
By the witness to Jesus of the prophets, Moses and Elijah.
You foreshadowed there what we shall be
When you bring our sonship to its perfection.
Grant that by listening to the voice of Jesus
We may become heirs with him,
Who lives and reigns with You and the Holy Spirit,
God, for ever and ever.'[3]

Here the Transfiguration is seen in the Patristic manner of an anticipated revelation of the church's glory in the New Age which Jesus has won for it. The prayer concludes with a fine application of the words from the cloud : 'Listen to Him.'   The Office Hymn at Morning Prayer is a trinitarian invocation that the church might be transfigured as radiant and glorious, being revealed more and more clearly as the Image of the Eternal Word, The Reconciler of all. The English version loses something of the original's grandeur of metre, but the impressive substance is preserved :

'More ancient than the primal world
And older than the morning star,
Before the first things took their shape,
Creator of them all, You are.

> Your Image is the Lord of Life,
> Your Son from all eternity ;
> All that must perish , he restores ;
> In Him all reconciled will be.

Transfigured Christ, believed and loved,

In You our only hope has been ;

Grant us in Your Unfathomed love,

Those things no eye has ever seen.

> O Father, Son and Spirit blest,
>
> With hearts transfigured by Your grace,
>
> May we Your matchless splendour praise
>
> And see the glory of Your face.[4]

In the Eucharistic Liturgy, the Preface of the day is a represent-
ation of thoughts expressed in Leo the Great's Homily :

> 'Father, all powerful and ever-living God,
>
> we do well always and everywhere to give you thanks,
>
> through Jesus Christ Our Lord.
>
> He revealed his glory to the disciples
>
> to strengthen them for the scandal of the cross.
>
> His glory shone from a body like our own,
>
> to show that the church,
>
> which is the body of Christ,
>
> would one day share his glory.'[5]

The Liturgical texts used in the Eastern church may be found translated in **The Festal Menaion** .[6] There is here the same consistent
proclamation of Christ's luminous deity in a resurrection glory that
has become a grace for his church. The Aposticha of Great Vespers
presents a meditation on the restoration by the Logos of the glorious
image of God in man :

'He who once spoke through symbols to Moses on Mount Sinai[7] saying
'I am He who is', was transfigured today upon Mount Tabor before
the disciples ; and in His own person He showed them the nature
of man, arranged in the original beauty of the Image.' [8]

The remainder of Matins is largely composed of two Canons by
Ss. Cosmas and John of Damascus respectively.[9] The recurring
theme of the prayers of the Office is that the Lord will illuminate

the souls of his faithful with the radiant light of his person:
'Thou wast transfigured upon Mount Tabor, O Jesus, and a shining
cloud, spread out like a tent, covered the apostles with Thy glory.
Whereupon their gaze fell to the ground, for they could not bear
to look upon the brightness of the unapproachable glory of Thy face,
O Saviour, Christ, our God who art without beginning. Do Thou
who then hast shone upon them with Thy light, give light now to
our souls.'[10]

The liturgical cycle of all Christian feasts revolves round
but one celebration, that of the unique mystery of Christian religion
- the paschal revelation of God in the person and presence of the
risen Christ. In the Christian cult the Transfiguration is therefore
celebrated as part of Christ's resurrection power, an aspect of the
soteriological effect of his economy. The aspect this festival connotes is especially the theosis (deification) of our race achieved in
the death and resurrection. The penetration of the human body
of Jesus with divine light so that no longer can a distinction be
made between received and emitted radiance is a perfect symbol
of the gift of adoptive Sonship communicated in grace to the church.
In the paschal mystery the life of the Christian is lifted up into
divine grace, and becoming more and more engrossed in the beauty
of God, thereby becomes more and more beautiful with his beauty,
a beauty it even appropriates as its own.

And yet the Transfiguration as a liturgical feast signifies
more than just a moral transformation into evangelical standards
of behaviour, or our aspirations to those standards; it signifies almost
a sacramental endowment of the believer, analogous to the metamorphosis of the eucharistic elements. We have a symbol here,
like the Eucharist, where even matter itself (in the form of Jesus'
radiant body and garments) is lifted into the divine presence and
consecrated. The metamorphosis in the cult and meditation of the
church is tantamount to a profession of belief in the reconciliation
Christ has effected between God and man, a reconciliation that
has broken down the dividing wall between the Lord of the Universe

and his creation. Christ stands as the absolute figure of reference for this concept of reconciliation. He is the God who stoops down to his children (synkatabasis) but also the faithful man lifted up to communion with God. He is at once the humbled Lord and the exalted servant, as Barth eloquently expressed it.[11] In his own person he stands as the sacrament demonstrating the suitability of matter as a true expression of the deity. His body is the Temple of the deity, the musical instrument of the Logos, and in this we receive the great sign that matter itself is now reconciled and bound up in a Christocentric mystery, renewed even as the chalice of divine presence. The radiance of that day of Transfiguration becomes, in Christian cult, the day when every atom of existence was revealed to be suffused with the light and energy of God's presence. To this extent the Transfiguration is the church's symbol of hope for what it knows has already been mysteriously achieved in God's economy, and which even how would be discernible to all if only one had the heart to see, but is, in fact, presently available as a vision of reality only for the saints. It is as Hopkins expressed it:
'These things, these things were here and but
the beholder
Wanting; which two when they once meet,
The heart rears wings bold and bolder
And hurls for him, O half hurls earth
for him off under his feet'.[12]
The church has rightly found in the Metamorphosis, a symbol of the whole of matter suffused with divine light and energy, and thus it stands as a primary example of Christ's redemptive work and the inner meaning of his incarnation; what the fathers from Irenaeus onwards never tired of repeating: 'He became man that we might become God'.

In the liturgical and prayer life of the Christian church, therefore, the Transfiguration has always assumed the role of an extension of the doctrine of the incarnation. It reminds one of the reconciliation effected, but also advances the believer's understanding to the point where he contemplates the ultimate fulfilment of God's economy - when the process of deification will have been accomplished perfectly throughout the whole universe, when God will be all in all, and all will be full of his glory . Transfiguration light has become in both the Eastern and Western church a particular mark of the great saints. Seraphim of Sarov and Paul of the Cross may be mentioned as two examples. Those who have been transfigured by the beauty of Christ and have entered fully into his grace, themselves become radiant symbols of Christ and therefore symbols of the true nature of man.

The Christian mystery of Transfiguration, therefore, offers the doctrine that the human person is in essence a creature touched by the divine energies, and is consequently in the root of his being fundamentally radiant and beautiful.

In a world still racked by war and cruelty, and disfigured by ignorance and selfishness, it is an optimistic symbol of hope, at once a consolation and an encouragement , and a worthy subject for our deepest contemplation.

4.2.   The Transfiguration: Fact and Meaning.

The Patristic interpretation of the Transfiguration of Jesus can be seen to offer different nuances of approach from those of the evangelists. The question that addresses itself to most observers, especially those who are perhaps unfamiliar with the results of modern biblical scholarship, yet more familiar with the traditional patristic interpretations that have been offered to them in homiletic form, is the inevitable, though innocent, question about historicity. What actually happened during the life of Jesus that came to be written up later in the Gospels and in the Fathers as Christian theological reflection on the Transfiguration? Put even more innocently and more naively: Did the Transfiguration really happen?

Like all naive questions, at one and the same moment it contains a force and directness of truth that demands an answer, and yet it starts from premises that need to be contextualised in a far wider range than is usually operative: a range it has been the aim of this study, in part, to provide.

And yet the earlier part of this chapter has already made the transition from questions of history to questions of meaning. It is my own belief that in the Transfiguration narrative we are dealing with a genuinely historical witness to the life of Jesus but not one that is straightforwardly historical in itself. In other words what is reflected in this narrative owes more to the experience of Jesus' resurrection in the apostolic church than it does to the reminiscences of his preaching ministry. However, it is also true that those early witnesses who shaped and fashioned the story of the Transfiguration were insistent that one only rightly interpreted the life of Jesus of Nazareth in the light of the mysteries experienced after his death and therefore the first apostolic preachers, and the evangelists following them, regarded the Transfiguration story as fundamentally an authentic comment on the ministry and character of Jesus.

In the biblical narrative of the Transfiguration we should notice that we have here no Logion tradition; no word of Jesus addressed to us. We see Jesus as mysterious event, given only to the most faithful of his disciples, those who had already come to embrace his truth by their personal allegiance to the master. In the Markan text, the most primitive of the texts that survive for us, we can see yet more primitive traces of what we may probably identify as a sermon of Kephas. In his sermon Kephas tells us that he saw Jesus transfigured on the mountain (and how many times he had been with his master on the hills of Galilee and Judaea) and he was radiant with the very Shekinah light of God himself. Such is his way of telling the story, and in doing so he draws every parallel with the Sinai covenant narrative for, like his master, Kephas was a Jew and versed in biblical idiom in a way that unfortunately escapes many in the church today. What is the fact? We are dealing with the apostolic preaching. We hear the words and tales of Jesus only through this medium of the apostolic preaching, and so when his greatest disciple tells us he saw his master on the mountain so radiantly beautiful how should we respond?

In the modern age we can no longer rightly ignore the Midrashic manner of biblical narratives, and we should return as best we can, by studious scholarship, to as full an understanding as we can achieve of the idiom of Peter and Mark the evangelist. But when our studies are done, the issue of our response is not set aside, only more clearly delineated for us. We see to what extent the symbolistic haggadah of ancient storytelling has influenced the detailed terms of the narrative; and that we acknowledge. In just the same way we see and also acknowledge the way in which the idiom of the hellenistic church has re-formed the same story in the hands of subsequent theologians from the second century to the fourteenth. This very study on the issue is just as bound up with its own inherent concerns, methods and value judgements as any of the earlier studies - never is fact and hermeneutic wholly separate, the search for meaning always inserts itself. What, then, is the relationship of fact and meaning in the Transfiguration story? Put crudely, if we went back in time to the first century, to stand on the mountain with Peter, what would we have encountered there? The answer to this question was suggested long ago, by Peter, by Mark, by Origen, and a host of fathers that followed: To have seen Jesus as Peter, James and John saw him would only have been possible for those who had the love and faith and persevering constancy of those disciples. The vision of Jesus radiant is not given cheaply or indiscriminately. The vision of Jesus in glory, (just as is true of the visions of Jesus in Resurrection glory) is not a vision afforded to those curious spectators outside his discipleship. For those without, even those seekers after answers to urgent questions of great merit who approached him, Jesus gives only enigma and invitation. Not until the invitation to 'Come and see' has been accepted does that preparation of the heart for the truth of Jesus take place. Only after it has taken place and been consolidated so that the disciple trusts his Lord, and the Lord trusts his disciple, is there any revelation of the true beauty of his face. 'My secret is mine and for mine own', as one of the great mystics put it.[13]

All this must be at best frustrating, and at worst utter nonsense for all the students of the history of religion. Yet it is written in utmost seriousness of intent in the hope that it will be recognised as a statement of truth, a statement of reality that is, by those who have already experienced its truth. This is the strange beauty of Christian theology: for those who do not know the answer it will not give the answer; for those who already know the answer it merely announces that someone else has known the answer too, This is because Christian theology does not initiate into truth, this is the sole prerogative of Him who is Truth; for ultimately the heights of Christian theology are not propositional but personal, and are gained no longer by intellectual acumen but rather by mystical initiation.

It is our conclusion, then, that yes Jesus was transfigured on the mountain, on the hills of Galilee. He was transfigured, as the Fathers rightly say, in everything he ever did. As an old man in the capital of a foreign power Peter told his congregation long after his master's death that he was transfigured even before his resurrection, for his memory of his master's face was for him a vision of such beauty that it could not be dimmed by the passing of the years. Christian disciples will only know the truth of his narrative now in so far as they find in his Homily an echo of a truth they have already known. We look today into the face of Our Lord through many glasses; liturgy, prayer, the questioning and inviting faces of men and women, the manifold mysteries of suffering and joy, compassion and love, that in the end all come to the same thing - His presence in the Spirit as Risen Lord of the world, a presence to the disciple that evokes an encounter with Jesus of Nazareth and issues the same invitation as the first disciples heard:

Come and See; a presence that not only transfigures the disciple, but transfigures the world for him too. When one does see the true face of Jesus its wholly radiant beauty is self-authenticating. He is his own apologia and vindication, as he always was during his earthly life. He invited, he commanded, but he never cajoled or courted. He explained his deeper meanings only to his chosen disciples.

Faith, then, did not make up the Transfiguration story. Nor is it strictly accurate to invert that sentence. The vision of Jesus transfigured did not create faith. It is the release of the Spirit of God's glory in Jesus' Resurrection that creates faith in him and the Resurrection, therefore, must be the only beginning place of authentic Kerygma for the church, as the evangelist himself tells us (Mk.9.9.). The Transfiguration is, for this reason, not part of the Kerygmatic core which the church preaches to the world. It finds no place, for example, in that list of basic salvation events narrated in the creed. This is because it is not meant as a kerygma for those outside the church, but a didache for those within. Transfiguration, as such, occurs only for the disciple who has passed through faith to knowledge of Jesus, and it is then a confirmation of that faith, and a confirmation of the knowledge the disciple already has, that the face of the rabbi of Nazareth is radiant with more beauty and majesty than one can ever hope to portray with sufficient grace, or urgency, or accuracy.

4.3.   Conclusion

To interpret the spiritual meaning of Transfiguration is the aim of all the Patristic homilies and commentaries that follow. The tenor of their approach is analysed in the preceding chapter. Contemporary Eastern Christianity develops on their premisses and continues their reflection on the event as a mystery of deification effected by the Logos within the world.[14] The Logos in the flesh is seen as the One who has made all things radiant with his presence. The Transfiguration of his own flesh is the sacrament of the Transfiguration of all things into the all pervading dominion of Christ. The Transfiguration, in this sense then, is an epitome of the Gospel of divine incarnation. This final comment intends to restate in summary form only two points gleaned from the narrative; the first is an insight offered by the evangelist Mark, and the second runs like a clear stream through the Fathers.

The Markan redaction of the story, and the Pre-Markan source, are both concerned with the question of authority - the authority of the Master as centre of faith and leader of the New Covenant, and the authority transmitted to his church.[15] The evangelist, in his Transfiguration narrative, has interpreted for us the glorious authority of Christ in one of the most striking and spectacular episodes of the whole Gospel text. Here all is glory, all is light, and the power and majesty of God's beloved Son is made manifest. The evangelical context, however, that surrounds the whole episode is the kerygma of his humiliation and death. The voice of God that commands us to 'Listen to Him' is directing us to hear the prophecies of the Passion that the church then, as now, frequently does not wish to hear. This suggests to me that Mark saw the most sublime manifestation of the glory of Christ in his voluntary acceptance of suffering and degradation in wholehearted obedience to his beloved Father. Having preached to his disciples the imminent inbreaking of the glorious Kingdom, his eventual coronation was in reality a far cry from his disciples' expectations. He was given a crown of thorns not gold, and his death took place to the sounds of mocking hilarity rather than reverential hymns. It is Jesus' utter faith in the fidelity of his Father, manifested above all in his faithfulness even to the cross, which is the window through which there breaks his radiant beauty over the church. It is a faith and obedience epitomised in his death. Having come to the cross and seen his church abandon him he realises that the Kingdom that formed the inspiring spur to all his ministry had not been resolved in his lifetime. He dies in absolute faith that God had not given him his mission in vain, no matter that all the facts of his career, and now the circumstances of his final end, all conspired to say he had been deluded. Jesus' faith in his Father does not waver in circumstances where the faith of any other could not have survived. His dying prayer is the psalm of distress he had learned by rote as a child, which begins with the tragic lament of desolation: 'Eli Eli lama sabacthani', and yet concludes with the most glorious hymn of trust in the faithfulness of Yahweh, and in the future of his church:

'Those who seek the Lord will praise him.
Long life to their hearts.
The whole earth, from end to end, will remember and come back to Yahweh;
All the families of the nations will bow down before Him.
For God reigns, the ruler of nations.
Before Him all the prosperous of the earth shall bow down,
Before him shall bow all who go down to the dust.
And my soul will live for Him, my children serve Him;
Proclaim the Lord to generations still to come,
His righteousness to a people yet unborn.
These things the Lord has done.'[16]

Such a faith of Jesus, worked out in the process of a growing apathy and opposition to his preaching, worked out in the end in nakedness and abandonment on the cross, is truly exalted by God in the victory of the Resurrection.[17] But his glory did not really begin on Easter Day; that was its manifestation in a transcendent and universal manner. His glory, as the theologians have taught us, was his faithful heart in all its responses to his Father, and above all in his perfect and pure faith on the Cross. The Transfiguration, as the evangelists portray it, is intrinsically related to that cross and occurs in the process of his last fateful journey to Jerusalem. In this lies a mystical pattern for the church of

Jesus. The Christian's transfiguration to heavenly glory is being worked out here and now, as one looks upon the face of the master and, entranced by his beauty, longs to learn of his ways. It is a glory that radiates in a darkened and torn world, a world that thinks it has passed through and beyond Christianity, but in fact has yet to make its encounter with Jesus; for it must learn to look for the Transfigured Christ not in the neon lights of stardom and the loud voices of success but in the smallness of humility and constant fidelity, in the smallness of true and integrated personality - the compassionate heart of the true human being in which alone the glory and radiance of the Christ can dwell, the only heart in which the Father shall be well-pleased. Such is the Transfiguration considered as a hymn to the glory and power of the Christ of humility.

The second observation, learnt from the Fathers, is the Transfiguration considered as an ascetical symbol. To find glory in the humility of Christ, to discover the utmost power of God in the gentleness of his compassion and the strange force of his mercy, calls for a sensitivity and strength of soul similar to that possessed by Christ himself. For most of us this sensitivity is just not there for it has been loaded over with cares and concerns often far removed from integrity and truth. Our hearts are conditioned by the society in which we live far more than by the Gospel. It is what the Fathers call the clouding of the Image of God in the soul by the passions; and what we might describe in contemporary terms as the evident loss of integration in the human heart. To rediscover integration is a painful process of healing and the pain is true asceticism - not that deviant asceticism so often encountered. It is our sharing in the sufferings of Jesus which of itself evokes a transformation to a new sensitivity to the ways of God who demands justice and mercy on the face of the earth. It becomes a purification of mind and heart that makes mercy and justice not only clearly the right thing to do, but also the thing one wishes to do with all one's energies, and affections. It is an ascetical purification that makes one aware of the presence of God, and for the first time capable of receiving the vision of God. The Transfiguration of Christ on the mountain, then, is not only a vision of the divine stature of Jesus, it is a vision of his stature as a man - a vision of what man really is. It is the New Man in a new nature founded on Christ himself. When the disciple comes before the mystery of the Transfiguration he sees an image of his true face that he has known but long since forgotten. This is an image of hope, because the sorrow of realising how far removed he is from the Transfigured life of Christ shall give way, the longer he looks upon this scene of numinous beauty, to a growing and irrepressible certainty that he too shall day by day grow into the Image of the Lord. We inevitably become that which we love; and that which we love ensures it.

NOTES TO CHAPTER FOUR

1.   J. Tomajean: **La Fête de la Transfiguration, 6 Août.** **L'Orient Syrien,** No.5., 1960, 479-82; A. M. Ramsey: **The Glory of God.** pp.128-129; K. Rozemond; **Les origines de la fête de la Transfiguration.** **Studia Patristica** 17, vol.2. 591-593 Oxford. 1982.

2.   **Roman Breviary.** (English Text) London 1974. Vol. 3. p.156* The Office of Readings presents parts of a Homily attributed to Anastasius of Sinai, but different to the one offered in part 2 of the study. cf Breviary. vol. 3. pp.161-163*

3.   Ibid. p.156*

4.   Ibid. p.164*. Cardinal Newman published his poetical works in 1867, within which there are two renderings of the Roman Liturgy's Hymns from Matins and Lauds: The **Quicunque Christum Quaeritis,** and the **Lux Alma Jesu;** cf **Verses on Various Occasions,** (Burns and Oates) pp.187-8.

5.   Roman Missal: **In Festum Transfigurationis.** (August 6th). The Liturgical Collects of the Anglican Tradition are presented in Appendix 2 of A. M. Ramsey: **The Glory of**

God and the Transfiguration of Christ. London 1949, 152-3

6.   (English Translation) Mother Mary and Kallistos Ware, Faber, London (1969) 1977 pp.468-503.

7.   Ex.3.14 - the revelation in the burning bush at Horeb which in its illuminated radiance is taken as a type of Jesus' radiance on Thabor.

8.   **Festal Menaion** p.476.

9.   The work of the former is not represented in our present study - cf. **Festal Menaion,** pp.482-494.

10.   **Festal Menaion,** p.478.

11.   K. Barth. **Church Dogmatics IV.**

12.   G. M. Hopkins. From 'Hurrahing in Harvest.' **Complete Poems,** Oxford 1970, p.70.

13.   Symeon the New Theologian; **1st Theological Discourse,** ET. J. McGuckin, **Cistercian Studies 41,** Kalamazoo, 1982, cf. p.118 fn.43.

14.   Kallistos Ware, **Festal Menaion,** London 1977, p.61-63.
PT. Bilianuk, **A Theological Meditation on the Mystery Of Transfiguration. Diakonia,** vol.8 No.4. 1973, 306-331
W. Teasdale, **The Spiritual significance of the Transfiguration. Diakonia** vol.14. No.3. 1979 203-212
A. Bulgakov, **Du Verbe Incarné.** Paris 1943.
V. Lossky, **The Mystical Theology of the Eastern Church.** ET. 1957. Ibid: **The Vision of God.** Faith Press 1963.
Ibid: **In the Image and Likeness of God.** London. 1975.

15.   An ecclesial authority which Mark outlines in the same way in his text at 10.41-45.

16.   Ps.22.26-31.

17.   cf. Phil. 2.6-11.

PART TWO

CHAPTER FIVE
THE GREEK FATHERS: TEXTS IN TRANSLATION

IRENAEUS OF LYONS

CLEMENT OF ALEXANDRIA

ORIGEN

METHODIUS OF OLYMPUS

EUSEBIUS OF CAESAREA

EPIPHANIUS OF SALAMIS

BASIL OF CAESAREA

GREGORY NAZIANZEN

GREGORY OF NYSSA

JOHN CHRYSOSTOM

CYRIL OF ALEXANDRIA

PROCLOS OF CONSTANTINOPLE

THEODORET OF CYR

ANTIPATER OF BOSTRA

PS. ATHANASIUS

PS. DIONYSIUS

ANASTASIUS I OF ANTIOCH

MAXIMUS THE CONFESSOR

ANDREW OF CRETE

JOHN OF DAMASCUS

GREGORY PALAMAS

IRENAEUS OF LYONS. (Born circa 140 AD).[1]

1.   **Adversus Haereses.** 4.20.2.

'Having the key of David, he shall open and no man shall shut; he shall shut and no man shall open.'[2] For no one either in heaven or on earth, or under the earth was able to open the book of the Father or to gaze upon him except the Lamb who was slain, who redeemed us with his own blood, who received power over all things from the same God who had made all things by the Word and adorned them by (his) Wisdom, when the 'Word was made flesh'.[3] This was so that just as the Word of God had the sovereignty in the heavens, so he might have the sovereignty on earth since he was the righteous man 'who did no sin, and neither was guile found in his mouth.'[4] It was so that he might have pre-eminence over the things that are under the earth, being made 'the first-begotten of the dead'[5], and that, as I have said already, all things might behold their King. It was so that the Father's light might join with and rest upon the flesh of Our Lord, and then come to us from his resplendent flesh. In this way man could attain immortality, being invested with the Father's light.

2.   **Adversus Haereses.** 4.20.5-6.

Man does not see God by his own powers. God is seen by men only when he pleases, only by those he has chosen, only when and how he wills it. God is powerful in all things and he has been seen in times past in a prophetic manner through the Spirit; he has also been seen in an adopted manner through the Son, and he will be seen as Father in the Kingdom of heaven. The Spirit shall indeed prepare man in the Son of God[6], the Son lead him to the Father, and the Father grant incorruption for eternal life which comes to everyone who looks upon God. For as those who see the   light are within the light and share in its brilliancy, even so, those who see God are within God and receive of his splendour. His splendour gives them life and so those who see God are brought to life. It was for this reason that although he is incomprehensible, boundless and invisible, he made himself visible and comprehensible and within the capacity of those who believe, in order that he might bring to life all those who receive him and look upon him through faith. Just as his greatness is past finding out, so is his goodness beyond telling. Granting the vision in his goodness, he then bestows life on all who see him. It is impossible to live apart from life, and the means of life is found in fellowship with God, and fellowship with God is to know God and to enjoy his goodness. (6) Man, therefore shall see God in order that he may live, being made immortal by the vision and attaining even to God.

3.   **Adversus Haereses.** 4.20.7-8

From the very beginning the Son of the Father declares him, since he was with the Father from the beginning. It was he who showed the human race prophetic visions and various gifts, as well as his own ministries and the glory of the Father; all in regular and connected order at the fitting time for the benefit (of mankind). For where there is a regular succession there is stability, and where there is stability it is suitable for the time, and where there is suitability there is also utility. This is why the Word became the dispenser of the Father's grace for the benefit of men, for whose sake he made such great dispensations. He truly revealed God to men, but also presented man to God, all the while preserving the invisibility of the Father so that no man should ever come to despise God, but should always have something to strive forward to. And yet he revealed God to man by many dispensations in case man should fall away from God altogether and so cease to exist. For the glory of God is a man who is alive; and the life of man is the vision of God. If the revelation of God which comes through the creation gives life to all things on earth, then how much more will the revelation of the Father which comes through the Word give life to those who see God. (8) The Spirit of God pointed out things to come by means of the prophets, to form us and adapt us in advance that we should be made subject to God, but it still lay in the future that man through the good-pleasure of the Holy Spirit, should see God. Since the prophets had been the instruments that announced future things, intimating that men would see God, it was fitting that they themselves should see God; not only that God and the Son of God (both Son and Father) should be announced by the prophets, but that he should also be seen by all his members who are sanctified and instructed in divine things. This was so that man might be disciplined and exercised beforehand to prepare for his reception into that glory which will be later revealed in those who love God. The prophets did not only give prophecy in words, but also in visions, and their manner of life, and by the actions which they performed according to the impulse of the Holy Spirit. It was in this invisible manner then that they saw God, as Isaiah tells us: 'I have seen with my eyes the King, the Lord of Hosts.'[7] He points out that man should look on God with his eyes, and also hear his voice. It was in this same way that they also saw the Son of God, as a man conversant with men, even while they prophesied what was to happen. For they told us that the one who had not yet come was present, and proclaimed that the impassible was subject to suffering, and declared that he who was then in hea-ven , had descended into the dust of death.[8]

4. Adversus Haereses 4.20.9.

The Word spoke to Moses appearing before him 'just as a man might speak with his friend'[9]. But Moses wanted to see the one who was speaking with him openly and so it was said to him: 'Stand in the cleft of the rock, and I will cover you with my hand. But when my splendour shall pass by, then you shall see my back parts but my face you shall not see; for man shall not see my face and live.'[10] This tells us two things: that it is impossible for man to see God; and that through the Wisdom of God man shall see him, in the last times, in the cleft of a rock (that is in his coming as man). It was for this reason that he conferred with him (Moses) face to face on the top of a mountain, when Elijah was also present as the Gospel tells us. And so in the end he made good the ancient promise.

CLEMENT OF ALEXANDRIA c.150-215[11]

1.   **Stromata 6.16.140.**

The Lord who ascended the mountain as the fourth[12] becomes the sixth[13] and is illuminated all round with spiritual light by laying bare the power proceeding from him as far as those selected to see were able to behold it. By the voice, that is the seventh[14], he is proclaimed the Son of God so that the (disciples) might be convinced about him and so come to rest[15];while he by his birth(indicated by a six conspicuously marked) becoming the eighth, might appear to be God in a body of flesh by displaying his power. He was numbered as a man indeed, but was concealed as to who he was.

2.   **Excerpts from Theodotus 4-5.**

It was because of his great humility that the Lord showed himself as a man rather than as an angel. Even when he was shown in glory to the apostles on the mountain he did not give the revelation for his own sake but for the sake of the church, 'the chosen race',[16] that it could learn about its[17] advancement after it passed from the flesh. He is the light on high, and he is that light revealed in flesh. What became visible here was not secondary to the light on high, nor was it separated from on high when it was among us as if it changed from one place to another or left one (place) to occupy the other. No, this was the (light) which is everywhere, and even as it was with the Father, so it was also here, for it was the power of the Father. Indeed the Saviour's words were to be fulfilled when he said: 'There are some standing here who shall not taste death until they see the Son of Man in glory.'[18] So it was that Peter, James and John saw and then fell asleep.[19] (5) Why was it that they saw the radiant face but were not struck with terror, yet when they heard the voice they fell to the ground? Doubtless because ears are less believing than eyes; and this unexpected voice greatly astounds them. John the Baptist heard the voice[20] but he was not afraid because he heard it in the spirit and was accustomed to it. But any other man who merely heard of this would find it amazing, and this is why the Saviour orders them: 'Tell no-one what you have seen.'21 The disciples had not looked upon the light with fleshly eyes for there is no affinity or intimacy between the light and the flesh except in so far as the Saviour's own power and will empowers the flesh to behold. In this case he allowed the flesh to participate in seeing what the soul could see, since it is conjoined to it. But the (command) 'Tell no-one' is also given in case men should come to understand who the Lord really was and so draw back from laying hands upon him[22], for then the Economy would not be fulfilled and even death would draw back from the Lord recognising the futility of trying to achieve an impossible task. In fact the voice on the mountain came for those chosen ones who already understood. Even so they were amazed at this witness to the one in whom they believed. When the voice came over the river[23] it was for those still on the way to faith, and then it was forgotten by them for they were bound up in the prescriptions of the scribes.

ORIGEN 185-253.[24]

1.   **Contra Celsum** 1.48

On the occasion of the vision on the mountain, he commanded his disciples: 'Tell no-one what you have seen until the Son of Man is risen from the dead,'[25] so it would not be in keeping with him to have told his disciples what John saw and heard at the Jordan. It can be seen that it was a trait of Jesus' character always to avoid unnecessary talk about himself; this is why he said: 'If I speak about myself, my witness is not true.'[26]

2.   **Contra Celsum** 2.64-65

Jesus was only a single person but he was nonetheless more things than one, according to the different standpoint from which he was assessed.   Not everyone who looked at him saw him the same way. It is clear that he was more things than one from the saying: 'I am the Way, the Truth and the Life;'[27] and again 'I am the bread' and again 'I am the door', and innumerable others.   When men looked at him he did not appear the same way to all who saw him, but rather according to their individual capacity to receive him.   This will be clear to those who notice that he did not admit all his disciples when he was about to be transfigured on the high mountain, only Peter, James and John, because they were capable of seeing his glory on that occasion, and of looking at the glorified aspect of Moses and Elijah, and listening to their conversation and the voice from the heavenly cloud.   I also think ... that he did not appear as the same person to the sick and those who needed strength, as he did to those who were strong enough to ascend the mountain with him ... The following saying shows that he did not always have the same appearance, when Judas who was about to betray him said to the crowds accompanying him who did not know Jesus: 'Whoever I kiss, that is the one.'[28]   And I think the Saviour himself indicates the same thing by the words: 'I sat every day in the Temple, teaching, and you did not lay hold of me.'[29] We hold, then, these lofty views on Jesus, not only in regard to the deity within, which lay hidden from the view of the crowd, but even with respect to the transfiguration of his body which took place when ever he wished, for whoever he wished. We conclude that before Jesus had put off the principalities and powers[30], and so long as he was still not dead to all sin, then all men were capable of seeing him; but when he had put off the principalities and powers and no longer had anything which was capable of being seen by the multitude, then all those who had formerly seen him were now incapable of seeing him. And therefore, to spare them, he did not show himself to all men after his resurrection from the dead.

(65)   Why do I say 'to all' because even with his own apostles and disciples he was not present all the time, and he did not show himself constantly even to them, for they were not able to receive his divinity without interruption. His deity was more resplendent once he had finished the Economy. Peter, called Kephas, the first-fruits as it were of the apostles, was able to see this, and along with him the Twelve (for Matthias was substituted in place of Judas); and after them he appeared to the five hundred brethren at once, and then to James, and subsequently to all the others besides the twelve apostles, perhaps also to the Seventy, and lastly to Paul ... No one could reasonably blame Jesus for not having admitted all his apostles to the high mountain at his transfiguration when he was about to manifest the splendour that appeared in his garments, and the glory of Moses and Elijah talking with him. He ony admitted the three we have spoken of. In the same way no one can reasonably object to the apostles who tell us that the vision of Jesus after his resurrection was not given to all men, but only to those he knew to have received eyes capable of seeing his resurrection.

3.   **Contra Celsum** 4.16

There are different appearances, as it were, of the Word according to the manner he shows himself to each of those who come to his doctrine. This corresponds to the condition of one who might be just becoming a disciple, or someone who has made some progress, or one who has advanced further, one who has almost attained virtue, or one who has already attained it. And so it is not the case, as Celsus and those like him would have it, that our God was transformed and, ascending the high mountain, showed his real appearance was something different, far more excellent than those who remained below, being unable to follow him on high, were able to see. The ones who were below did not possess eyes capable of seeing the transformation of the Word into his glorious and more divine condition. It was only with difficulty that they were able to receive him as he was. Those who were unable to behold his more excellent nature might well say of him: 'We saw him and he had neither form nor comeliness. His form was dishonourable and beneath that of the sons of men.'[31] Let these remarks be an answer to the speculations of Celsus who neither understands the changes and transformations of Jesus as related in the histories, nor the mortal and immortal nature he had.[32]

4.   **Contra Celsum** 6.68

So if Celsus were to ask us how we think we know God, and how we shall be saved by him, we would answer that the Word of God, who enters into those who seek him, or who accept him when he appears, is the one who can make known and reveal the Father. Before the appearance of the Word no man saw the Father. For who else is able to save the soul of man and conduct it to the God of all things except God the Word, who 'was in the beginning with God'[33]? He became flesh for the sake of those who had clung to the flesh, and had become as flesh, so that those who could not see him as the Word, with God, God himself, might be enabled to receive him. And so he spoke in bodily form and announced himself as flesh in order to call to himself those who are flesh. He did this in the first place to effect their transformation according to the Word that was made flesh, and secondly, to lead them on high so that they can see him as he was before he became flesh. And they received this benefit and rose up from their great introduction to him in the flesh and said: 'Even if we have known Christ after the flesh, henceforth we know him so no more.'[34] And so he became flesh, and having become flesh, he tabernacled among us'[35], not dwelling outside us. And after tabernacling and dwelling within us he did not continue in that form in which he first presented himself, but made us ascend the lofty mountain of his word, and there showed us his own glorious form and the splendour of his garments. He showed us, as well as his own form, the form of the spiritual law, which is Moses, seen in glory alongside Jesus. He also showed us all prophecy, which even after his incarnation did not perish but was received up into heaven, which is symbolised by Elijah. The one who saw these things could say: 'We behold his glory, the glory of the only-begotten of the Father, full of grace and truth.'[36]

5. Hom. In Genesim l.7.

Just as the sun and moon illuminate our bodies, so does Christ and the Church illuminate our minds. But we can only be illuminated if we do not have the minds of the blind men. Even when the sun and moon shine on the physical eyes of the blind they still cannot receive the light. And Christ manifests his light to our minds in the same way. He will only illuminate us if no blindness of mind obstructs. But if at first this should be the case, then those who are blind ought to follow after Christ shouting and calling out: 'Son of David have pity on us', so that they can receive their sight from him and then might be able to be lit up by the splendour of his light. Of those who see, not all are illumined by Christ in an equal degree. Each one is illumined according to his capacity, to the extent that he is able to receive the power of the light. Our bodily eyes are not illuminated by the sun in equal degree for if a man climbs to higher places and contemplates the origin of the (sun's) appearance by a reflective scrutiny then he perceives the force of its splendour and its heat so much more. And it is the same when our mind approaches Christ in a higher and more lofty manner. We come closer to the splendour of his light and so we are lit up more significantly and more brilliantly by his light. This is just as he himself said through the prophet: 'Come close to me and I shall come close to you; says the Lord.'[37] And again he says: 'I am a God who is near, not a God far off.'[38] Still, all men do not come to him in similar ways but each one according to his own virtue. When we come to him among the crowds he refreshes us with the parables in case we should faint on the way through having too little to eat. When we sit at his feet ceaselessly and constantly, our sole occupation being to listen to his word, not distracted by many ministries but 'choosing the best part' which shall not be taken away from us[39] - those who come to him in this way attain his light so much more abundantly. And indeed if we are like the apostles and never leave his side but remain with him through all his tribulations, then he will secretly explain to us all he has spoken to the crowds, unravel it and illuminate us so much more brilliantly. And if a man even comes to be like those who can climb the mountain with him, like Peter, James, and John, then he will not only be illuminated by the light of Christ, but even by the voice of the Father.

6.   Comm. In Matthaeum 12.36-43

36.   Now after six days, according to Matthew and Mark, he took with him Peter and James and John his brother, and led them

up a high mountain apart, and was transfigured before them. Before we start the exposition of the things that strike us in relation to this let it be granted that this took place long ago, and as it is written. It seems to me then that those who are taken up by Jesus onto the high mountain and are found worthy of seeing his transfiguration apart (from the others) are intentionally brought up six days after the discourses he has just spoken[40]. Six is the perfect number and the whole world was made in six days, a perfect work of art. This is why, I think, the man who transcends all the things of the world is represented in the words: 'after six days Jesus took up with him' certain men. Such a man no longer beholds visible realities which are temporal, but already beholds realities that are invisible since they are eternal. And so if any one of us wishes to be taken by Jesus up the high mountain and found worthy to behold his transfiguration apart, he must pass beyond the six days. For then he will no longer look on visible things or love the world and the things of the world[41]. Such a man no longer lusts after worldly (that is bodily) lusts or the riches of the body or any fleshly glory, or any of those things whose nature it is to distract the soul and drag it down from higher, more divine things and fix it fast to the deceit of this age in wealth and glory and all the other lusts which are the enemies of truth. And when he has passed through the six days, as we have said, he will keep a new sabbath. He will rejoice on the high mountain as he sees Jesus transfigured before him. The Word has different forms and he appears to each as is expedient for him to see. He is never revealed to any man beyond his capacity to see.

(37)   Perhaps you will ask, when Jesus was transfigured before those he led up the high mountain, did he appear to them in the form of God[42] in which he previously was, so that for those below he had the form of a slave but for those who had followed him to the high mountain after the six days he did not have that form but the form of God? But hear these things, if you can, and pay attention spiritually for it is not said simply: 'He was transfigured'

because Mark and Matthew have also recorded a certain necessary addition, for they both say: 'He was transfigured **before them.**' And so, according to this you will say that it is possible for Jesus to be transfigured before some people in this transfiguration, but even at the same time not to be transfigured before others. If you wish to see how Jesus was transfigured before those he had led apart with him up the high mountain, then first see with me Jesus in the Gospels, for there he is more simply appreciated, and we might say 'known according to the flesh'[43] by those who do not go up the high mountain by means of uplifting works and words, yet 'known no longer according to the flesh' by means of all the Gospels, for there he is known in his divinity and seen in the form of God according to their knowledge. It is before such as these that Jesus is transfigured, not before any of those below. And when he is transfigured his face shines like the sun so that he may be revealed to the children of light who have put off the works of darkness and put on the armour of light and are no longer children of darkness or night, but have become the sons of day and walk uprightly as in the day[44]. Being revealed to them he will shine on them not only as the sun, but as one seen to be the sun of righteousness.

(38)   He is transfigured before the disciples, but there is something more. It is not only the fact that his face shines like the sun. There is more because his garments appeared as white as light to those whom he led apart up the high mountain. The garments of Jesus are the sayings and letters of the Gospel with which he clothed himself. And I think that even the sayings in the Apostles which indicate truths about him are also the garments of Jesus which become white to those who go up the high mountain with him. But since there are even degrees among white things, his garments become as white as the brightest and purest of all white things, that is light. So when you see a man who has a thorough understanding of the theology concerning Jesus and can clearly interpret the Gospel sayings, you should not hesitate to say that

for him the garments of Jesus have become as white as light. When you understand and see the Son of God in his transfiguration in such a way that his face is like a sun and his garments white as light, then to the man who sees Jesus in this form there will immediately appear Moses (the Law) and Elijah (by synedoche not just one prophet but all the prophets) conversing with Jesus. This is the meaning of the words: 'talking with him.' Luke has it: ' Moses and Elijah appeared in glory' - and so on to the words - 'in Jerusalem.' So if anyone sees the glory of Moses, he will have understood that the teachings of the spiritual law are in harmony with Jesus, and will have understood the wisdom in the prophets that is hidden in a mystery[45]. Such a man sees Moses and Elijah in glory when he sees them with Jesus.

(39)   It is necessary now to expound the passage given in Mark :- 'And as he was praying he was transfigured before them.'[46] And we say that perhaps it is possible to see the Word wonderfully transfigured before us if we have done these things we have spoken of and gone up into the mountain, seen the absolute Word speaking with the Father and praying to him for those things that the true High Priest might well pray for to the only true God. In order to have this fellowship with God and pray to the Father, he goes up into the mountain and then, according to Mark, 'his garments became white, radiant as the light, as no fuller on earth could whiten them.' Perhaps the earthly fullers are the wise men of this world, so careful about the language which they consider to be bright and pure so that even their base thoughts and false dogmas seem to be made beautiful by their fulling, so to speak. And the one who shows his own garments radiant and even brighter than their fulling could make them, to those who have ascended, is the Word who when his clothes become white and dazzling, as Luke tells us, demonstrates the radiance of thought in the scriptural sayings which are despised by many.

(40)   Next let us see what was in the mind of Peter when he answered Jesus: 'Lord it is good for us to be here. Let us make

three tabernacles' and so on. These words call for very special examination because Mark in his own person has added 'for he did not know what to say,' and Luke says: 'he did not know what he was saying.' Consider, therefore, whether he spoke these things as if in a trance, filled with a spirit that moved him to say these things which could not have been a holy spirit because John taught in the Gospel that no one had the Holy Spirit before the resurrection of the Saviour. He said: 'For the Spirit was not yet since Jesus was not yet glorified.'[47] So if the Spirit was not yet, and Peter spoke under the influence of some spirit, not knowing what he said, then the spirit which caused these utterances must have been one of those spirits that had not yet been conquered through the cross or put on show along with them, of whom it is written: 'Having put off from himself the principalities and powers, he made a show of them openly, triumphing over them in the cross.'[48] Perhaps this spirit was the same one that Jesus called 'stumbling block' and which is called Satan in that passage: 'Get behind me Satan, you are a stumbling block to me.'[49] I well understand that these things will offend many who come across them because they suppose that it is contrary to good sense that (Peter) should be so convicted when only a little while before Jesus had called him blessed because the Father in heaven had revealed to him things about the Saviour, that is that he was truly Jesus and Christ, the Son of the living God. Such a person should look more carefully at what is said about Peter and the rest of the apostles, and how they even made requests as if they were alien to him who would redeem them from the enemy and purchase them with his own precious blood. For if anyone would have it that the apostles were perfect before the passion of Jesus, let them tell us why 'Peter and those with him were heavy with sleep.'[50] I will anticipate something else that follows and apply it to the subject in hand, and in turn will raise the following questions: Is it possible for anyone to find in Jesus an occasion of stumbling apart from the working of the devil who caused him to stumble? Is it possible for anyone to deny Jesus, indeed even in the presence of a little maid and a doorkeeper and the most worthless of men, unless a spirit had been with him in this denial that was hostile to that Spirit which God gives to men, according to their merits, to help them to confess? No one who has learned to refer the roots of sin to the father of sin will deny that it was through him that the apostles were made to stumble, and that Peter denied Christ three times before that famous cock-crow. If this is so, consider whether at this point he also has a mind to make Jesus stumble, as far as is in his power, to turn him aside from an economy marked by suffering that would bring salvation to men, one that he undertook with great eagerness, trying to fulfil everything that contributed to this end. Does he, by deceit as it were, wish to draw Jesus away, as if he were calling upon him to stop condescending to men, not to come to them, or suffer death for them, but rather to remain on the high mountain with Moses and Elijah? He also promised to build three tabernacles, one apart for Jesus, and one for Moses and one for Elijah; as if one tabernacle would not have been enough for the three if they had found it necessary to be tabernacled on the high mountain. Perhaps he was acting with an evil intention even in this when he incited the one who 'did not know what he was saying.' Perhaps he did not wish Jesus, Moses, and Elijah to be together, and wanted to separate them from one another under the pretext of the three tabernacles. Similarly it was a lie to say: 'It is good for us to be here' for if it had been good they would have stayed there. But if it was a lie you will doubtless try to find out who caused this lie to be spoken, especially as John tells us: 'When he speaks a lie he speaks of his own, for he is a liar and the father of lies.'[51] And just as there is no truth apart from the working of him who says: 'I am the Truth,'[52] so there is no lie apart from him who is the enemy of truth. These paradoxical qualities, then, truth and falsehood, were still in Peter. From truth he said: 'You are the Christ, the Son of the living God,'[53] but from falsehood he said: 'Heaven preserve you Lord, this must not happen to you;'[54]

and also 'It is good for us to be here.'[55] If any one does not admit that Peter spoke these things from an evil inspiration, but says that his words were simply his own choice, I would ask them how they interpret the texts: 'He did not know what he was saying,' and 'he did not know what to answer'.

(41)   We have said all this merely by way of scrutinising the letter. We have hardly exhausted our energy in interpreting the figurative meaning of these things. Accordingly, then, let us consider Peter and the Sons of Thunder who were taken up the mountain of the dogmas of truth to see the Transfiguration of Jesus. Did they wish to build tabernacles in themselves for the Word of God who was going to dwell in them, and for his Law which they had seen in glory, and for that prophecy which spoke of the death which Jesus would accomplish ? In this context Peter would have said: 'It is good for us to be here,' for the benefit of those who desired the contemplative life, since he loved it himself and preferred its delights to life among the turmoil of the crowd. But because 'love does not seek after itself'[56] Jesus did not do what Peter thought was good. This is why he came down the mountain to those who were not able to climb it and look upon his transfiguration. (He came down) so that they might see him in the kind of form that was within their capacity. It is fitting, then, for a righteous man who has that 'love which does not seek after itself' to be free of all things but still bring himself under bondage to all those below in order to gain more of them.[57] Perhaps there is someone who does not accept this interpretation of ours, referring to what we have alleged about the trance and the working of an evil spirit in Peter concerning the words 'he did not know what he was saying.' Such a one might say that there were some people mentioned by Paul who want to be teachers of the Law but do not know what they are talking about and make bold statements about things they do not understand, while they cannot either clearly expound the nature of what is said, or comprehend the meaning.[58] Peter's eagerness was itself of such a kind that he did not perceive

what was good in reference to the economy of Jesus and those who appeared on the mountain - Moses and Elijah - and this is why he says: 'It is good for us to be here,' although 'he did not know what he was saying' because 'he did not know what to say.' For if the 'wise man understands the things of his own mouth and carries prudence on his lips'[59] it follows that he who is not wise does not understand the things of his own mouth and cannot comprehend the nature of what he speaks.

(42)　　　　Next we come to the words: 'While he was still speaking behold a bright cloud overshadowed them.' Now I think that God wished to dissuade Peter from making three tabernacles in which, if it had been left to him, he was going to live. And so he showed a better tabernacle, as it were, a much more excellent one, the cloud. It is the function of a tabernacle to overshadow and shelter whoever is inside it, and the bright cloud overshadowed them. And so God was making, as it were, a more divine tabernacle which, in so far as it was bright, might be a pattern of the resurrection for them. For a bright cloud overshadows the just who are at once protected, illuminated and enlightened by it. What is this bright cloud that overshadows the just? Is it perhaps the Father's power from which the voice of the Father proceeds to bear witness that the Son is beloved and well-pleasing, and to exhort those who are under its shadow to listen to him and no one else? As he speaks of old, so he speaks always, through what he wills. And perhaps the bright cloud that overshadows the just and prophesies of the things of God is the Holy Spirit who works within it and says: 'This is my beloved Son in whom I am well-pleased.' But I would also venture to maintain that Our Saviour is a bright cloud. So when Peter said 'Let us make three tabernacles here' ... (Text mutilated here) ... one from the Father himself, one from the Son, and one from the Holy Spirit. The bright cloud of the Father, Son and Holy Spirit overshadows the genuine disciples of Jesus. Or else the cloud perhaps overshadows the Gospel and the Law and the Prophets and then becomes bright to the man who can see its light in the

Gospel, Law and Prophets. Perhaps the voice from the cloud is saying to Moses and Elijah: 'This is my beloved Son in whom I am well-pleased. Listen to him,' because they had desired to see and hear the Son of Man and to look on him in glory. Perhaps it teaches the disciples that he who was the Son of God in a literal sense, the beloved one in whom God was well-pleased, the one to whom they had to listen, was the very one they were looking at transfigured, whose face shone like the sun and who was clothed in garments as white as light.

(43)   After this it is written that when they heard the voice from the cloud bearing witness to the Son, the three apostles could not bear the glory of the voice and the power that rested on it, and so fell on their face and prayed to God, terrified at the supernatural vision and the things spoken from the vision. But consider whether you could also say this about these details of the text, that the disciples had understood that the Son of God had been speaking with Moses and (realised) that it was he who had said: 'Man shall not see my face and live,'[60] and reflecting on God's testimony to him, they could not bear the radiance of the Word and so humbled themselves under the mighty hand of God[60]. When the Word had touched them they raised their eyes and saw Jesus alone; no one else. Moses (The Law) and Elijah (The Prophet) became as one with the Gospel of Jesus. They did not remain what they had been as three, but the three became one. Consider these things with me in relation to mystical matters; for in regard to the basic meaning of the letter, Moses and Elijah appeared in glory and talked with Jesus and then went back again to the place they had come from - perhaps to share the words Jesus had spoken to them about those who were to gain his benefits almost immediately afterwards, that is the time of his passion when the tombs were opened for many of the saints who had fallen asleep and they were to go to the true holy city (not the Jerusalem over which Jesus wept) and appear then to many people.[62] But after the economy on the mountain they came down the mountain again in order to come to the multitudes

and minister to the Son of God regarding the salvation of the people. It was then that Jesus commanded his disciples: 'Tell the vision to no man until the Son of Man should rise from the dead.'[63] This saying is like the one we investigated previously when he commanded the disciples to tell no man that he was the Christ.[64] Consequently the things we said on that text will be useful to us for this passage here. Jesus, accordingly, does not want his glory to be spoken of before his glory after the passion. For it would have been harmful for those who heard, especially the crowds, when they saw him crucified who had been so glorified. And since his glorification in the Resurrection is akin to his Transfiguration and that vision of his face like the sun, this is why he wishes the apostles to speak of these things after he rose from the dead.

METHODIUS OF OLYMPUS (d.circ 311.)[65]

1. De Resurrectione

(12)   The Transformation is the restoration into an impassible and glorious state. For now the body is one of desire and humiliation[66] and this was why Daniel was called a 'man of desires'[67]; but then it will be transfigured into an impassible body, not by the change of the arrangement of its members, but by it no longer desiring carnal pleasures. Origen, therefore , thinks that the same flesh will not be restored to the soul, but that the form of each, according to the appearance by which the flesh is now distinguished, shall arise stamped upon another spiritual body; so that everyone will again appear the same in form; and that this is the resurrection which is promised. For, he says, the material body being fluid and in no way remaining in itself, but wearing out and being replaced around the appearance by which its shape is distinguished, and by which the figure is contained, it is necessary that

the resurrrection should be only that of the form.

(13)   So, Origen, you maintain that the resurrection of this body that is changed into a spiritual body is to be expected only in appearance; and you set forward the vision of Moses and Elijah as a most convincing proof of it, saying that they appeared after their departure from life keeping the same appearance as that which they had from the beginning, and such will be the resurrection of all men.   But Moses and Elijah rose up and appeared with this form you speak of before Christ suffered and rose.   How then can Christ be celebrated by prophets and apostles as the 'first-born of the dead'?[68]   For if we believe that Christ is the first-born of the dead, he is such because he has risen before all others.   But Moses appeared to the apostles before Christ suffered, having this form which you maintain fulfils the resurrection.   And so, there is no resurrection of the form without the flesh.   For either there is a resurrection of the form, as you teach, and then Christ is no longer the 'first born of the dead' by the very fact that souls appeared before him having this form after death; or he is truly the first-born, and it is quite impossible that any should be thought fit for resurrection before him, so that they would not die again.   But if no one rose before him, and Moses and Elijah appeared to the apostles not having flesh, only its appearance, then the resurrection in the flesh is clearly manifested.   For it is most absurd that the resurrection should be set forth only in form, since the souls, after their departure from the flesh, never appear to lay aside the form which, according to him, rises again.   So if that remains with them, so that it cannot be taken away, as with the soul of Moses and Elijah, and does not perish as you suppose, and is not destroyed, but rather is everywhere with them, then surely that form which never fell cannot be said to rise again.[69]

EUSEBIUS OF CAESAREA c.263-339.[70]

1.   **Comm. In Lucam.**   ch.9.

'He took up Peter, James and John.'

In the Transfiguration only three are found worthy to look upon the Kingdom of heaven revealed to them in power. But in the fulfilment of the age, when the Lord comes with the Father's glory, then it will not only be Moses and Elijah who shall attend him, and it will not only be the three disciples who are there, but all the prophets and patriarchs and just men. And it will not be up a high mountain, but up to heaven itself that he will lead the worthy by his godhead. And then his godhead will not shine like the sun but will shine as a light beyond any created light that can be conceived either by the senses or the mind. For he himself is the 'light which enlightens every man coming into the world'.[71] And then he shall even reveal his face. It will not be as of old when he said to Moses: 'You shall see the hinder parts but my face you shall not see'[72]. This will not be the case on that day for he shall reveal himself to the saints so that all will be able to say: 'but we with unveiled faces behold the glory of the Lord and are transfigured into the same image, from glory into glory.'[73] On that day the cloud will not speak out, nor will the Father bear witness to the Son through a cloud, but he shall do so himself, without any over-shadowing or any interpreter. In truth shall he glorify his only begotten Son above all his saints, enthroning him at his side and showing him forth as co-ruler, and setting him above every principality. On that day it will not be only the three disciples who hear the voice on the mountain and fall down on their faces, but 'every knee shall bow, in heaven, on earth and in the under-world.'[74]

'And a voice came from the cloud ...'

The Father's voice comes through the cloud, for this is the way God appears, and bears witness to the Sonship of the Christ. It was not fitting that it should be only from Peter that we should know that he was the Christ the Son of the living God, or that our understanding of him as coming from the heavenly Father should have come solely from Peter's testimony; and so the Father's own voice sets the seal of truth upon this confession and witnesses that he is the Son of God, commanding us to listen to him.

EPIPHANIUS OF SALAMIS c.315-403[75]

Adversus Haereses. 1.3

Of old, Christ entrusted the Law to Moses, so if he and the prophets were quite alien to him then why did he allow them to appear by his side in the moment of his own glory? Look at this miracle because he did not choose to reveal them at his tomb or his cross but only when he wished to reveal to us a share in his glory, a pledge as it were. And then, I tell you, he summoned to himself the saints Moses and Elijah, in order to demonstrate that they were the co-inheritors of his Kingdom.

BASIL OF CAESAREA c.330-379.[76]

Comm. In Isaiam. 4.(138)v.5.

'And he shall come to be in every place on Mount Zion. He will overshadow all her surrounding regions by day with cloud that is

like smoke, and by radiant light at night. He shall shelter it with
all glory, and he shall be as a shade from the heat and as a shelter;
a hiding place from harshness and rains.'[77]

     After all things have been cleansed by washing and the
purification of repentance, there shall come the time, it says, when
'every place shall be reckoned with Mount Zion'[78]; that is raised
high and worthy to be considered heavenly. Afterwards, the 'seven
women will lay hold of the man'[79] and the 'Lord's design shall shine
gloriously'[80] so that 'he might exalt and glorify the remnant of
Israel'.[81] 'On that day they will be called saints when he has washed
away the sins of the daughters of Israel and cleansed them of the
blood in their midst.'[82] On that day he will overshadow the surrounding regions of Jerusalem with cloud by day to give them shade
from the heat and shelter from harshness and rain . The night will
be filled with radiant light, glory like smoke hanging over all things.
It is our opinion that these things are promised here to those who
will be found worthy of 'rest'.[83] For 'there are many mansions in
the father's house'[84] and different legacies are kept in the
inheritance of the earth, which is the inheritance of the meek.[85]
It follows then that some are destined to be within the splendour
of the vision[86] of God, some will find their rest in the shelter of
the heavenly powers, and others shall be concealed in the glory of
the light as if in smoke. But perhaps the light is to shine on Zion
herself, and by day the cloud (shall shine) on her surrounding regions.
This cloud takes its origin only from the light itself. Just as smoke
rises from the fire so does this cloud take its being from the light.
Those who live under it shall enjoy great glory for here they are
illuminated. In the heat it will spread out over their heads to bring
them pleasant restfulness in its shade. When harsh rainstorms pour
down it will supply cover and shelter. It will give sure protection
to those in need; its impenetrability will set them apart from all
visible reality. Of such a kind was the luminous cloud which
enveloped the disciples at the transfiguration of the Lord. On that
day the stillness and solitariness of the cloud was a sign of the

serenity to come. The overshadowing of the cloud indicated what our future state of restfulness will be like.

2. Hom. In Ps.44.5.

So gird your sword upon your thigh mighty one, in your graciousness (that means in the fulness of time) and your beauty (which is the godhead we contemplate with our minds). For he who is good exceeds all human intelligence or ability and can be contemplated in mind only. The disciples knew his beauty when he privately explained the parables to them; but Peter and the Sons of Thunder saw his beauty on the mountain more radiant than the very radiance of the sun, and they were found worthy to see with their eyes the preliminaries of his glorious advent.

GREGORY NAZIANZEN c. 330-389[87]

1. Oratio. 40.5-6.

God is light; the most high, the unapproachable , the ineffable. He cannot be conceived in the mind nor spoken by the lips. He gives life to every rational creature. He is to the world of thought what the sun is to the world of sense; and he presents himself to our minds in the degree that we are cleansed. He is loved in the degree that he presents himself to our minds and he is conceived in the degree that we love him. He contemplates and comprehends himself, and pours himself out on all that is external to him. I speak of that light which is contemplated in the Father, the Son and the Holy Spirit, whose richness is their unity of nature, and their one brightness that flashes out. A second kind of light is the Angel, an outflow or communication, as it were, of that first light, which draws its illumination from its inclination and obedience to the light. ... A third kind of light is man, a light which is visible to external objects. They call man light because of the faculty of speech in us.[88] And the name is applied again to those of us who approach God more intimately than others. I also acknowledge another light by which primeval darkness was driven away and pierced. It was the first of all visible creation to be called into being, and it radiates through all the universe, the wheeling orbit of the stars and all the beacon fires of the heavens.

(6)   Light was also the firstborn commandment given to the first-born man; 'for the commandment of the Law is a lamp and a light.'[89]   Or again: 'for your judgments are a light upon the earth.'[90] ... To mention more lights - it was light that appeared out of the fire to Moses when it burned the bush but did not consume it[91] in order to demonstrate its nature and the power it contained. It was light that was in the pillar of fire that led Israel and tamed the wilderness[92]. It was light that carried Elijah up in the chariot of fire, yet did not burn him as it carried him[93]. It was light that shone around the shepherds when the eternal light was mingled with the temporal[94]. It was light that was the beauty of the star that went before the wise men to Bethlehem to guide them on their way, and to be the escort of the light that is above us when he came down among us. Light was that godhead which was shown to the disciples on the mountain - a little too strong for their eyes. Light was that vision which blazed out upon Paul[95] and healed the darkness of his soul by wounding his eyes. Light is also the brilliancy of heaven to those who have been purified here when the righteous shall shine forth as the sun[96] and God shall stand in their midst[97], gods and kings, deciding and distinguishing the ranks of the blessed-ness of heaven. Besides these things the illumination of Baptism is also light in a special sense, about which we are now speaking for it contains a great and marvellous   sacrament of   our

salvation.

2. **Carmina.** 20

His eighteenth miracle: He changed a divine form, appearing to his
friends more radiant than the sun.

3. **De Moderatione in Disputando.** Orat.32.18.

They went up the mountain so that he might radiate in his (bodily)
form and reveal the godhead, laying bare the one who lay hidden
in the flesh.

4. **Oratio.**29.19.

For the Jews, he had: 'Neither beauty nor form'[98] but for David
he was: 'gracious and beautiful beyond the sons of men.'[99] And
he flashed like lightning on the mountain and became brighter than
the sun, intimating mysteries of the age to come.

GREGORY OF NYSSA c.335-394[100]

Contra Eunomium. 4.1.

I proclaim that the Lord is Son of God because the Gospel which
was given from heaven through the bright cloud, so proclaimed him.

For, he says: 'This is my beloved Son.' But although I was taught that he was the Son, the name did not drag me down to think that 'Son' had any earthly significance. I know that he is from the Father and I also know that he is not from passion . And I can add to these statements the fact that I also know of a bodily generation that is pure of passion, so that even on this point Eunomius' physiology of bodily generation is proved false, if, that is, a bodily birth can be found which does not admit of passion.

JOHN CHRYSOSTOM c.347-407.[10]

l.   **Ad Theodorum Lapsum.** l.ll.

To show that my words are not empty boasts let us turn our minds to the mountain where Christ was transfigured and let us look upon him shining in radiance. And yet he did not show us here the full radiance of the age to come. The splendour here was a con-descension rather than a true manifestation of what it will be like, which is clear from the words of the evangelist. For what does he say? 'He shone as bright as the sun.' But the glory of incor-ruptible bodies does not emit such light as this corruptible body, nor such as could be contained by mortal eyes, for incorruptible and immortal eyes are necessary for this vision. On the mountain only so much was revealed to them as was possible to see without damaging the eyes of those who looked on, and even then they could not bear it and fell on their faces. Tell me, if someone brought you into a certain splendid place where everyone sat dressed in golden garments and in the middle of the throng showed you someone else whose garments and the crown upon his head were made purely from precious stones, and then he promised you that you would be enrolled in the number of that people - would you not do all in your power to achieve such a promise? So open the eyes of your mind and look into that theatre, not that frequented by ordinary men but by those who are more noble in gold, and precious stones and sunbright rays, and every kind of splendour that can be seen; and not only men but those who are far more noble than them, the angels, archangels, thrones, dominions, principalities and powers. As for the King, no one can say what he is like for his beauty and comeliness, his radiance and glory and great magnificence wholly escape all speech and thought. And so, tell me, are we to deprive ourselves of such good things in order to avoid a short time of sufferings? Even if we had to endure a thousand deaths each day, endure Gehenna itself, in order to see Christ coming in his glory, and be reckoned in the assembly of his saints, would not all these things be worth enduring? Listen to what the blessed Peter says: 'It is good for us to be here.' So if he, seeing an obscure image of the things to come, immediately cast out everything from his soul, for the sake of the delightfulness of what he saw being placed in his soul, then what can be said when the very truth of these things comes about; when the kingly halls are thrown open and the King himself can be seen no longer in riddles or through a mirror, but face to face; not by faith any longer but before our very eyes?

2.   Hom.21. Ecloga de Imperio Potestate et Gloria.

When you hear the saying of the prophet: 'I saw the Lord'[102] you should not suppose that he saw God's essence, but rather a condescension, and even then (he saw it) much less clearly than the heavenly powers. This is made clear by the apostles for as it is said: 'Jesus went up the mountain and was transfigured before them.' What does 'transfigured' mean? It means that he opened out a little of the godhead and showed them the indwelling deity. 'And his face was as radiant as the sun and his garments became as white as light. 'The evangelist, wishing to show us this radiance of his, tells us how radiant he was. And how radiant was he? Immensely radiant. But tell me in what manner? Like the sun. Like the sun you say? Yes. Why was this? Because I do not have any other star so splendid and so brilliant. He was as white as snow for I do not have any other material that is whiter. For he did not really become radiant in this way, as we can see from what follows: 'And the disciples fell to the ground.' If he was as radiant as the sun the disciples would not have fallen down, for they saw the sun every day and did not keep falling down. But since he was radiant far beyond sun or snow, this was why they could not bear the radiance and fell down. But what else could I do? I am a man and I speak as a man. I have an earthly tongue and I ask the indulgence of the Master for I did not use these words from foolishness but because of the poor limitations of our nature and our speech. Be merciful Lord for I did not say these things in foolishness but because I had no other (words). Nonetheless I do not remain standing in the poverty of these expressions but rise up on the wings of understanding.

3.   Hom.56. In Matthaeum 17. (passim)

(1)   Why did he bring Moses and Elijah among them? One could say that there were many reasons, but the chief one is this: because some of the crowds were saying he was Elijah, and others - one of the ancient prophets; and so he brought forth the leading prophets so that they could see how great a difference there was between slaves and the Master. Peter was rightly praised when he confessed him to be Son of God. We can say more because people frequently accused him of being a transgressor of the Law and thought of him as a blasphemer, one who appropriated the glory of the Father which did not belong to him. They said: 'This man is not from God because he does not keep the sabbath.'[103] And

again: 'We do not stone you for any good work, but for blasphemy because being a man you make yourself God.'[104] It is for this reason then that he brings among them the ones who excelled in respect to both matters, to show that both charges arose from malice and that he was innocent of them both. He was not a transgressor of the Law neither did he attribute to himself a glory that did not rightly belong to him when he said that he was equal to the Father. It was Moses who gave the Law and the Jews would therefore understand that he would never have willingly suffered this behaviour which they considered transgression; nor would he have ever served anyone who transgressed the Law or was an enemy of Him who gave the Law. And Elijah too was filled with zeal for the glory of God, and if Christ really had been an anti-god, calling himself God, making himself equal to the Father, while not being what he said he was, then he too would never have been present and never have given him obedience.

(3)   Luke tells us next that Peter and the others were seized with great fear, and he says: 'They were heavy with sleep, but staying awake they saw his glory.'[105] Here he calls 'sleep' that great heaviness which came upon them from the vision. For just as the eyes are darkened by excessive radiance, so did it happen to them at that time. It was not night but daytime, and the splendour of the rays pressed heavily on the weakness of their eyes. And what happened? Peter said nothing, nor did Moses or Elijah, but one who is greater and more trustworthy than all of these, the Father himself, sent out a voice from the cloud. Why from a cloud? Because God has always appeared in this fashion; for 'cloud and darkness are all around him'[106] and again 'He who puts the cloud as his footstep'[107], or 'The Lord sits upon a light cloud'[108], and 'A cloud took him up from their sight'[109] or, 'As the Son of Man comes upon the clouds'.[110] It was so they should believe that the voice came from God. This is why it came from a cloud - a bright cloud too.

(4)   There is nothing more blessed than the apostles, especially

these three, who were judged worthy to dwell with their Master in the cloud. But if it is our desire, then we too shall see Christ. Not in the way that these saw him on the mountain, but in a much greater splendour. He will not come like this in the future. For then he spared the disciples by only showing so much of his splendour as they were able to bear. But in the future he will come in the very glory of the Father, not only with Moses and Elijah, but with all the infinite armies of the angels, with the archangels and cherubim, and with these infinite multitudes. He will not come with a cloud over his head, he will open up the very heavens.

CYRIL OF ALEXANDRIA d.444[111]

1.   Hom. Diversae 9
Skilful competitors are gratified by the spectators' applause and urged on by the hope of prizes towards the victory that honours them. And those who long to gain the divine graces and thirst for communion in that hope which has been prepared for the saints, willingly undertake the struggle for the sake of righteousness in Christ. They live an admirable life. They do not prefer sloth that brings no reward, nor are they in love with an unmanly cowardice, but they bear themselves manfully against every temptation and reckon all the assaults of persecutors as of little matter, considering it as their riches to suffer for Christ's sake. Such men remember the text of the blessed Paul which says: 'The sufferings of the present time are not worth comparing to the future glory that is to be revealed in us.'[112]   And so look closely into this most beautiful economy which Our Lord Jesus Christ has now arranged for the benefit and upbuilding of the holy apostles. He said to them: 'If anyone wishes to come after me let him deny himself, and take up his cross and follow me. For whoever wishes to save his life

will lose it, but whoever shall lose his life for my sake, he shall find it.[113] This teaching is our salvation, and is most fitting for the saints for it prepares heavenly glory and makes our lot one of gladness of heart. Because to suffer for Christ's sake is truly not without reward for it brings about our communion in eternal life and glory. The disciples, however, had not yet received power from on high and were still likely to fall into human weaknesses, such as to think to themselves 'how can anyone deny himself?' or 'how can a man who loses his life find it again?' or 'what would be a fitting reward for those who suffered this?' or 'what will be the gifts in which they share?' And in order to remove such thoughts and words as these from them and refashion them as men of courage he inspired within them the desire of his glory; for he said: 'I tell you there are some of you standing here who will not taste death until they see the Kingdom of God.' Surely he did not mean that such a span of life would be drawn out for them that they would survive even into those times of the consummation of the ages, when he would descend from the heavens and restore to the saints the kingdom that had been prepared for them? Even this, however, was possible for him; for he can do all things and there is nothing that cannot be done, nothing that cannot be accomplished by his all powerful nod. But the Kingdom he spoke of was the vision of his glory in which he will be seen in that time when he will shine out upon all men on earth. For he will come in the glory of God the Father and no longer in our human pettiness. So how did he make them see this wonder, those who had received his promise? Going up the mountain he took three chosen ones from among them and then he was transfigured into a certain extraordinary and godlike radiance, so that even his garments seemed to shine at the touch of this light. Then Moses and Elijah stood around Jesus talking to one another about his passing which he would fulfil in Jerusalem[11], that is the mystery of the economy in the flesh and the saving Passion which was to be upon his honourable cross. It also came about like this because the Law of Moses and the words of the holy Prophets foreshowed the mystery of Christ. The one consistently wrote about it in types and shadows, as if on graven tablets, the others preached it in many different ways. But in the proper time it is seen now within our own form. And for the sake of the life and salvation of all men, he did not shrink from suffering death upon the tree. This is why Moses and Elijah were present and spoke to one another. It was in order to show that the Law and the prophets were the attendants of Our Lord Jesus Christ, whom they foreshowed to be the Lord both of the Law and the Prophets. By the harmony of the Law and the Prophets he was preached in advance. For the prophetic words are not at variance with the Law. This is why, in my opinion, the most sacred Moses and the greatest of the prophets, that is Elijah, were talking with one another. There is something else to consider here, for some of the crowds were saying that he was Elijah, and others that he was Jeremiah or one of the prophets. For this reason he brought out their leading figures to let them see the difference between a slave and the Master.[115] There is still something else to consider here, for they constantly accused him of transgressing the Law and reckoned him a blasphemer as if he attributed to himself a glory that was not rightly his, the glory of the Father. So they said: 'This man is not from God, because he does not keep the sabbath;'[116] and again 'We do not stone you for any good work but for blasphemy because being a man you make yourself God.'[117] And to show these charges rose from malice and that he was innocent on both counts (that he had neither broken the Law, nor attributed to himself a glory that was not rightly his when he had said that he was equal to the Father) - then he brought forward the very ones who excelled in respect to both matters. For it was Moses who gave the Law and the Jews would therefore understand that he had never neglected or scorned the Law as they suspected, and never broken it, but rather followed it and was opposed to all who set it aside. And Elijah was filled with zeal for the glory of God and if Christ really had been an anti-god calling himself God, making himself equal to the Father while not being what he said he was and not doing this legitimately, then he too would never have stood with him or been subject to him. Apart from these things we have said so far, there is still something else to speak of. What is it? Well, (they came) so that the disciples might learn that Christ has the power of life and death and rules over those who are above as well as those who are below. For this reason he brings forward the one who was still living, and the one who was dead. And when they appeared they were not silent but spoke about the glory which he was to fulfill in Jerusalem, that is his Passion and Cross, and by implication the resurrection also. The blessed disciples were somewhat sleepy here, just as they took their ease when Christ was praying. This economy fulfilled human needs so that when they were wide awake they were able to behold this venerable and wonderful transformation. Thinking perhaps that the time of the Kingdom of God had arrived, the great Peter was glad that they were there talking on the mountain and he spoke out for three tabernacles to be built. He did not know what to say. For then it was not the time for the consummation of the age; nor in the present time are these saints to take their share in that hope which was promised to them. As Paul says: 'He shall refashion the body of our lowliness to make it conform to the body of his glory,'[118] Christ's no less. Since the economy was still in its early stages, not yet finished, how was it possible for Christ, who had come into the world for the sake of love, to draw back from his great desire to suffer on behalf of the world? He saved that nature which is under heaven by offering it to death according to the flesh, setting it free by his resurrection from the dead. This is why Peter did not know what to say. Moreover, apart from the marvellous and ineffable vision of Christ's glory, something else happened that was both useful and necessary to confirm their faith (and not only for the disciples but for us as well) for from the cloud the voice of God the Father came down from heaven saying: 'This is my beloved Son in whom I am well pleased. Listen to him.' And it says that while this voice was speaking Jesus was found alone. What can the stiff-necked Jews say to these things - who will not be guided, the disobedient ones whose hearts suffer no admonition? For behold in the presence of Moses, the Father commands the apostles to listen to Christ. If he had wanted them to follow in the commandments of Moses surely he would have said 'Keep the Law since you trust in Moses'. But God the Father does not say this. In the presence of Moses and his prophet Elijah he orders them to listen to Him. And in order that no one might mis-represent the real meaning of the saying and (pretend) that the Father really ordered them to obey Moses and not Christ the Saviour of us all, this was why it was necessary for the evangelist to make a special note saying that when the voice came Jesus was found to be alone. And so when God the Father commanded the holy apostles from the cloud on high to 'Listen to him', Moses had gone away, Elijah was no longer present. Christ alone was there. God ordered them, then, to listen to him, for he is the end[119] of the Law and the Prophets. For this reason he also spoke to the Jewish people in these words: 'If you believed Moses you would have believed me, for Moses was writing about me.'[120] But since they had dishonoured the commandments of the most wise Moses and constantly nullified the words spoken through the prophets, rightly were they cast out and cut off from the good things promised to their fathers. As it is written: 'Obedience is better than sacrifice. To listen is better than the fat of a lamb.'[121] This shows what happened to the Jews. But for us who recognised his appearing, all things in all manner are made good through him and with him who is the Christ, through whom and with whom, to God the Father, be glory and sovereignty, with the Holy Spirit, through the ages of ages, Amen.

2.   Com. In Lucam.9.[122]

(col.652D). He went up the mountain, taking the three chosen ones, to show that an earth-bound mind would never be suitable for contemplation, only a mind which has spurned earthly things and gone beyond all bodily matters to stand alone in stillness[123] beyond all the cares of this life; one that can be said to be higher than the oppressive passions. For then it is transformed into a certain elect and godly radiance so that even its garments are illumined in the beams of that light, and they too seem to flash with light.

(col.653D) Since they had heard that our flesh had to rise again, but did not know in what form it would be, he changed his own flesh in order to give an example of the transformation, and to confirm our hope. And so he was transfigured before them. It is my belief that his transfiguration did not happen by a laying aside of the human form of the body, but rather by certain luminous glory clothing him, which therefore changed the dishonourable character of the flesh into a far nobler appearance. As the divine Paul so beautifully put it: 'It is sown in dishonour but raised in glory.'[124] For now this same flesh is naked, not clothed in any glory or adorned in any natural splendour. It has nothing more than the obscurity and weakness of its own nature. But in the time of resurrection a kind of divine transformation will take place, a change in glory rather than a change in form, and then the body clothed in divine glory will be radiant and the 'just will shine like the sun in the Kingdom of the Father'[125] as the Saviour said. And so we see that the transfiguration was an example of that glory that is to come, given to the disciples and revealed in a bodily way to fall under the scope of mortal eyes, even though they could not bear the immensity of the radiance.

PROCLOS OF CONSTANTINOPLE. d.446. [126]

Oratio 8.

Come my friends, today let us attentively apply ourselves
to the Gospel treasures so that we can draw out, as usual, a source
of riches that can be freely divided out and never used up. Come
to that wisest of good guides and let us follow Luke once more
to behold Christ going up the high mountain, taking with him Peter,
James and John as witnesses of the divine transfiguration. For it
says that the Master took Peter and his companions and ascended
a high mountain on which Moses and Elijah conversed with Christ;a
high mountain on which the Law and the Prophets conversed with
Grace; a high mountain on which Moses sacrificed the paschal lamb[127]
and sprinkled the doorposts of the Hebrews with its blood ; a high
mountain on which Elijah dismembered the ox with those others,
and consumed the sacrifice with fire passing through the water[128];
a high mountain on which Moses stood who opened and closed the
waters of the Red Sea; a high mountain where Elijah stood who
opened and shut the clouds of rain[129]; a high mountain so that Peter,
James and John might learn that He was the one 'to whom every
knee shall bend, in heaven, on earth, and in the underworld.'[130]
For the Master ascended the mountain taking only three with him.
He did not take them all, and he did not leave them all behind.
He did not begrudge the glory to the others, nor did he consider
them to be inferior, nor did he do it to distress the other nine.
He is the Just One, and all he does is justly done, and he reckoned
all of them as one, and made no distinctions among them in his
love , for he had made them as one. But because Judas, who was
to become the traitor, was unworthy of the divine vision and that
awesome appearance, then because of him he left the others behind
too so that Judas would not be the only one left behind, and that
future accusations might be forestalled. He brought up these
three independent witnesses to his transfiguration, in accordance
with the Law, and so that he might make it known spiritually to
the others in these three. For he had said:'Righteous Father,guard
them that they too may be one just as we are one.'[131] So when
Judas saw Andrew,Thomas, Philip and the others kept off the

mountain as well as himself, but not complaining or annoyed or pro-
testing about it but rather rejoicing and thinking that they were
sharers in the same heavenly grace as those who had gone, then
he had absolutely no grounds for complaint that he had ever been
slighted in any of the miracles. Nonetheless it was he who kept
the purse, and not only was he angry without reason at the woman
who anointed Jesus, but he even handed the Master over, shame-
lessly, to his enemies.

2.   Why is it said: 'And he was transfigured before them and
there appeared to them Moses and Elijah conversing with him?'
Peter, so eager and quick to speak, as always, sees men he had
never seen before, conversing with him. And he does not weigh
up the immensity of this wonder, and he does not have regard to
the marvel of this divine radiance, but cries out that this desert
place is good. Then the fishermen become tabernacle-builders;
saying to the Saviour: 'Let us make three tabernacles here; one for
you , one for Elijah and one for Moses; not knowing what he was
saying.' How kindly does the most-wise Luke excuse him by adding:
'not knowing what he was saying.'But Peter, you prince of disciples
and leader of the apostles, why did you want to fall down to these
mean thoughts and insult divine realities with your human words
- talking this way about erecting three tabernacles in the wilderness,
and offering the same honour to slaves as to the Master by setting
the shrines of the other two on the same level as the tabernacle
to Christ? Surely Moses was not conceived of the Holy Spirit as
he was? Surely a virgin-mother did not give birth to Elijah as the
all-holy virgin Mary gave birth to him? Surely no one knew Moses
as an infant in his mother's womb as the Fore-runner[132] knew him?
Surely the heavens did not herald the birth of Elijah nor the Magi
worship the swaddling bands of Moses? For Moses and Elijah never
performed such miracles as these; casting out legions of demons from
men, casting out spirits from the recesses of men. For when Moses
was angry he struck the sea with his staff and it divided. But Jesus,
your Master, walked over the sea and made the depths passable

for you, Peter.[133]   Elijah entreated and increased the widow's meal
and raised her son from the dead; but the one who took you from
being a fisherman to be a disciple, fed thousands from a few loaves
and went into Hell to despoil it and carried off those who had lain
there throughout the ages.   And so, Peter, do not say: 'Let us make
three tabernacles here'.   Do not say: 'It is good for us to be here.'
Think nothing base, nothing earthly, nothing creeping. think rather
of the things that are above, not the things of earth, as Paul tells
us to do.[134]   For how is it good for us to be here where the hurtful
serpent wounded the first man, and then closed up Paradise; where
we heard that our bread is to be eaten in the sweat of our face;
where we learned from Cain to groan and tremble on the face of
the earth; where there is nothing lasting; where all things are
shadows; where all things pass in a moment - so how is it good
for us to be here?   If Christ intended to leave us here then why
did he bend down the heavens and come down?[135]   If Christ intended
to leave us here why did he share in our flesh and blood?   If Christ
intended to leave us here why did he stoop down to one who had
fallen and raise up his prostrate form?   If it is good for us to be
upon the earth in vain are you called the Keybearer of Heaven.
For what use would you have for the keys of heaven?   Moreover,
if you long for this mountain then say farewell to the heavens.
If you want to build tabernacles you must renounce the title and
role of the foundation of the Church.   It was not without reason
that Christ the Lord was transfigured, but so that he might reveal
to us the transfiguration of our natures that is to come, and his
second coming, in light, upon the clouds with all the angels.   For
it is he who 'is girded with light as in a robe;'[136] he who is the
judge of the living and the dead[137].   This is why he brought Moses
and Elijah in among them to stand as seals of the ancient revelations.
3.   What more does the great evangelist have to say?   'While
they were still talking, behold a bright cloud overshadowed them
and behold a voice came from the cloud saying: This is my beloved
Son in whom I am well-pleased.   Listen to him.'   He says that while

Peter was still speaking, the Father confounded him from heaven to this effect: What indeed is all this Peter? Why are you confusing yourself so, and why are you blurting out these nonsenses, saying that this is a good place? Are you out of your mind? Or are you envious of them and do not know what to say? Have you still not learned anything? or understood the unshakeable knowledge of the Sonship? Were you not the one who said: 'You are the Christ, the Son of the living God'? You have looked on so many wonders, Bar Jonah, and are you still a Simon? He set you as the Keybearer of Heaven and have you not yet laid aside your fishing tunic? Look, this is the third time that you have run counter to the Saviour's will, not knowing what to say. For he said to you: 'I must suffer,' and you said: 'This must never happen to you.'[138] Again he said: 'All of you will be scandalised;' and you said 'If all others are, I will not be scandalised.'[139] And see, now do you want to build a tabernacle for Christ, the same as that for Moses and Elijah? A tabernacle for Christ who stretched out the heavens with me?[140] A tabernacle for him who laid the foundations of the earth with me? A tabernacle for him who gathered the sea and fixed the firmament? A tabernacle for him who lit the stars, who set fire in the skies, and made all things with me before the ages? A tabernacle for him who is of me, and also of you? A tabernacle for a man who is fatherless, and for a god who is motherless? A tabernacle for him who chose his own tabernacle and accepted a virgin's womb? And so, because you wished to build three tabernacles, not knowing what to say, I used a bright cloud as my own tabernacle and overshadowed all who were present. I cry out then from the heavens: This is my beloved son in whom I am well-pleased - not Moses or Elijah, but him. Not the one or the other, only this one. This is the one in whom I am well pleased. Listen to him.

4.   Moses I justified but in this one I am well-pleased. Elijah I assumed, but this one I sent out into the virgin, as into heaven; and out from the virgin I sent heaven to him. For as he said: 'No

one has gone into heaven except the one who came down from heaven.'[141] In vain, then, would he have come down upon the earth if he intended to remain always upon the earth. In vain would he have emptied himself, assuming the form of a slave[142] if he had become what you are while not remaining that which he was. And if he had not taken up the Cross, like you, and for the sake of all of you, to redeem the world by his own blood, then the whole Economy would be made futile and the ancient uncertainties of the prophetic words would still be in force. So desist Peter and do not think the thoughts of man, but the things of God. For this is my Beloved Son in whom I am well-pleased. Listen to him. Twice have I spoken in this voice about him, when you were present; on this mountain and in the presence of John in the river Jordan. This was so that the ancient prophet might be proved right who cried out: 'Thabor and Hermon rejoice in your name.'[143] Whose name? - 'This is my Son the Beloved.' For as Paul says: 'He has given him the name above every name.'[144] Perhaps, my dear, you are wondering what it means: Thabor and Hermon shall rejoice in your name? Well learn this sensibly. Thabor is the mountain on which Christ wished to be transfigured, where the Father bore witness to the Son, as you have just heard. And Hermon is a mountain somewhat near the Jordan[145], from which Elijah was taken up. It is right next to the waters of the Jordan where Christ desired to be baptised, where the Father bore witness again to the Son. On both these mountains the undefiled Father confirmed the Sonship, at both times crying out: This is my beloved Son in whom I am well-pleased. Listen to him. For whoever hears him hears me also. Those who are ashamed of him and his words, I shall be ashamed of them in my glory with the holy angels.[146] Listen to him without deceit or wickedness; without reservations and without indulging curiosity. Seek faith, do not search for phrases. Take up faith, do not bandy words with The Word. That great Paul crushed curiosity well enough when he taught them all, crying out without hesitation: 'Oh the depths of the riches of the wisdom and knowledge of God; How

incomprehensible are his judgements and how inscrutable his ways;'
to him be glory to the ages of ages. Amen.

THEODORET OF CYR c.313-466.[147]

l.   **Epist.** 145

The most celebrated Athanasius was five times exiled from his flock
and forced to live in foreign lands. His teacher, Alexander, had
to fight for the same doctrine. So did Eustathius and Meletius and
Flavian, those luminaries of the East; and Ephraim, the Harp of
the Spirit, who day by day watered the Syrian nation with the springs
of grace. So also did John and Atticus, the great-sounding heralds
of the truth; as well as the ancients Ignatius, Polycarp, Irenaeus,
Justin and Hippolytus, most of whom not only shone as High Priests,
but also graced the choir of Martyrs. There is also the one who
now governs Great Rome, the most holy Leo, who spreads out the
rays of right teaching from the West to every region, who in his
own writings has set out for us this rule of faith. All of these
have clearly taught that the only begotten Son of God is One, being
Son and God before the ages, ineffably begotten from the Father,
and that after the incarnation he is also called Son of Man, and
Man, not as changed into this since he has an unchangeable nature,
but as assuming what is ours. (They have taught that) the same
one was impassible, and as God was immortal, yet as man was both
mortal and passible; but that after the resurrection he received impas-
sibility and immortality even in his manhood. For the body remained
a body but it is impassible and immortal; and being a divine body
it is glorified with a divine glory. The blessed Paul teaches us this
most clearly when he says: 'Our citizenship is in the heavens from

where we expect Our Lord and Saviour Jesus Christ, who will transform the body of our lowliness to make it conform to the body of
his glory.'[148] And he does not say 'to his glory' but 'to the body
of his glory'. The Lord himself said to the apostles: 'For there
are some standing here who will not taste death until they see the
Son of Man coming in the glory of the Father'[149] and six days later
he took them up a very high mountain and was transfigured before
them. His face became like the sun and his garments as radiant as
light. By these things he taught them the manner of the second
coming, and although the assumed nature is not uncircumscribed,
since this is solely the property of deity, nevertheless he emits the
sparkling radiance of divine glory and beams out rays of light which
are beyond the capacity of the eyes' senses. In this glory he
ascended, and in this way the angels said he would come again.
This is what they said: 'The one who was taken from you into
heaven, so shall he return as you have seen him going into
heaven.'[150] And after the Resurrection he was seen by the divine
apostles and he showed them his hands and his feet - and to Thomas,
even his side and the wounds of the nails and lance. He kept these
marks of nails and lance intact because of those who openly deny
the assumption of flesh, and because of others like them who say
that after the Resurrection the nature of the body was changed
into that of godhead. He left the signs of suffering in his own body,
he who set bodies free from every blemish, so that he might convict
of their error, by means of his sufferings, those who deny the
assumption of a body, and so that by the marks of the nails he
might instruct those who think that his body was changed into
another nature that in reality it remained in its own form.

ANTIPATER OF BOSTRA (fl. Mid 5th Century).[151]

Contra Apologiam pro Origene.

When the divine scripture talks of being changed or re-fashioned it does not in any way speak of the composition of the physical form, but of those parts that are being changed either to greater honour or dishonour. We can see this from one of many places in divine scripture, as for example when it is said of the Master that 'he was transfigured before them,' and was transfigured from a mean form into a more glorious one. The evangelist immediately explains the manner of the transfiguration for us, that his face shone as bright as the sun and his garments became like light. The aspect of his face was changed. This does not tell us that the whole arrangement of his face was changed, only its glory. And this, his transfiguration in glory, was said by the Lord to be like his future coming from the heavens. For he spoke to them about this vision saying: 'There are some standing here who will not taste death before they see the Son of Man coming in glory;'[152] or according to another evangelist, 'until they see the Kingdom of God coming in power.'[153] He said this in reference to Peter, James and John. For the former evangelist immediately adds: 'It came to pass eight days after these words', and having numbered them he continues: 'He took with him Peter and James and John,' and in the following verses he tells about their vision. The evangelist who says 'after six days' is only counting the days in between. Let them desist, therefore, who make so bold as to stretch out their hands to misinterpret the sense of these divine things. Let them abide in the tradition of the apostles which is handed down from the beginning, and let them be fellow-citizens in the mind of the churches who hold and teach the resurrection of men: knowing nothing else by the word 'men' than that which it normally means to be a man. And whatever does not correspond to this definition of being a man, let it not be recognised or taught.

PSEUDO-ATHANASIUS fl. mid 5th Century [154]

Ep. De Incarnatione. 4

For there is but one person, both before the Incarnation and after
the incarnation, the uncircumscribed God in the flesh, the impassible
in the sufferings of the flesh, who overcomes death and rises on
the third day. It is this one who ascended to heaven in a glory
that was his by nature not by grace, and he will come again openly,
in his own godhead, radiating an ineffable glory from that holy body
of his which he took from Mary, just as he revealed it in part on
the mountain in order to teach us that he is the same - previously
and now;not deified later in time, which is the blasphemy presently
causing trouble.

PSEUDO-DIONYSIUS fl. c.5OO. [155]

De Div. Nom. l.4.

We have also been initiates in all the other divine enlightenments,
which the secret tradition of our inspired teachers has granted to
us by mystic interpretation in accordance with the scriptures. We
have apprehended these things in this present life, according to our
powers, through the sacred veils of that loving kindness which in
the scriptures and hierarchical traditions wraps up spiritual truths
in terms drawn from the world of sense, and hyper-essential truths
in terms that are drawn from essence; clothing shapeless things that
are formless in shapes and forms and fashioning manifold attributes
for the supernatural imageless Simplicity by a variety of separable
symbols.   But hereafter when we are incorruptible and immortal

and attain that blessed lot of being like Christ, then, as scripture tells us, we shall all be for ever with the Lord.[156] We shall be fulfilled with his visible theophany in holy contemplations, and it shall shine round about us with radiant beams of glory just as of old it once shone round the disciples at the divine Transfiguration. And then, with our mind made impassible and spiritual, we shall participate in a spiritual illumination from him, and in a union that transcends our mental faculties. There, amidst the blinding blissful impulses of his dazzling rays we shall be made like to the heavenly intelligences in a more divine manner that at present. As the infallible scripture says, we shall be equal to the angels and shall be sons of God, being sons of the Resurrection. [157] But as for the present we employ, so far as in us lies, appropriate symbols for divine realities.

ANASTASIUS I OF ANTIOCH   c.559-599.   [158]

Hom. De Transfiguratione. 3-9.

3.   And it came to pass after six days Jesus took up Peter, James, and John his brother, and led them up a high mountain by themselves. And he was transfigured before them. His face shone like the sun and his garments became as white as snow. And behold there appeared to them Moses and Elijah, talking with him. These are not things we should hear lightly. And we should not think that there is no meaning behind these words, or that they only signify what the text says, for they open to us mystical secrets, of how we shall come in the future to enjoy the repose of good things - or rather the saints, not us. And so, when six days had passed after had had given a promise, he fulfilled that promise which

he spoke to his disciples. His promise was this: There are some of you standing here who will not taste death before you see the Kingdom of God which must be revealed after the consummation of this dull-witted world. This is why after six days he took up those who were destined to know the divine mysteries of the Kingdom before they tasted death. For after six days comes the seventh which is that holy repose on which no work is to be done, since God made heaven and earth in six days and rested on the seventh, and made it holy. So, on the first day came the promise, and again on the first day comes the fulfilment of that promise. The number six, then, has a bearing on this dull-witted world which was composed from the fulfilment of its proper days, six being a symbol of creation and having in itself male and female whose inter- course makes a bodily creation. But after their creation there comes the seventh day: 'in which they neither marry nor are given in marriage, but are as the angels of God in heaven.'[159] This is why the number seven is called the 'Virgin', just as the seventh day is holy causing all servile work to cease and making everyone sit down each in their own place.[160]

(4)   Then after this he took with him the three chosen disciples, for it was not fitting for Judas to be a witness of such great mysteries; but then again he alone could not be left out of this vision so that no excuse might be given him for his betrayal, if for example he thought that all the others had been given prefer- ence over him.[161] So it was that Jesus took with him only the three and he led them up a high mountain (but what is higher than his own glory?) by themselves. The immaterial life is all of one kind. This leading them up on high from the low places does not take place in geographical terms but in God's terms.   That is he makes them capable of receiving his transcendent illuminations.   Then he was transfigured before them.   Of old Jesus the Saviour was trans- figured, not in the presence of men, but in the presence of his own father when he did not think it a thing to be grasped to be equal to God, but emptied himself out, taking the form of a slave, he

who was in the form of God[162]. And so, he formerly covered up the divine form when he was transfigured into the form of a slave but now he restores that form of the slave to its natural state, not laying aside the servile nature but rather brightening it with divine properties. Thus he was transfigured before them to show them that in this way 'he will refashion the body of our lowliness then and make it conform to the body of his own glory.'[163] And it says that 'his face shone like the sun and his garments became as white as snow.' These things are written not because he can be compared to the sun or the snow (for to what can you compare the incomparable?) but because there is nothing among material things that is brighter than the sun or whiter than snow, and he wished to give a suitable description of the immensity and splendour of the light by reference to something we know about.[164] The radiance of his garments signifies the change of our bodies; for we shall become a garment for him, since he put on the vesture of our flesh. Or perhaps 'his face shone like the sun' symbolically designates his own body and 'his garments became as white as snow' signifies those who are cleansed by him through his refashioning and transforming power, because this spiritual garment can also be likened to snow since it too is refashioned and evaporates from water to become snow. And because our own nature became his garment, and shall be so again, so we hear Isaiah speaking to him in the person of God: 'For you shall put on all of these as vesture, and gird yourself in them as a bridal ornament.'[165]

(5)   And so he was transfigured before them and his face shone like the sun and his garments became as white as snow, and there appeared to them Moses and Elijah talking with him. The disciples became much more clear-sighted in as much as they went up the mountain with Jesus, for they had scarcely recognised who it was that was talking with Jesus when Moses and Elijah were transfigured with him. For if they had not been transfigured with him they would not have been talking with him. According to Luke, however, they talked with Jesus about his death which he would fulfil in

Jerusalem.[166] So it was that the disciples heard from them what they had not understood when Jesus spoke to them, when Peter thinking the things of man rebuked Jesus for saying that he would be killed by men and on the third day would rise from the dead. So, as I have said, Moses and Elijah spoke with Jesus (that is the Law and the Prophets) for when the minds of the disciples were transfigured and the shadows of the Law moved away, then they believed that Moses, that faithful servant, had written everything about Christ and in his own words clearly depicted his death[167] which he would fulfil in Jerusalem. But with regard to how, or whence, or by what signs the disciples recognised the prophets – does not seem to me to be a suitable question, or one that is worthy of investigation. For if they were set apart on so great a height to be made worthy of such a vision, a vision that the one who was revealed as transfigured with the prophets had called the 'Kingdom of God' in their very presence, then how would it have been possible for them not to have recognised their fellow saints?[168] At all events the apostles too were prophets, and when prophets meet with prophets they have one and the same knowledge; and all the more so in the presence of Jesus who enlightened their souls[169] and formed their minds after his own divine form. 'And Peter answered Jesus saying: Lord it is good for us to be here. If you wish we shall make three tabernacles here, one for you, one for Moses, and one for Elijah.' Peter sensed what a great distinction there is between spiritual and sensible realities, and he chose the better things in preference to the worse. But he had not yet fully understood what it was they were seeing, otherwise he would not have thought that spiritual beings had any need of tabernacles. Perhaps he was anxious for the Master because of the death he had foretold, and even those he saw were talking with Jesus about this same thing. Both of them agreed that the death would take place at Jerusalem; so perhaps Peter asked the Lord if it would not be a good thing to remain there and in no way surrender himself to the Scribes and Pharisees who were his enemies. Perhaps he thought that none of the plotters would come against Jesus on the mountain and it would all turn out differently to Jerusalem, and that in a different place these things would not happen. This is why it is good for us to be here with Moses and Elijah rather than to go to those unholy and god-murdering priests. And so, if you agree with what I say, let us make here three tabernacles, he says, one for you, one for Moses and one for Elijah. But in trying to spare the Master he did not realise that he was becoming an obstacle to the salvation of the world. Luke reflects on this when he says: 'He did not know what he was saying'; but Mark says 'For he did not know what to say', or to think either. Those who went up with Jesus stood in a higher place.

(6)   While they were still speaking etc. (Mt.17.5-8).

So while Peter was still speaking these words of affection for his Master, a certain luminous cloud overshadowed them from on high and a voice came from the cloud to correct Peter, and perhaps also the other disciples who wanted the same things as he did, and were also saying that he should remain on the mountain. They were corrected so that they should think nothing contrary to the beloved Son but rather listen to him and follow his will. For he is the salvation of all men. What we are to understand by this cloud we can find from similar sayings in the scripture. We discover, for example, that Moses too went into the cloud when it covered Mount Horeb in the desert. And it witnesses that he came into the darkness where God was.[170]   And again, in ancient times a cloud covered the Tent of Witness in a different way and from it God was heard speaking with Moses.[171]   Yet again a column of cloud went before the people giving them rain by day and fire by night. Isaiah too foretold that the Lord would come into Egypt upon a light cloud.[172] We also hear in Solomon that when he had built and dedicated the Temple the cloud filled the house and the priests were not able to go in from the face of the cloud to offer sacrifice.[173]   These and many more instances can be gathered from the whole of scripture as clear explanations for our minds that we can know what this cloud was, overshadowing all those who were seen as well as those who saw them. From the cloud there was also heard the voice saying: 'This is my beloved Son, in whom I am well-pleased. Listen to him.'

(7)   These clouds we have spoken of are to be understood as related to one another. Indeed we should not scruple to say that they are all but one cloud; and this is not to be thought of as any vaporous emanation of the earth, or any evaporation of water or condensation of air, or anything atmospheric of any kind of physical nature; but rather something that we can attain to, a harbinger for us of the knowledge of the divine nature, which as David appropriately calls it, is 'magnificence'.[174]   For since the comprehension of the divine nature is impossible to those who were born and are corruptible, then he appears to us in ways that we can receive and in those things that after his own self, have the closest relation to him.   So it was he spoke to us through the prophets and we heard a man saying: 'I am the Lord your God,' not that we believe that the man (Isaiah for example)[175] is really God, but rather that the one who is speaking in him is God.   And so if the voice appeared as that of the cloud from whence it was heard, nonetheless it was clearly coming from the Father witnessing to Jesus' Sonship and thundering out his Logos-nature through the surrounding countryside. For there are indeed awe-inspiring clouds which give forth a voice and interpret the word; as it is written: 'The clouds give forth a voice'[176] and they are ordered   not to pour out rain upon that vine which produces thorns, the somatic House of Israel.   What I am talking about is the prophets, who give the rain of the word, and water those who need to drink.   This cloud, however, excels and overshadows all others, in the same way that we say that Providence presides over all things.   And thus it is said: 'This is my beloved Son in whom I am well pleased.   Listen to him.'   It does not say 'The Son whom I love' but rather 'My beloved'.   For not everyone we love is our beloved although anyone who is our beloved must also be loved by us.   For the beloved is wholly so by nature, but

the one that is loved is not wholly so by nature but by God's favour. Because the Son is the one he is also the other; that is he is the beloved and then I can also say that he is the one whom God favours, for he took up something of a different naure to himself, and assumed something of a different substance into the manifestation of one hypostasis. And this is why the Father showed us these different substances in his testimony, not as separating what had been united (for how can one separate what God has joined together?) but as teaching the union of the different natures, and that he who is composed of these natures is the One Son and Christ and Lord; the one beloved Son he is well-pleased that all creation should worship and hear.[177]

(8)   And when the apostles heard this magnificent voice, 'they fell upon their faces', subjecting themselves to this voice   sent out from on high, and 'they were exceedingly afraid.' Perhaps this was because of their former disobedience, on learning that their thoughts were contrary to the good-pleasure of the Father when they had tried to prevent the death of the Son, since in this the salvation of all men had been pre-destined according to the ancient counsel of the Father. But as they grew afraid and lay upon the ground 'Jesus drew near and touched them saying: Rise up and do not be afraid.' No one else could dispel that cringing fear except the Son who always told those who came to him to take courage.

(9)   Trusting in him, they raised their blinded eyes, perhaps tearfully, 'And raising their eyes they saw only Jesus.' The enigmatic demonstration of the Kingdom of Heaven had then come thus far. 'And as they came down from the mountain Jesus commanded them - Tell no one what you have seen until the Son of Man has risen.' For what reason did he forbid them to tell of what they had seen, or reveal to anyone the mystery of the resurrection? It was because it was necessary first of all for the First-Born to rise from the dead[178], and by that deed to confirm faith in the Resurrection; and only then to make known the common resurrection of all men by that witness. For who would have believed it if such

things had been proclaimed, when even the chief apostles did not believe? (And Peter had even had blasphemous thoughts in what he had said about the Saviour's death). And they did not believe until they heard the voice crying out from on high, bearing witness to the beloved Son and ordering obedience. For the voice said: Listen to him and consider everything that he says as an unquestioned law. This is why it was necessary for him to command the disciples to be silent about what they had seen until the time he should go forward to overcome death. It was so that their listeners should not become accustomed to disbelieve their words. And after the resurrection of the First-Born they then boldly made known the resurrection of all men, and the transfiguration from crass to spiritual bodies. And they authoritatively proclaimed to all men that just as 'Christ rising from the dead will die no more and death has no dominion over him.'[178] then so will he make us conformed to his glory;[179] and refashion our bodies as spiritual and incorruptible. And if we shall walk in newness of life[180] we shall be carried off in the clouds to meet the Lord in the heavens, and so we shall be always with the Lord[181]; To whom be glory and dominion to the ages of ages. Amen.

MAXIMUS THE CONFESSOR c.580-662.[182]

Ambiguorum Liber. (Excerpts)

1. (PG 91.1125-8 passim):

And so some of the disciples of Christ, because of their diligence in virtue, went up with him and ascended the mountain of his manifestation. They saw him transfigured and unapproachable by the light of his face. They were struck with wonder at the radiance of his garments, and they knew that he had become even more venerable for he was graced by having Moses and Elijah on each side of him. So it was that the disciples passed over from flesh to spirit even before they had ended their life in the flesh, by a change in the sensible operations which the Spirit effected in them, lifting the veils of the passions from their intellectual powers. Then, being purified in the senses of both body and soul, they were taught the spiritual meanings of the mysteries that were revealed to them. They learned mystically that the brilliance of his face which flashed with truly blessed radiance, overcoming the power of all eyes, was a symbol of his Godhead which is beyond all mind or sense or essence or knowledge. He had 'neither form nor beauty'[183] nor did they know the Logos in the flesh, but in this way they were led to understand that he 'was beautiful beyond the sons of men,'[184] and that he 'was in the beginning and was with God and was God,'[185] and they were brought up to the glory of the only begotten Son of the Father, 'full of grace and truth'[186] by means of an apophatic theological gnosis that sings of him as wholly uncontained. The white garments are a symbol of the words of holy scripture which became luminously clear and evident for them;[187] all difficult problems and figurative shadows taken from their minds, laying open the meaning of all that lay hidden therein. For they had a knowledge of God that was sweet and true and had been freed of their attachments to the world and the flesh. It was also a symbol of the creation itself after the abolition of all the bad things that in this present time seem to be visible in it.

2.   (PG.91.1160).

As it was said earlier, then, the thrice blessed apostles on the mountain, were mystically led (in a way that cannot be known or expressed) by the luminous splendour of the Lord's face, to the very power and glory of God, which is wholly beyond the capacity of all beings. And they learned that the light which appeared to their senses was a symbol of a mystery obscurely hidden. For just as here the flashing of the light that came upon them overcame the power of their eyes, remaining incomprehensible to them, just so does God transcend all the power and working of the mind, leaving no trace on the mind of any man who attempts to think about him.

ANDREW OF CRETE c.660-740. [188]

Oratio 7. In Transfigurationem. (passim).

1.   If you lift off the veil of foolishness about the Kenosis of the Logos, and raise your minds from the earth, and come to be taught how to think of the things above, then come confidently to me because I am offering you a spiritual banquet of words. Let us go up the high mountain of the Transfiguration in the presence of the Logos and lay aside the garments of this material and darkened life, and put on the garment woven on high, garments that radiate with rational virtues. For we are already dressed in white in our lives, and in our thoughts, and in the pure inspirations of the Spirit who lifts us up on wings. Christ himself wishes us to make this ascent with him, he who is all-pure, the hyper-essential Word of the Begetter, who came down from heaven for our sake and became poor in our flesh because of his love for man. This is clear from the fact that he took chosen apostles with him who were already closer than the others in intimacy, and led these up the high mountain. What was he doing ? What was he teaching ? He was showing the radiance of his own godhead that transcends all brightness. A little earlier he had done this more mystically but now he does it quite evidently in his Transfiguration, refashioning

that nature of which we had heard: Dust you are, and unto dust you shall return.[189] And so, today we celebrate this feast, the deification of our nature, its transformation to a better condition, its rapture and ascent from natural realities to those which are above nature. How and whence does such immense and wonderful grace come to us? Clearly from that which overcomes all human reason, the very godhead itself which incomparably transcends all thought and speech.

2. I would say that if anyone wants to be raised up like a disciple with the Logos on that mountain of lofty contemplation to behold the unapproachable glory of that kingdom, and be found worthy of his visible and intelligible theophany, then he should listen to what Christ has just said earlier about his Kingdom coming very soon (for this is what the Transfiguration really is in which the unchangeable one shone brighter than the sun for our sake and the sake of all that is ours) and then he should give food and drink to Christ who hungers and thirsts for the salvation of us all.

3. What of his face that is so immensely brilliant? Is it that inconceivable beauty, the highest and most precious of all things that are desirable, which brings ceaseless joy to all who look upon it, and seems to be revealed to the extent it can be received? Or is it something secret, even more divine? Something completely new which no mind or tongue could ever begin to see or express? For if his garments become like this because of the brilliant light pouring out from within, then what will he be like who is covered up and hidden in these garments, since he is beyond all sight and knowing? If he was revealed as he is in himself, all the coverings removed, what could I say then? But even through that one holy garment, woven from the Virgin's blood which he mystically took to himself through the Spirit, who could see him as they saw him manifested then? There is nothing, no nothing of all that can be seen in creation, that could contain the immensity of this radiance. For if all beings participate in the Good, this does not mean that it can be grasped completely, in its essence, but only in the measure

202

and the manner that it is accessible to those who participate in it. This happens by virtue of its supreme goodness reaching out and pouring forth on all things with its illuminations and boundless graces. This can be demonstrated by that blessed and celebrated affection which overcame the apostles on the mountain when the eternal and unapproachable light transfigured his own flesh and shone forth in a manner transcending all essence in the immensity of its radiant brightness. Being unable to bear the rays that came through this blameless flesh, in a manner beyond nature, rays that emanated from the godhead of the Logos who was hypostatically united to the flesh, they fell upon their faces. What a wonder, wholly beyond nature.

JOHN OF DAMASCUS c.675-740.[190]

1. Akrostich.[191]

Moses in prophetic vision of old, saw the glory of the Lord on the sea and in the cloud and in the pillar of fire. He cried out: To our God redeemer let us sing.

His body deified, sheltered by a rock, Moses the gazer on God perceived the Invisible One and cried out: To our God redeemer let us sing.

You were seen by Moses on the mountain of the Law and again on Thabor; formerly in the darkness but now in the unapproachable light of godhead.

At first you overshadowed your glory in the tent and spoke with Moses your servant. Master, this was an ineffable type of your radiant transfiguration on Thabor.

Only begotten, Most High Word, the chief apostles came with you on the Mount of Thabor, and in their company stood Moses and Elijah, all servants of God. But you alone are the Lover of Man.

You who are wholly God became wholly mortal; commingling manhood and the whole godhead in your person, which Moses and Elijah saw in two natures on Mount Thabor.

From your flesh rays of godhead issued forth over the prophets and apostles, and so the chosen ones sing out loud: Glory to your power Lord.

You kept the bush untouched by the encircling fire, Master, and revealed to Moses your flesh lit up by divinity. This is why he sang: Glory to your power Lord.

With the godhead hidden in the rays of the sensory sun, as on Mount Thabor, he sees you transfigured my Jesus: Glory to your power Lord.

As the apostles saw Moses and Elijah, so they saw that fire that did not burn your bodily form, even though it had no form. For you Lord, are one, out of two, in two perfect natures.

The most eloquent tongue could not tell of your greatness for as the Lord of Life and Master of Death you summoned Moses and Elijah to Mount Thabor to witness your godhead.

O Christ, with invisible hands you formed man in your image and in this craft most beautifully revealed the original type; not as if in an image, but in its very self; for you are God by nature and man at the same time.

Mixed unconfusedly, you revealed to us the live coals of the godhead burning up sins and illuminating souls on Mount Thabor. Moses, Elijah and the chief disciples are all astounded.

How great and awesome is this vision today. For on Mount Thabor the intelligible sun of righteousness flashes out. From heaven it is sensed; on earth it is beyond compare.

The weakened shadows of the Law have passed away and Christ the truth has come into full view. Moses cried out on Thabor, perceiving your deity.

Moses' column is the transfigured Christ; the cloud is clearly the grace of the Spirit;the overshadowing ,a revelation of utmost clarity. Now the apostles see things that cannot be seen: the godhead shining out from the smallness of the flesh on Thabor. They cry out: Blessed are you Lord our God unto the ages.

The apostles are gripped with fear, panic stricken before the glory of God's kingdom on Mount Thabor. They cry out : Blessed are you Lord our God, unto the ages.

Now they hear things that cannot be heard. The Son who came fatherless from the Virgin receives glorious witness from the Father's voice that he is God and Man; one and the same throughout the ages.He is beloved Son, not by adoption from the Most High, but by nature, pre-existing and turning to us without shadow of change: Blessed are you Lord our God, unto the ages.

When the disciples heard the Father's witness,Master,and saw something greater than a human vision,they could not stand the radiance of your face and fell upon the earth, singing out fearfully :

> Children bless him, priests sing his praise,all you people exalt him through the ages.

You are the most beautiful King and Lord of all Lords, Blessed Prince dwelling in unapproachable light, in which the disciples are struck with fear and cry out :

> Children bless him,priests sing his praise,all you people exalt him through the ages.

They gather round you,Christ, Master of Heaven, King of all the earth,holding dominion over the underworld : from earth the apostles, from heaven Elijah the Tisbite, from among the dead Moses , and all ceaselessly sing :

> Children bless him, priests sing his praise, all you people exalt him through the ages.

The apostles choose to leave behind all the trivial cares of life as they follow after you, O Lover of Man, towards that heavenly city lifted above the earth.Here they sing out,made worthy,perhaps,of your theophany,for they saw the Most High God standing in the midst of the gods[192],standing in unspeakable light on Thabor with   Moses and Elijah, so that the mystery of the Second Coming might clearly be revealed. And so, Christ, we all magnify you.

Come to me, and trust me, all you people climbing the holy and heavenly mountain, and we shall stand in the city of the living God, in the radiance of the only begotten Son, to gaze by mind on the formless godhead of the Father and the Spirit.

You have entranced me with desire, O Christ, and have been transformed in your divine love to burn my sins with formless fire and replace them with your delights. Good Lord make me worthy to glorify your two comings without cease.

2. Oratio, De Transfiguratione.

l. Come you God-loving congregation and let us celebrate this day. Come and let us keep today's festival with the heavenly powers who delight in the feasts, for they have come here with us to celebrate it. Come let us rejoice, our lips resounding like cymbals. Come let us exult in spirit, for whose is this feast and celebration? for whom is this pleasure and delight except for those who fear the Lord, who worship the Trinity, honouring the Son and co-eternal Spirit with the Father; those who confess with soul and mind and tongue the godhead made known indivisibly in three hypostases; those who know and proclaim that Christ is the Son of God, God, one person made known in two natures without division or confusion, each with their own natural properties. All rejoicing and every festive joy is ours. Christ instituted the feasts for us, for joy is not for the impious. Let us cast off every cloud of grief that hangs over our minds and prevents us from lifting them up on high. Let us scorn every earthly thing for our citizenship is not on earth. Let us lift up our minds to the heavens from where we wait for our Saviour Christ the Lord.[193]

(2) This day on Mount Thabor an abyss of unapproachable light shone upon the apostles; today shone a boundless flood   of

divine radiance. Today Jesus Christ was recognised as the Master of the Old and New Covenants, he who is my friend in name and deed; the sweetest one desired above all else and surpassing the understanding of all sweetness. Today on Mount Thabor, Moses the leader of the old covenant, the divine law-giver, stood before Christ the Law-Maker as a servant before his master, and was illumined by his economy, of which in ancient times he had initiated the mysteries in types. As I said before, this was because the nether parts of God were revealed and he distinctly saw the glory of the Godhead, sheltered in the cleft of a rock, as scripture tells us. But that rock is Christ, God made flesh, the Word and the Lord, as the divine Paul clearly teaches us: 'But the rock was Christ'[194] who opened up his own flesh as a little cleft and shone upon those standing by with an exceedingly great light, too powerful for any to behold. Today the great prince of the new covenant, who clearly proclaimed that Christ was the Son of God when he said: 'You are the Christ the Son of the living God'[195], saw the leader of the old covenant standing beside him who set the laws of both; and he gave a piercing cry: 'This is he who is[196] who raised me up as prophet and sent me out as a man and a prince of the new people. He who is above me, and yet for me, holding dominion over all creatures. This is he who set out both covenants for my sake and yours, the old and the new.' Today the virgin of the old covenant gives the good news of the virgin Lord who came from the Virgin to the virgin of the new covenant.[197] Come then and, led by the prophet David, let us 'sing psalms to our God, sing psalms to our King, sing psalms.'[198] For God is King of all the earth sing psalms wisely; let us sing with rejoicing lips; let us sing psalms with under-standing minds that savour the taste of the words. For the wise man said: As the mouth tastes food so the mind discerns words.[199] And let us sing psalms to the Spirit who searches out all things, even the inscrutable depths of God in the light of the Father, to that Spirit that enlightens all things that they may see the unap-proachable light of the Son of God. Now are things seen that are beyond the eyes of man – an earthly body radiating the divine splendour; a mortal body pouring forth the glory of the godhead. For the Word is made flesh[200] and flesh is made Word, though neither departs from its wonderful nature. O Wonder exceeding all thought. Glory did not come to this body from without but from within, by the Word of God uniting it hypostatically to his own supreme deity in a manner past all telling. How are these things joined that cannot be joined, yet abide without confusion? How can irreconcileables be reconciled as one without transgressing the respective properties of their natures? This act of union happens hypostatically so that the things that are united are one, and form but one hypostasis in a distinction without division, and with the unconfused union of the conjunction of hypostases safeguarded, and the duality of natures preserved through the immutable incarnation of the Word, and the incomprehensible and unchanging deification of the mortal flesh. And so, by way of communication, the things of man become the things of God, and the things of God become the things of man; all in an unconfused interpenetration[201] of one another, and a constant union of hypostasis. For he is but one; both that which is from all eternity and that which came to be later in time.

(3)   Today the ears of men heard things never heard before. For he who had been seen as man was witnessed to be the beloved only begotten and consubstantial Son of God. This testimony is not false. Its declaration is true for it is the voice of the Father who begot him that declares it. Let David come and play the godly-sounding lyre of the Spirit and sing now, in a clearer and more expressive voice, that which long ago in the beginning he foresaw from such a distance with prophetic and pure eyes, when he prophesied the coming of God the Word to us in flesh saying: 'Thabor and Hermon shall rejoice in your name'.[202]   For in the first place Hermon clearly heard the name of Sonship witnessed to the Christ by the Father and it rejoiced when the Forerunner[203] set out for the Jordan like a mediator between Old and New, in order to baptise.

He was that treasure hidden in the desert who was sent out in order
to bring into the open that unapproachable light shining in the darkness (that is the world) unknown to the eyes of the blind; and then
in the midst of the Jordan, the water of forgiveness, there stood
one who was not purified by those waters, the one who purified
the whole world; and then the voice of the Father cried out from
heaven witnessing that the one being baptised was the beloved Son,
while the Spirit in the form of a dove pointed him out. In the
second place Thabor rejoiced and was glad, the divine and holy
mountain, highest of mountains[204], no less in glory and splendour
than in its soaring heights. How rightly it now rejoices, for it
abounds in heavenly grace. In that place the chosen apostles saw
him radiant in the glory of his kingdom whom the angels cannot
gaze upon. In this place the resurrection of the dead was confirmed,
for he is shown to be Lord both of the living and of the dead, for
he takes Moses from the dead and brings Elijah forward as a living
witness, who of old was carried off from earth to a heavenly life
in a chariot of fire. In this place even the chief prophets give
prophetic revelation about the Master's death on the cross. This
is why Thabor rejoices and is glad, and skips like a lamb, for it
has heard the Father testify from the cloud (which is the Spirit)
to the sonship of Christ the Life-Giver. For this is 'that name
above all names'[205] in which Thabor and Hermon rejoice: 'This is
my beloved Son'. This is cause for rejoicing for the whole creation.
It is the honour of mankind and a glory that shall never be taken
away. For it is to a man that this testimony is given, though one
who is not merely a man. What cause for rejoicing has been given
us that far surpasses our understanding. What blessedness above
every hope. What gifts of God surpassing our desires. What graces
beyond the measure of our asking. What a liberal and prodigal giver
who has such overflowing munificence. O Gift worthy not of the
recipient but rather of the giver. What an unheard of exchange.
O the power of the giver and the weakness of the recipient. How
wonderfully he showed lost[206] mankind the way when he who is

without beginning came to be a creature in the body. For if man is made God, by God being made man, one and the same is shown to be both God and man. So the same one, being man, is without beginning in his Godhead, and yet being God, comes to be in his manhood.

(4)   Of old on Mount Sinai, violent storms, smoke and terrifying fire veiled his great condescension[207], proclaiming that there was no approach to the Law-Giver, the one who had only revealed his back and by his works showed that he was the supreme artificer. But now everything is light and splendour for he who is the Lord and Maker of all things, himself comes forth from the bosom of the Father, and while not leaving his own place, which is reclining on the bosom of that Father, he stoops down to his slaves, and being fashioned in the form of a slave he becomes a man in nature and appearance so that , revealing the brilliance of God in and through his own person, mankind could reach God who lies beyond their reach. For God created man by the communion of his own grace and, making him from clay, he breathed into man the spirit of life. He gave him a share in his own power and honoured him with his own image and likeness. He raised up the society of Eden and let man consort with the angels. But because we darkened and suppressed the likeness of the divine image by the grime of the passions then he took pity on us and renewed a second communion with us, much more steadfast and wonderful than the first. For while remaining in the excellence of his own godhead, he took up what was inferior, recreating mankind in himself, joining the archetype and the image. And today in this image he shows forth his own beauty for his face shines like the sun because it is made one hypostatically with immaterial light and so becomes the sun of righteousness. His garments became as white as snow, because they were glorified by their temporary relation to him, not hypostatically by the union. A cloud of light overshadowed them, representing the radiance of the Spirit. And, as the divine apostle said, as the sea bears the image of water, so the cloud does of the Spirit.[208] For all things

are lit up and radiant for those capable of light who have not defiled their souls with sordid things in their consciences.

(5)   So come then and let us emulate the obedience of the disciples, and eagerly follow Christ who is calling us. Let us shake off the host of passions and confess, without shame, the Son of the living God. Being made worthy of the promises, let us go up to the mountain of virtues, which is love, and become the spectators of glory and hearers of ineffable things. For as the Lord said, blessed are those eyes of the onlookers because they see, and those ears because they hear the things many prophets and kings longed to see and hear, but could not.[209] Come then let us unfold the meanings of the divine words and set the table for our good guests who reach out for these divine things with all eagerness. Let us set a table of divine words, served up by the grace of the Spirit, not in the conceit of Greek oratory (since we have not been sufficiently initiated in this knowledge) but sustained rather by the grace of him who gave to the dumb man a tongue to speak out clearly.

(6)   In Caesarea Philippi (this is Paneas which was once known and highly celebrated as the city of the Caesar Philip, and called in divine scripture Dan, where it is said: 'For David counted the people from Dan to Bersabee;'[210] and the same place to which the Master came with his servants and dried up the source of bleeding for the woman with the haemorrhage) in this city then, he gathered the very first meeting of his disciples. He who is the Rock of life, set up his seat for a while on a certain rock there and questioned them: 'Who do men say that the Son of Man is?'[211] Not that he himself was asking as one ignorant with the ignorance of men, he who knows all things, but rather as desiring to dissipate the gloomy ignorance cast over their spiritual eyes, by the bright light of knowledge. And they began to tell him that some thought he was John the Baptist, others Elijah, and others Jeremiah or one of the prophets. For since they saw so many profound miracles they suspected him to be one of the ancient prophets raised up from the

dead and that was why he was endowed with such grace. This is clearly seen, for it says: 'For Herod the Tetrarch had heard of the reputation of Jesus and said to his servants - This is John the Baptist. He has been raised from the dead and this is why these powers are at work in him.'[212] So in an attempt to dissipate this rumour and give the true confession, as a gift excelling all gifts, to those who did not know, then what should he do who has the power of all things within his hands? As man he proposes the enquiry, but as God he secretly enlightens the one he first called and who first followed after him; the one he himself had predestined with his own foreknowledge to be the worthy leader of the church. He inspires, then, and speaks through this one. And what was the question? 'But you, who do you say that I am?' And Peter, burning with a fiery zeal and in the inspiration of the Holy Spirit says: 'You are the Christ the Son of the living God.' O blessed mouth. O truly happy lips. O God-bearing mind worthy of the divine initiation. Instrument through whom the Father speaks. How blessed are you Simon son of Jonah (and he who does not lie has said this) because not flesh and blood, nor human understanding, but my heavenly Father, has revealed this divine and ineffable theology to you. For no-one knows the Son except he alone who is known by him, that is the Father who begets him and the Holy Spirit who knows even the depths of God. This is that firm and immoveable faith on which the Church is founded as on a rock, and of which you (Peter) worthily bear the title. Against it the gates of Hell shall rail, by the mouths of heretics and the instruments of demons, but they shall not prevail. They will take up arms but will not overcome, for: 'The arrows of foolishness become their wounds, and so shall it be. Their mouths falter and shall be turned against them.'[213] For whoever stands against the truth prepares the weapons of his own destruction. The Lord has demonstrated this by his own blood and has entrusted this to you as his most faithful servant. By your prayers keep this (faith) safe from stormy waters here; for what can never be overthrown or shaken or plundered is our most secure confidence. This is the word of Christ, through whom

the heavens were made and the earth was established, to abide
unshaken. As the Holy Spirit says: 'By the Word of the Lord, the
heavens were made.'[214] And so let us ask that the storm may be
calmed, that the tumult may be broken, and tranquil peace may
be granted to us, safe from the storms of the sea. Entreat this
of Christ who is the spotless Bridegroom of Peace, he who has
appointed you, Peter, as the Keybearer; he who has granted you
the grace of binding and loosing; he whom you proclaimed with truly
divine voice to be the Son of the living God. O divine and ineffable deeds. For he himself preached that he was the Son of Man
and Peter (or rather the one who spoke in Peter) preached that he
was the Son of God. He is indeed both God and man. He is not
called 'son' as 'of Peter' or 'of Paul' or 'of Joseph' or of any other
father. He is called Son of Man for he has no father upon this
earth, just as he has no mother in the heavens.

(7)   And so because he wished to confirm this word by a deed,
he knew exactly what to do (for he is the omnipotent wisdom and
power of God in whom are hidden all the treasures of knowledge[215])
and so he said: 'There are some of you standing here, who will not
taste death before they see the Son of Man coming in his Kingdom.'
Now if he had said 'There is one of you standing here' as if referring only to one of them, then we could surmise that it meant the
same as that other saying: 'If I wish him to remain until I come,
what is that to you?'[216] which referred to John the Theologian,
who might abide without tasting death until the Parousia of Christ.
For already some of the wisest commentators have interpreted it
in this way. But because the saying refers to several onlookers,
then we should really follow this up, and no scope is given to those
who wish to accept the aforementioned interpretation of this saying.
He says: 'There are some of you standing here.' Why is it some
and not all of them that are called to this vision? Are they not
all disciples and apostles? Were they not all called in the same
way, and did they not all follow after him? Did they not all receive
the same grace of healing? So how were they not all worthy to
see this vision? Surely the Master was no respecter of persons?

Well, all were disciples, but not all of them were blinded by the disease of avarice. All were disciples but not all had lost their clear-sightedness under a film of malice. All were disciples but not all were traitors. All were apostles but not all were caught in the noose of despair trying to set evil to rights by evil[217]. All were lovers of Christ but one was a lover of money. This one was Judas Iscariot, the only one who was not worthy of the vision of the Godhead. For it is said: 'Take away the wicked one lest he see the glory of the Lord.'[218] And so he alone is set apart from the rest, that envious and malicious one who was burning up with an even greater madness. But since they would all look upon his sufferings it was fitting that they should all have looked upon his glory and for this reason he took with him the chief apostles to be the witnesses of his own glory and radiance. They were three in number and this intimates the sacred mystery of the Trinity. He took them also because 'every word shall stand by two or three witnesses'[219] and thus the crime of betrayal shuts out the traitor, while his own godhead is still revealed to the apostles. And because Judas remains below with Andrew and the others, he has no excuse to give for his crime, as for example that he had been incited to sell his Master because he had been refused this vision. It was for this reason that Andrew and the rest of the apostolic band remained below, but though separated bodily in that place they are united in the bond of love, and though detained below in the body they still follow the master on high by their desire and yearning soul.

(8)   'And after six days,' as the divine evangelists Matthew and Mark write; or 'it happened eight days after these words' as the most wise Luke says ... How rightly and truly are these six and eight days announced by these heralds of truth. There is no discord in this saying only perfect accord emanating from the same Spirit. For it was not them that was speaking but the Spirit of God speaking in them. For it is said: Because when he comes the Paraclete will teach you and remind you of all things.[220] And so, those who say 'after six days' have subtracted the extremes, that is, the first and

last day, only counting the middle period; but the one who counts eight days has included these in his computation. And these are the different ways that men usually reckon up. Six is taken as a primary and perfect number for it is composed of its own parts. Halved it is three, divided by three it is two, and its sixth part is one. Added together again all these restore it perfectly. This is why those skilled in these matters call the number six 'perfect'. Moreover, in six days God made the system of all things visible by his Word. In addition they are also perfect who beheld the glory of God which surpasses all things since he is above perfection and beyond all greatness; as it is said: Be perfect as your Father in heaven is perfect.[221] The number eight also bears a type for the age to come because this present life was drawn up within seven ages, but on the eighth the life to come will be proclaimed just as the great Gregory said in his theology when interpreting the saying of Solomon: 'Give them a seventh part (speaking of this present life) and even an eighth (speaking of the life to come).'[222] For in the eighth age, the things of that age are revealed to those who are perfect. This is just as the divine and prophetic Dionysius said: 'And so will the Master look upon his perfect servants'[223] which actually happened when he looked upon his apostles on Mount Thabor. So then, you now have the reckoning of the days.

(9)　　　Why then did he take up Peter, James and John? Peter, because he wished to show that the testimony he had given in truth about him was a testimony that came from the Father. He also wanted to confirm Peter's faith in what he had said, for the heavenly Father had revealed this witness to him as the leader who would assume the rudder of the whole Church. He took James as one who would be put to death for Christ's sake before all the other disciples, and as one who drank his cup and who for his sake was baptised with his own baptism. He took John as the virgin of theology and the purest of instruments, as one who beheld the eternal glory of God as he thundered out: 'In the beginning was the Word, and the Word was with God, and the Word was God.' This was why he was called the Son of Thunder.

(10)   Why does he lead his disciples onto a high mountain? Because divine scripture figuratively calls the virtues 'mountains'. And set as the pinnacle and citadel of all the virtues is love.   For in love is perfection defined.   For if anyone should speak in the tongue of men or angels, even if he had faith to move mountains, or all knowledge, and knew all the mysteries, and handed over his body to be burned, but did not have love, then he becomes as sounding brass or a tinkling cymbal and is reckoned of no account.[224] And so, then, it is necessary to leave earthly things behind on earth, to transcend this body of lowliness[225] and stretch out towards that sublime and divine mirror of love so as to see the things that cannot be seen.   For whoever arrives at the summit of love, as it were, stands out of himself and perceives the invisible one.   He flies over the covering darkness of the bodily clouds and comes into the clear sky of the soul and so can look more keenly into the sun of righteousness, even though he cannot contain the sight of the whole Godhead. Then he will pray by himself, for stillness[226] is the mother of prayer and prayer is the revelation of the divine glory.   For when we quieten the senses, and turn to ourselves and to God, and are freed from all the distractions of the outside world, we become inward to ourselves.   Then it is that we see clearly in ourselves the Kingdom of God.   For the Kingdom of heaven is that Kingdom of God which is within us, as Jesus our God told us.   But the servants and the Master pray in a different fashion.   The servants approach their master through petitions, in fear and longing.   Their prayer becomes a familiar friend of their mind through the journey to God and union with him, and it strengthens and nourishes it.   But that holy mind which is hypostatically united to God the Word - how shall it pray? How can the Master ever be in need?   Surely it is because he made our life[227] his own and wants to train us and show us the way to the ascent to God through prayer; to teach us that prayer is the ambassador of the divine glory.   He proves then that he is no rival to God for he honours his Begetter as his own source and cause,

and he admits the flesh as his own nature so that by it he might grow in strength and learn things, and come to be practised in the initiation of higher realities. He also wants to entrap in this way, the Tyrant who was watching carefully to see if he was God. This is announced by the power of the miracles; and for this reason he always mixed together divine and human works, as if hiding the fishook within the bait. In this way the one who tricked man from his hope of godhead would himself be tricked by the assumption of flesh, and seeing Jesus radiant in prayer should think of the glorified face of Moses. Moses, however , was glorified by a glory that came to him from without, but the Lord Jesus did not hold the elegance of this glory as a grace, but rather from the innate radiance of his own divine glory.

(ll)   What is the invocation the Prophet David taught you when he wisely spoke out:' For he shall call upon me saying You are my Father, my God who works my salvation.'[228] Indeed from before all ages he is truly the Father of God the Son who shines forth from the nature of his Begetter. Yet God is also the worker of his salvation in so far as he is made flesh and renews, in himself, our nature, and restores the image to its ancient beauty, and bears in himself the common character[229] of manhood. This is why the text goes on: 'And I shall set him as the First-born'.[230] For he was named the first-born of many brethren[231] who shared in flesh and blood just like us. Yet in so far as he is God the Word, eternally Son, he did not come to be later in time; only as man it is said that he came to be later, for his personal character of sonship bides changeless in him. And when he himself became flesh, it too became the flesh of the Son of God from the very first instant because of the hypostatic union, and he himself is said to have become flesh who being as God, became as man.

(12)   And so, on Mount Thabor he took up those who were eminent in the highest of the virtues and was transfigured before them. Before the disciples he was transfigured, yes, the very one who is eternally glorified and radiant in the splendour of the

godhead. For without any beginning he was begotten from the Father and possesses the eternal nature of the godhead's radiance. He did not come to be later in time, nor did he come to receive this glory, for he is of the Father, though without beginning and without time, and he has the brilliance of his own glory. The same one was made flesh and abides in the same divine brightness. As the flesh itself passes from non-being to being, it is glorified and the glory of the godhead is said to be even that of the flesh. For both are but one Christ, consubstantial with the Father, and also of our nature and race. And therefore that holy body was never at any time devoid of the divine glory, but from the first instant of the union was perfectly enriched hypostatically with the glory of the unseen God, so that the glory of the Word and that of the flesh are one and the same. However, the glory that may not be seen is covered over by a body that can be seen and it becomes invisible to the angels as well as to those in the bonds of flesh who cannot contain the invisible. That which he had assumed was transfigured therefore, and he revealed it to his own disciples, making known to them invisible realities: and from blind men making them able to see. This is the meaning of the phrase: 'He was transfigured before them.' For he remains ever as he was before he was revealed but now he appears visibly to his disciples.

(13) And his face shone like the Sun. Whose face was it that shone? The face of him who by his own immense power lit up the sun; he who created light before ever the sun was, and later illumined it to be a vessel of the light , he who is the true light eternally begotten from true and immaterial light, the enhypostatised Word of the Father, the radiance of the glory, the natural seal and substance of God the Father. What are you saying, then, Evangelist? To what can you compare these incomparable realities? What simile or precedent is there for things that have no precedent? Does the Master become radiant like the slave? Does the unbearable and unapproachable light itself become as something inferior to the Sun that lights us all? But the evangelist will reply: I do not equate

or compare the unique and only begotten Son, or liken his glory to any particular thing at all. I speak only as one under the bonds of flesh and suggest this corporeal paradigm of the thing that is the most beautiful and radiant of all. Not that it is a good simile since it is impossible for the uncreated to be properly described by reference to the created, and yet the sun has two natures: that of light which was produced first and that of the body that was later illumined in the creation; and through the whole of its body the light is inseparably united, and even while it remains in its own body the light is poured out through all the farthest regions of the earth. So it is with Christ. He is the light of light, without beginning and unapproachable, yet he comes to be in a created and temporal body. He is the one sun of righteousness, the One Christ made known in two inseparable natures. That holy body was limited for while it stood on Thabor it did not extend beyond the mountain; the godhead however, which is in everything and beyond everything, is not limited by place. The body shines like the sun for the radiance of that light truly belonged to the body and all things are held in common by the one God the Word made flesh, both the things of the flesh and the things of the unlimited Godhead. Yet it is one thing to say why the wonderful things of the glory are in common, but something quite different to say how the passions are understood to be common. For the Godhead is the conquering power and bestows its own radiance and glory to the body; while in the passions it abides without any trace of passion. Thus, His face shone like the sun, not because it was not really much more splendid than the sun, but because the onlookers could not have been able to bear anything more. If all the brightness of the glory had been revealed would they not have all been burnt up? His face shone like the sun for as the sun is for sensory creatures so is God for intellectual beings. And his garments became as white as light: for the sun is one thing being a fountain of light that cannot be seen clearly while the light itself is something quite distinct and comes to the earth from the sun: and so are the energies of the wisdom and philanthropy of God which are both seen and perceived since we do not live wholly devoid of these good things. In this way, then, his face shone as clearly as the sun, while the light made his garments white, adorning them by participation in the divine light.

(14)   When these things had passed, Moses and Elijah were brought forward in glory, like slaves before their master. They were seen speaking with him by their fellow servants. This happened so that he might be shown to be Lord both of the Old and the New Covenant, and so that the mouths of the heretics might be shut, whose throats are open like tombs, and that our faith might be strengthened towards the resurrection of the dead, and also that he might be believed to be the Master both of the living and of the dead; the one to whom the Father himself bears witness. It was only right, then, that seeing the boldness of these fellow-servants and ministers of God, the disciples should be amazed at the man-loving condescension of the Master and be stirred up with even greater zeal, and strengthened in the contest. A man who can see the fruits of his labours will come boldly into the contest, for the desire of gain usually leads men on not to spare their bodies, like soldiers and boxers and farmers and merchants who take up their labours with great eagerness. Sailors, for example, go boldly out to sea without a thought for pirates or wild beasts, setting off in search of the profits they long for. And just as these people put their work before their pleasure because of the profits they can see accruing to them, and thus are able to endure all their toils, then in the same way the spiritual standard-bearers of the Master (those boxers, farmers and merchants who do not seek after earthly gain or strive after transient goods) prepare themselves all the more for the contest when these things are set out as a hope before their eyes, when they see those who have laboured before them now enjoying the very delights of the good things they hope for. In their contest they are not ranged against men, they do not beat the air, nor do they put the plough-oxen under their yoke to turn over the furrows of earth, nor do they ply the waves of the oceans; their task is

to fight against the principalities and powers, against the world-powers of darkness. And they rejoice that these give way to them.[232] For we gather the spoils while they are stripped bare. Our contest is against the great waves of this world, and those spirits of evil that set them in motion and we hold out by means of the rudder of the cross. We chase away those who roar after their prey like wild beasts, by the power of the Spirit, and in the hearts of men we sow a word of piety, as in a furrow, so that they yield a rich crop for the Lord. However, let us return to our text in hand.

(15)   At this point I can imagine Moses speaking out as follows: 'O spiritual Israel, listen to the things that sensory Israel was not able to hear. The Lord your God is one Lord, made known as one God in three hypostases; for there is but one nature of Godhead: for him who bears witness, for the Son who receives that witness, and for the Spirit who overshadows him. The one who now receives the Father's testimony, this is the one, the life of men. But ungrateful men shall see him hanging on the wood and they will not believe in their life.' Then perhaps Elijah spoke, and said: 'This is the one I saw in ancient times, bodiless in the gentle breeze (which is the Spirit)[233]; for no man has ever seen God[234] as he is in his own nature. What I saw was made visible in spirit. It is 'The changing of the right hand of the Most High'[235]; it is 'what eye has not seen nor ear heard, things that have not entered into the heart of man.'[236] And so 'in the age to come we shall always be with the Lord'[237] looking upon Christ in the radiant light of the godhead.'

(16)   But what of Peter who becomes a spectator of this divine revelation? Like one inspired of the Spirit he says to the Lord: 'It is good for us to be here.' Does anyone else exchange darkness for light? See how beautiful is this sun, how charming, and delightful and desirable. How brilliant and radiant he is. This present life is so sweet and lovely that all men hang onto it and would give anything not to lose it. Well, how much sweeter and more desirable is the light himself from whom every light receives illumi-

nation, he who is life itself, in whom all life shares and takes its origin: 'in whom all of us live and move and take our being.'[238] How much more desirable and lovable is he. But our desire and our understanding are both unable to represent the true extent of his excellence, for it overcomes all comparisons and will not submit to measurement. How could the uncircumscribed be measured, or the boundless ever be grasped by thought? This light carries off the laurels against all other natures. This is life itself which conquers the world. How could it be other than good, then, to be in the presence of the good? Peter, however, did not speak foolishly. He said this because all good things have their proper season and because there is a season for every deed, as Solomon said.[239] He also said this because the good was not circumscribed on that day only for those who were present, but indeed for the sake of all those who would come to believe, and goodness was poured out and diffused so that even more men could become participators in that mercy that would be accomplished through his cross and passion and death. This was the reason why it was not good for Jesus to remain in that place since he was going to redeem, with his own blood, the work of his own hands for whose sake he had put on flesh. And if he had remained on Mount Thabor he could not have fulfilled his promise to you Peter and you could not have become the key-bearer of heaven; Paradise would not have been opened to the thief; the haughty tyranny of death would not have been overthrown; the kingdom of Hell would not have been given over to plunder; the patriarchs, prophets, and saints would not have been snatched from the depths of Hell; and our nature would not have been clothed in immortality; (all because Adam longed for deification before the proper time, but what he desired came afterwards). And so, Peter, do not seek for good things before the proper time. There will come a time when you shall enjoy this vision forever. The Master has not appointed you as overseer of tabernacles but of the world-wide church. Your disciples, those sheep that the Good Prince of Shepherds put in your care, began to carry out your words and build a tabernacle for the Christ, and for Moses and Elijah his servants. And this is the festival we now keep today. Peter spoke these things without thinking, nonetheless it was in the inspiration of the Spirit who was foretelling things to come. The most holy Luke tells us: 'He did not know what to say.' And Mark tells us the reason for this: 'because they were greatly afraid.' And while Peter was saying these things 'behold a bright cloud overshadowed them' and the disciples were struck with even greater fear, seeing Jesus the Saviour within that cloud with Moses and Elijah.

(17)   In ancient times that seer of God went into the divine darkness, which signified the obscurity of the Law. The Law was a shadow of things to come. It was not truth itself as we learn from Paul's writing[240]. At that time Israel could not look upon the glory of the face of Moses which was destined to fade; but we behold the glory of the Lord with faces unveiled, and are trans-figured from glory to greater glory by the Spirit who is Lord.[241] This is why the cloud comes. It is not a cloud of gloom, for it did not hang over them threateningly but overshadowed them with light. The mystery which had been hidden from the ages, and for generations, was made known[242] and eternal and everlasting glory was revealed. This is why Moses stood by with Elijah (they represented the Law and the Prophets) for Jesus had been found - the giver of life, the one whom the Law and the Prophets preached. Moses also represented the ancient saints who were asleep, and Elijah, those who still lived. This is because the one who was transfigured is Lord both of the living and of the dead. So it was that Moses finally came into the Promised Land. For Jesus[243] brought him into his inheritance. The things he saw in types in ancient times he now looked upon clearly. This is the significance of the bright cloud.

(18)   And a voice came from the cloud saying: 'This is my beloved Son in whom I am well-pleased. Listen to him.' The voice of the Father came from the cloud of the Spirit: This is my beloved Son. This is he who is; who is seen as man; who formerly became

man and was among you in humility but today his face is radiant.
This is my beloved son who is before all ages, the one who is only-
begotten from the One; he who comes forth eternally and timelessly
from me who begot him. He is from me and in me and with me.
He is eternally and does not come to be later in time. He is from
me as from a fatherly causation, being born of my own substance
and hypostasis, for he is consubstantial with me. He is in me as
one begotten without division or separation. He is with me as a
hypostasis subsisting in his own perfection. This is no word sent
out lightly: for he is my beloved. And who is the beloved son
except the only-begotten? In him I am well-pleased; for the only
begotten Word of the Father in his good pleasure has been made
flesh, and the Father's good-pleasure in his only begotten son has
effected the salvation of the whole world. The good-pleasure of
the Father has brought about the unification of all things in the
only begotten son. For man is a microcosm and bears, in himself,
the conjunction of natures both visible and invisible for he is both
one and the other. And accordingly is the Master of all things,
the Provident Creator, well-pleased in his only-begotten and consubstantial son, for he bears in himself Godhead as well as manhood
and thus effects the unification of all the creation 'so that God
might be all in all'.[244] This then is my Son, the radiance of my
own glory, the seal of my own hypostasis, through whom I made
even the angels; through whom the heavens were founded and the
earth made firm, who upholds all things by the word of his power
and the breath of his mouth (which doubtless means the Spirit, the
Lord and Giver of Life.)[245] Listen to him, for whoever receives
him receives me who sent him out,[246] not like a Lord but as a
Father. For as man he is sent out but as God he remains in me
and I in him. The man who does not honour my only begotten and
beloved son does not honour me, the Father who sent him. Listen
to him, for he has the words of eternal life.[247] This is the perfect
fulfilment of all accomplishments. It is the power of the Mystery.

(19)   And then what happened? He dismissed Moses and Elijah

to their respective places, and the apostles saw only him. So they came down from the mountain and told no-one anything of what they had seen or heard, as the Master had commanded them. And I shall tell why this was so. I think it was because of the fact that the disciples were still imperfect, as he knew, since they had not yet participated perfectly in the Spirit. And he commanded them to do this so that grief would not fill the hearts of the others or arouse the fury of the traitor's envy. And so we ourselves make an end of our discourse.

(20)   But you should take care always to remember these things I have said. Foster in your hearts the beauty of this divine vision, and always hear the Father's voice: This is no slave, no ambassador, no angel, but my beloved Son Listen to him. And so, let us listen to him when he tells us: You shall love the Lord your God with your whole heart. You shall not kill, or indeed even be angry at your brother, but first be reconciled with your brother and then come and offer your gift. You shall not commit adultery, or indeed even be curious at someone else's beauty. You shall not swear falsely: indeed you shall not even swear at all, but let your yes be yes for you, and your no, no, since anything beyond this comes from the evil one. You shall not bear false witness or defraud anyone, but rather give to any man that asks of you and do not turn away from the man who wishes to borrow from you; and do not prevent one who takes away your goods. Love your enemies, bless those who speak evil against you. Do good to those who hate you, and pray for those who calumniate and persecute you. Do not judge, that you may not be judged. Forgive and it will be forgiven you, so that you will become sons of your Father - perfect and merciful like your Father in heaven who causes the sun to rise upon the evil and the good, and the rain to fall upon just and unjust alike. Let us keep these divine precepts with every care so that we too may enjoy his divine beauty and be filled with the savour of his sweetness. This shall be so even now, as far as we can achieve it, being weighed down by this earthly tabernacle of the body; but afterwards

it shall be so even more clearly and purely when 'the just shall be as radiant as the sun'[248], when freed from the necessities of the body they shall be as incorruptible angels[249] with the Lord, in the day of the great and glorious revelation from the heavens of our Lord and God himself, Our saviour Christ Jesus: to whom be glory and dominion now and forever and to the ages of ages. Amen.

GREGORY PALAMAS c.1296-1359.[250]

1. Hom.34.

We give praise and stand in wonder before this great work of God; I mean the whole of visible creation. Even the Greek philosophers gave praise and stood in wonder at this when they conducted their investigations. We, however, look to the glory of the creator whereas they were against it. Like fools they worshipped the creation [251] instead of the creator. The voices of all the prophets, apostles, and fathers have shown this to be true. I myself have shown this for the benefit of my readers, and as a hymn to the Spirit who spoke through those prophets, apostles and fathers. In the times of wicked falsehoods the heresiarchs also tried to speculate on these matters, but it was for the ruin of all who trusted in them. Righteous truth was disregarded and they used the very voices the Spirit had given them to utter vile things against the Spirit. And yet, our god-bearing fathers, each in their own way, made the lofty doctrine of evangelical grace easy for us and suitable even for servile ears and minds. They made it perfectly suitable even for us who are imperfect just as mothers who love their chidren chew up the harder pieces of food and prepare it most usefully and agreeably while their infants are still at the breast. In the mouths of our physical mothers, then, food is liquified for babies, and in the same way in the hearts of our god-bearing fathers, intellectual realities become profitable food for those souls who hear and trust in them. The mouths of the wicked blasphemers, however, are full of deadly poison which they have mixed up even with the words of life to make them death-bearing for those who listen but do not take care. So let us flee from those who do not receive the patristic interpretations but instead try to introduce contrary things from themselves. They pretend to be concerned about the correct readings of texts while all the time disdaining a righteous understanding. Let us flee with more haste than we would from a snake. For when a snake strikes your body it brings a temporary death, separating it from the immortal soul, but when heretics seize the soul in their jaws they separate it from God, and for the immortal soul this is an everlasting death. So let us flee from such as these with all our strength and take refuge with those who teach righteous and salutary things in accordance with the patristic traditions.

Of such things will I now speak; and I commend these matters to your charity since today we celebrate the feast of the venerable transfiguration of Christ upon the mountain. We celebrate what it teaches us about its own light, on which subject there is now much controversy from those who are hostile to the light. Come then, and for a short while we will expound today's Gospel readings in order to explain the mystery and demonstrate the truth. 'After six days Jesus took Peter, James and his brother John and led them up a high mountain by themselves. And he was transfigured before them, and his face was as radiant as the sun.' The first things we need to understand about this Gospel is from which day does Matthew, the evangelist and apostle of Christ, begin to enumerate the six days? So which day was it? It was from that day the Lord was teaching his disciples and said: 'The Son of Man will come in the glory of his Father' and then he added, 'There are some of you standing here who will not taste death until you see the Son of Man coming in his Kingdom.' See how he identifies the Father's glory and his own Kingdom with the light of his own transfiguration. The evangelist Luke also suggests this, indeed clearly teaches it, when he says: 'It happened eight days after these words that he took Peter and James and John, and led them up a mountain to pray. And it happened in his prayer that the appearance of his face was changed and his garments became brilliant white.' But how do they concur with one another; the one who says openly that eight days passed from the promise to the day of his revelation, and the one who says six days? Listen and learn. There were eight upon the mountain, and six of them appeared. There were the three, Peter, James and John who came up with Jesus, and there they saw Moses and Elijah beside Jesus and talking with him. Altogether that makes six. But also with the Lord were the Father and the Holy Spirit who are altogether invisible. The first witnesses in his own voice that Jesus is his beloved Son, and the other shines alongside them through the bright cloud to show the intimate unity of the Son's light with himself and the Father. For their unity is very profound, and there is but one leaping forth of brilliance. Thus the eight are six, and there is no disagreement between the eight and the six. Likewise the evangelists do not disagree when one says 'after six days' and when Luke says 'It happened eight days after these words.' We should consider what kind of typology is given us by both these words on the mountain; mystically yet openly, for anyone who thus views the text correctly will know that these preachers of God concur with one another. Luke who says eight days, does not disagree with the one who says after six days, but rather counts in both the day when these words were spoken as well as the day on which the Lord was transfigured; which is exactly what Matthew gives us to understand when we look carefully, for the proposition 'after' clearly signifies the following day and while the one uses it, the other omits it. Luke does not say 'after eight days' as Matthew says 'after six days', but says that these things came to pass 'in eight days'. Thus, there is no difference in the accounts of the Gospel histories.

There is something else, however, something great and mystical that is intimated to us through their apparent disagreement. So apply your minds to what I shall say, to the very limits of your understanding. Why did one say after six days, and the other one adds on a seventh to mention the eighth? It was because the great vision of the light of the Lord's transfiguration is the mystery of the eighth day[252], that is the age to come, which follows after the sabbath-rest of the world made in six days. It is the subsequent illumination of our senses that work in a sixfold manner; for we have five senses but added to these in accordance with the senses, is the uttered word which activates that sixfold energy of our senses. But the Kingdom promised to the saints is not only above sense, it is even beyond speech, and for this reason - for after these sixfold senses have come to a happy end, and in that ending the worthy are enriched in the seventh (state), then is the Kingdom of God revealed in the eighth (state) in a power of even greater energy, which is the power of the Spirit of God, through whom the saints are found worthy of beholding the Kingdom of God. According to Saint Luke the Lord showed this to his disciples when he said: 'There are some of you standing here who will not taste of death until they see the Kingdom of God coming in power.' That is, he gave to those who can see, the power to look on invisible things, having previously cleansed them of deadly and soul-destroying defilement, which is sin. The taste of sin has its origin in thinking evil, but those who are cleansed of it in advance will not taste soul's death for their consciences will be kept undefiled, I think, in the power of the revelation that is to come.

'There are some standing here who will not taste death until they see the Kingdom of God coming in power.' The Lord of all things is everywhere and his Kingdom is everywhere, with the result that the coming of his kingdom clearly does not mean it should pass from one place to somewhere else, but that it should be revealed by the power of the divine Spirit. This is why he said: 'Coming in power.'

This power does not come near to anyone at random, but only to those who stand with the Lord, that is, to those who are steadfast in his faith and those like Peter, James and John who were first taken up the high mountain by the Word (which clearly means those who transcend our natural baseness). It is for this reason that God is revealed upon the mountain, as we are told, both as one who comes down from his own lofty regions, and as one who lifts us up from our earthly baseness. This is so that the incomprehensible one may (in proper degree and in so far as is safe) be comprehended by created nature. Such an appearance is not inferior to intellectual perception, but much greater and more exalted, for it takes place by the power of the divine Spirit. And therefore, that light of the Lord's transfiguration does not come to be, or pass away, nor is it circumscribed, nor does it fall under any sensory power. Although it is seen by bodily eyes, and in a short space of time, and on the puny top of a mountain, it is nonetheless as the saying goes: The initiates of the Lord pass from flesh to spirit in an exchange of senses, which the Spirit works in them.[253] So it was that they beheld him who graced them with so great a power of the divine Spirit, that ineffable light.

And today there are some who fail to understand this and become as blasphemers against it. They maintain that the chief apostle saw the light of the Lord's transfiguration by a sensory and created power, and for this reason they try to pull down to a creaturely level not only that light (the glory and Kingdom of God) but even the power of the divine Spirit through which these divine things were revealed to these ones. Clearly such men have not heard or believed Paul who says: 'Things which eye has not seen, nor ear heard, which have not entered into the heart of man, things which God has prepared for those that love him, he has revealed to us through his Spirit.' For the Spirit searches the very depths of God.[254] But at the beginning of the eighth day, as it is said, the Lord took Peter, James and John,and led them up a mountain to pray. He always prayed alone separating himself from everyone else,

even these apostles, just as when he fed the five thousand men
women and children with five loaves and two fishes. On that day
he immediately dismissed everyone and ordered all his disciples to
get into the boat, while he himself went up a mountain to pray.
And again, when the time came for his saving passion, he took with
him only a few of the more eminent disciples and said to the rest:
'Stay here while I pray.' Then he took with him Peter, James and
John. So, taking only these three with him, he climbs the high
mountain, apart, and he was transfigured before them, that is, before
those who beheld him. What does 'transfigured' mean? As
Chrysostom the theologian says: 'He revealed, as it pleased him,
a little of the godhead and showed the indwelling deity to the
initiates.'[255] For it happened that in his prayer, as Luke says, his
appearance was changed; as radiant as the sun, as Matthew writes.
He says 'like the sun' not so that light should be understood as
anything sensory. Away the blind minds of those who can understand
no powers greater than those revealed to them in the senses ! No,
it was so that we might understand that just as the sun is for all
those who live in the senses and perceive through them, so is Christ
our God for all those who live by the Spirit and perceive in the
spirit. There is need of no other light for those whom God has
granted this divine vision. For these, he alone and no other is light
eternal. For those who have the greatest of all lights what need
is there for a second light? In his prayer, then, Christ was radiant,
and ineffably revealed to the leading apostles that ineffable light
when the chief prophets were also with them. This was in order
to show that prayer is the mother of that blessed vision, and so
that we might learn that when we draw near to God by virtue and
find intellectual union with him, then that radiance draws near and
is revealed to all those who have the grace to see it; those who
ceaselessly reach out to God by the diligence of good works and
the purity of their prayer. As it is said: The true and most lovely
beauty which encircles that divine and blessed nature is seen only
by the one who has a pure mind.[256] And he who gazes upon its

flashing graces receives from it just as a brightly coloured flower is coloured over again in a man's eye. So it was that Moses' face was glorified when he spoke with God. And do you see how Moses was also transfigured going up the mountain there to see the glory of the Lord? But Moses suffered a transfiguration, he did not effect one in himself, as it is said: The light of truth brings me in this measure to see and suffer the radiance of God.[257] But Our Lord Jesus Christ possessed that radiance as his very own. His body did not radiate with divine light as a result of his prayer, rather he was demonstrating how the radiance of God comes from it to the saints and how they can see it. For even the just shall be as radiant as the sun in the kingdom of their father[258] being wholly transformed into divine light. Just as they were born from divine light so shall they behold Christ in all his divine and ineffable radiance whose glory proceeds naturally from his godhead and on Thabor is revealed as common even to his body because of the oneness of hypostasis. Because of this light his face was as radiant as the sun. Our opponents, however, who proudly rely on Hellenistic thought and wisdom of this world, who do not wholly trust spiritual men in regard to the words of the Spirit, but who were predestined to rebel, when they hear about the light of the Lord's transfiguration on the mountain, which the eyes of the apostles beheld, then immediately they reduce it to a sensory and created light and drag down to this level that immaterial and everlasting light that never sets, which is not only above all sense but is even above all understanding. These are men who lie prostrate on the ground, incapable of understanding anything that is above earthly things. And yet, he himself, who formerly shone in this light and showed that it was uncreated, calls it 'the Kingdom of God'. The Kingdom of God is not servile or creaturely but alone of all things it is without master and unconquerable. It reaches beyond all time and all ages, and as it is said: It is not right to confine or subject the Kingdom of God to ages or times.[259] For this, we believe, is the inheritance of all who are saved.

As the transfigured Lord was radiant and chose to reveal that glory and radiance and light, so will he come again just as he was seen by the disciples on the mountain.[260] Was it that he took up some light, to have it through the ages, which he did not have before? Away with such blasphemy. For the man who says this reckons there are three natures in the Christ; the divine, the human and that of the light. Therefore he revealed nothing external, only that radiance which he had mystically; for he had the radiance of the divine nature hidden under the flesh. It is therefore the very light of the godhead and it is uncreated. According to the theologians, Christ was transfigured not by receiving something he did not have before, nor by being changed into something he previously was not, but as manifesting to his disciples what he really was, opening their eyes and from blind men making them see again. Do you see how eyes are blind to that light which see by only natural means? So evidently that light is not sensory, and it is clear that those who see it do not do so with sensory eyes, only as transformed by the power of the Spirit. And so, they themselves were changed, and were therefore able to see this change taking place. This was not something new that happened for it derived from his assumption of our condition, which was thereby deified by this union with the Word of God. So it was that she who mysteriously conceived and brought him forth in virginity was able to recognise her child as the flesh-bearing God. And so did Simeon who took the infant into his arms, and the aged Anna who met with them. For the divine power shone through these who had kept the eyes of their hearts in purity, like the rays of the sun through a pane of glass.

What was the reason for him to pick out the leading apostles from the others and lead them up on their own? It was clearly to intimate something great and mystical. But how could a vision of merely sensory light be something so great and mystical that these elect should be brought up first, leaving the others below? Why would they need the power of the Spirit which enabled (or rather changed) their eyes to see this light, if it were only sensory or created?

How can a sensory light be the glory and the Kingdom of the Father and the Spirit? How shall Christ come in this glory and Kingdom in the age to come when he will have no need of air or light or space and suchlike, but as the apostle says will be God for us beyond all.[261] And if beyond all then certainly beyond light. So it is demonsrated yet again that this is the light of the godhead. John, the greatest of the Gospel theologians, reveals in the Apocalypse that the future and abiding city has no need of the sun or the moon to illumine it for the glory of God shines upon it and its lantern is the lamb.[262] Does he not clearly show us Jesus here who now on Thabor is divinely transfigured, who has as a lantern the body, and reveals on the mount, to those who had come up with him, that glory of the godhead which is beyond light. The evangelist also speaks of those who dwell in that city as 'they who have no need of the light of a lantern or the light of the sun, for the Lord God shines upon them and there will no longer be night.'[263] What is this light , then, in which there is no alteration or shadow of change?[264] What is this unchangeable light that never sets? Surely it is the light of the godhead. How also would Moses and Elijah (the more so Moses who was present in soul not embodied) be able to be seen or glorified in a sensory light? For they too were 'seen in glory speaking about his death which he would accomplish in Jerusalem.' So how did the apostles know them, whom they had never seen before, except in the revelatory power of that light?

But not to overtax your attention too much let us keep the rest of the Gospel sayings for the time of the most holy and divine sacrifice. Let us keep on believing as we were taught by those who had been enlightened by Christ, those who alone can know for certain. For God says through the prophet: My mysteries are for me and for mine.[265] Let us, then, believe rightly as we have been taught, and understand the mystery of the Lord's transfiguration. Let us make our way towards the illumination of that light, and filled with the desire for the beauty of this changeless glory let us cleanse the eye of our mind of earthly considerations. Let us scorn what is pleasurable and beautiful, all these things that seem sweet but do not last, for in fact they are the harbingers of eternal pain. Even if these pleasures bring happy times to the body, they wrap the soul in the foul robe of sin. And this was the reason why he was bound hand and foot who did not have the proper garment for the incorruptible feast, and was cast out into the fire and the darkness. But we are all freed from this fire and darkness by the illumination and the knowledge of the immaterial and eternal light of the Lord's transfiguration. To him and to his eternal Father, and to the Life-giving Spirit be the glory, who have but one and the same brightness and godhead and glory and Kingdom and power, now and forever, and to the ages of ages. Amen.

2. Hom. 35. (Passim)

(a) PG 151.437.

So now I beseech you, reach out and lift up the eyes of your mind towards the light of the Gospel preaching so that you may be yourself transfigured in the renewal of your minds,[266] attracting the divine rays from on high and becoming conformed to the likeness of the glory of the Lord[267] whose face on the mountain shone today as radiant as the sun.

(b) PG 151.439

His garments, since they were near to his body, themselves became luminous; and from this is shown what is the vesture of glory in which those who are near to God shall be clothed in the age to come. Such are the garments of innocence of which Adam was despoiled through his transgression.

(c) PG 151.445

The bright cloud was shining and the voice of the Father sounded from the cloud, and then it says that the disciples fell upon their faces. They did not fall down because of the voice, since this had happened frequently before, not only over the Jordan but also in the time of the saving Passion at Jerusalem when the Lord said: 'Father glorify your name. And then a voice came from heaven: I have glorified it and will glorify it again.'[268] And all the crowd heard this but none of these fell down. And so it was not only the voice but also that incomprehensible light which shone out with the voice; and as all the god-bearers have known it was really because of this wonderful and extraordinary light (not because of the voice) that the disciples fell down upon their faces. Indeed as Mark tells us, before ever the voice came, they were filled with fear, caused solely by that vision of God.

(d) PG 151.448.

We, however, shun the heretics of ancient and modern times. We believe, as we were taught, that the saints beheld and had fellowship not with the essence of God but rather with his kingdom and glory, his radiance, his mystical light and his divine grace. We press on towards the radiance of that light of grace so that we might know and venerate the threefold light of the deity that ever shines as one; a mystical ray of one nature in three hypostases. And we lift up the eyes of our mind towards the Word who now sits with his body above the vaults of heaven, sitting in glory at the right hand of the majesty.

NOTES TO CHAPTER FIVE

1. Text of Irenaeus, **Adversus Haereses** cf. PG 7.1032-38. For an ET of the works of Irenaeus cf. **ANCL.** vol. 5.

2. Rev.3.7.

3. Jn.1.14.

4. I Peter.2.23.

5. Col.1.18.

6. Some Mss. read 'In filium' viz: 'fashion man into a Son of God.'

7. Is.6.5.

8. Ps.22.15

9. Num.12.8

10. Ex.32.20-22.

11. Clement: **Stromata.** 6.16.140.3 cf. PG 9.368. (ET,ANCL 4,12) **Excerpta ex scriptis Theodoti** cf. PG 9.655-656

12. That is the Lord is the fourth to go up after the three disciples. The 'Fourth' is the mystical symbol of the Sabbath commandment which he will apply later.

13. The sixth is a perfect number for being rooted in itself as his previous exegesis demonstrated. It is therefore a fitting symbol of the divine power he will reveal on this occasion. Christ has become the 'sixth' by the appearance of the two prophets. In other words from being the 4 he has demonstrated his 'root' (2) and manifested its divine power, (6). A typical but subtle use of number symbol.

14. The voice is the seventh character to appear in the narrative. Seven is the symbol of the Divine Sabbath and is attributed to God himself. See the following note:

15. When Clement mentions the Sabbath symbol it is suitable that he should find here a symbol of rest: **Anapausis** . When Creation had reached its first fulfilment after seven days God imposed sabbath rest on all his people. In the Fathers the symbolism is used to refer to the seven ages

of the first creation which will give way after a period of 'rest' (the sleep of the saints, or alternatively their paradisial bliss before Judgement) to the New Creation, that entirely new eighth age.

16.   I Peter.2.9.

17.   The text could read **His** advancement (Prokope) ie. that of Jesus himself after his bodily death, but the reading chosen here is the more common theme in the patristic tradition that follows and so has determined my choice.

18.   Mt.16.27.

19.   Meaning death. It is a biblical pun on the double meaning of death/sleep. cf. Lk.9.32; Jn.11.11.-14.

20.   Jn.1.33.

21.   Mt.17.9

22.   ie. in the Passion.

23.   Mt.1.17.

24.   Origen: **Contra Celsum** 1.48. cf PG 11.752. (ET ANCL.23).
Origen: **Contra Celsum** 2.64-5. cf PG 11.896-900
Origen: **Contra Celsum** 4.16. cf PG 11.1048.
Origen: **Contra Celsum** 6.68. cf PG 11.1401.
Origen: **Hom. In Genesim:** 1.7. cf. PG 12.151-152
Origen: **Com. In Matthaeum** 12.36-43 cf. PG 13.1059-1086
Origen: **Philocalia** 15.9, PG 14.1312-1313
See also H. Smith **The Ante Nicene Exegesis of the Gospels.** London. 1927, vol.3. pp.185-192.

25.   Mt.17.9.

26.   Jn.5.31.

27.   Jn.14.6. (followed by Jn.6.35 and 10.7).

28.   Mt.26.48.

29.   Mt.26.55.

30.   cf. Col.2.13-20. (viz. before the complete fulfilment of the economy of salvation at the Cross and Resurrection). The Colossians passage also gives us the context that explains his references to being 'dead to sin'.

31.   LXX Is.53.2

32.   cf also **Contra Celsum** 6.75-77 which parallels this exegesis. CC 6.77 reads as follows: 'But there is also something mystical in this doctrine, which announces that the varying appearances of Jesus are to be referred to the nature of the divine Word, who does not show himself in the same manner to the multitude as he does to those who are capable of following him to the high mountain which we have mentioned; for to those who remain below as yet, and are still not prepared to ascend, the Word has 'neither form nor beauty' because to such people his form is 'without honour', and inferior to the words given out by men (who can be figuratively called the sons of men). For we might say that the words of the philosophers who are 'sons of men'- appear far more beautiful than the Word of God who is proclaimed to the multitude.'

33.   Jn.1.1.

34.   2 Cor.5.16.

35.   Jn.1.14a.

36.   Jn.1.14b.   Origen also applies Jn.12.42 to the Transfiguration.

37.   Zech.1.3.

38.   Jer.23.25.

39.   Lk.10.40. cf. Similar exegesis in his **Comm. In Joannem** 12.41. cf GCS.40.163f.

40.   Mt.16.28.

41.   1 Jn.2.15.

42.   Phil.2.6.f

43.   2 COr.5.16.

44.   Rom. 13.12-13.

45.   1 Cor.2.7.

46.   The reference is, in fact, not to Mark but to Luke 9.28f.

47.   Jn.7.39.

48.   Col.2.15.

49.   Mt.16.23.

50.   Lk.9.32.

51.   Jn.8.44.

52.   Jn.14.6.

53.   Mt.16.16.

54.   Mt.16.22.

55.   Mt.17.4.

56.   I Cor.13.5.

57.   cf. I Cor.9.19.

58.   cf. I Tim.1.7.

59.   Prov. 16.23.

60.   Ex.30.20.

61.   cf. I Peter.5.6.

62.   cf Mt.27.52.f

63.   Mt.17.9.

64.   Mt.16.20.

65.   Methodius: **De Resurrectione.** Fragment preserved in Photius, **Bibliotheca,** Cod.234, Part 3, section 2. chs.12-13. ET in **ANCL,** vol.6.pp375-6, adapted here.

66.   cf.Phil.3.21.

67.   Dan 9.23. (marginal gloss).

68.   cf. Rev 1.5.

69.   Cf. A.H.C. Van Eijk, **Only that can rise which has previously fallen. The history of a formula.** JTS, 22,1971,517-529.

70.   Eusebius: **In Lucam 9,** cf. PG 24.549-50.

71.   Jn.1.9.

72.   Ex.33.20-23.

73.   cf 2 Cor 3.18.

74.   Phil.2.10.

75.   Epiphanius: **Adversus Haereses** 1.3.   Haer.42.   Scholia 17-
        18, PG 41.735-738.   See also **Adv.Marcionitas** . PG 42.328.

76.   Basil: **Comm. In Isaiam** 4.5. cf. PG 30.341-44.
        Basil: **Hom. In Ps.44.5.** cf PG 29.400.

77.   cf. LXX Is.4.5.

78.   Is.2.1-3.

79.   Is.4.1.

80.   Is.4.2.

81.   Is.4.3.

82.   Is.4.4.

83.   The LXX text of Is. reads: 'The Lord will come and rest;'
        The Heb. reads 'come to create'.   Rest (Anapausis) is
        a central eschatological symbol in the Fathers for the
        stage before   the New Creation.   Cf. fn.15.

84.   Jn.14.2.

85.   Ps.37.11; Mt.5.5.

86.   Literally **Epiphaneia:** appearance or revelation.

87.   Gregory   Nazianzen: **Oratio   40   De   Baptismo.**   5-6,
        cf, PG,36,363-366.
        Gregory Nazianzen: **Carmina 20.** PG 37.491-2.
        Gregory   Nazianzen: **Orat.32.18**   (De Moderatione).
        PG 36.193-196.
        Gregory Nazianzen: **Orat.29.19** (3rd Theol.Orat.) PG 36.100.
        (ET.**NPNF.**7).

88.   φως   :   from   the   supposed   etymological   root   φαω   ,
        which   appears   in   φημι   (I   speak)   and   modified in:φαινω,
        (I shine): (Note by C G Browne in **NPNF** vol.7. p.361).

89.   Prov.6.23.

90.   Ps.119.105.

91.   Ex.34.2.

92.   Ex.13.21.

93.   2 K.2.11.

94.   Lk.2.9.

95.   Acts.9.3.

96.   Mt.13.43.

97.   Wis.3.7.

98.   Is.53.2.

99.   Ps.44.3.

100.   Gregory Nyssa: **Contra Eunomium.** 4.1.   PG   45.625. (ET.NPNF.5).

101.   Chrysostom: **Ad Theodorum Lapsum,** 1.11 cf. PG 47.291. Chrysostom: Hom.21.**Ecloga de Imperio,Potestate et Gloria,** cf PG. 63.700. (A parallel treatment can be found in **De Capto Eutropio,** PG 52.404-405.) Chrysostom: **Hom. 56.**1,3-4 **(In Matthaeum** 17) cf. PG 58.550f.

102.   Is.6.1.

103.   Jn.9.16.

104.   Jn.10.33.

105.   Lk.9.32.

106.   Ps.96.2.

107.   Ps.103.3.

108.   Is.19.1.

109.   Acts.1.9.

110.   Dan.7.13.

111.   Cyril of Alexandria. **Hom.Diversae.9.** cf PG 77.1009-1016. Cyril of Alexandria. **Com. In Lucam.9.** cf PG.72.653-656.

112.   Rom.8.18.

113.   Lk.9.23.

114.   Lk.9.31.

115.   Cyril is clearly dependent on Chrysostom here.

116.   Jn.9.16.

117.   Jn.10.33.

118.   Phil.3.21.

119.   Telos: end or fulfilment.

120.   Jn.5.46.

121.   I Sam.15.22.

122.   The **Commentary on Luke** is the earlier text from which the homily has been taken. The exegesis makes two points that are not found in the **Homily,** however, and accordingly they are reproduced here.

123.   Hesychia.

124.   I Cor.15.43.

125.   Mt.13.43.

126.   Proclos of Constantinople: **Oratio** 8. cf PG 65. 763-772.

127.   Ex.12.3

128.   I K. 8.33.

129.   cf. Ex.14.11, I K.17.1.

130.   Phil.2.10.

131.   Jn.17.11.

132.   viz. John the Baptist. Lk.1.41.

133.   Mt.14.25.

134.   Col.3.2.

135.   Ps.17.10.

136.   Ps.103.2.

137.   Acts.10.42.

138.   Mt.26.22.

139.   Mt.26.31-33.

140. Is.44.24.

141. Jn.3.13.

142. Phil.2.7.

143. cf Ps.88.13.

144. Phil.2.8.

145. It is a source for the Jordan but very far from the scene of the Baptism.

146. Lk.9.26.

147. Theodoret of Cyr: **Epist.145.** cf PG 83.1384-5. (ET.**NPNF.**3).

148. Phil.3.20f.

149. Mt.16.28.

150. cf. Acts.1.11.

151. Antipater of Bostra: Text preserved in John of Damascus' **Sacra Parallela.**cf.PG.96.497:**Contra Apologiam Pro Origene.**

152. Lk.9.27.

153. Mk.8.39.

154. Ps.Athanasius. **Ep. De Incarnatione.** cf PG.28.96.

155. Ps. Dionysius: **De Divinis Nominibus** 1.4. PG.3. 592. (The ET. of Rolt is adapted here.) See also **Div.Nom** 4.5-6 for the Dionysian Theology of the divine light that was to have such an effect on the later Hesychast school.

156. I Thess.4.6.

157. Lk.20.36.

158. Anastasius of Sinai (Anastasius I of Antioch): **Hom.7. De Transfiguratione, 3-9.** cf PG.89.1365-76.

159. Mt.22.20.

160. He parallels Clement's number symbolism as in the **Stromata.**

161. Paralleling Chrysostom's exegesis on why Judas did not ascend the mountain.

162.   cf. Phil.2.6-7.

163.   Phil.3.21.

164.   Again showing signs of dependence on Chrysostom's exegesis.

165.   LXX Is.49.18.

166.   Lk.9.31.

167.   A word-play on death/exodus as in Luke 9.31 linking the death of Christ with the **Exodus** typology of the lamb.

168,   Lit. Συμμυστας.

169   Hegemonikon.

170.   Num.16.43.f

171.   Ex.13.21.

172.   LXX Is.19.1.

173.   2 Chron.5.13.

174.   Ps.145.3f et al.

175.   eg Is.48.17.

176.   Ps.144.5.

177.   The exegetical argument is that the voice calls Jesus Beloved Son, which refers to his unique relation with God the Father as God the Word - a natural relation. The voice calls him 'The favoured one' to refer to his human nature in which he is the leader of many brethren - favoured by the grace of God. The first part of the witness demonstrates an ontological Christology, the second a grace Christology.

178.   Rom.6.9.

179.   Phil.3.21.

180.   Rom.6.4.

181.   I Thess.4.16.

182.   Maximus Confessor: **Ambiguorum Liber.** cf PG 91.1125-28 passim.   Also PG. 91.1160.

183.   Is.53.2

184.   Ps.44.3.

185.   Jn.1.1.

186.   Jn.1.14.

187.   An evident reference to Origen's exegesis.

188.   Andrew of Crete: Oratio.7. **De Transfiguratione** (Passim) cf. PG.97.932-57

189.   Gen.3.19.

190.   John of Damascus: **Akrostich Hymn,** cf PG.96.847-850. **Oratio De Transfiguratione,** PG 96 545-576.

191.   The Akrostich form means that the first letter of each stanza if read together produces a message. In this case the first letters produce: 'Moses saw the Face of God on Sinai'.

192.   cf. Ps.82.1.f

193.   Phil.3.20.

194.   I Cor.10.4.

195.   Mt.16.15. The following reported speech is figuratively set in the mouth of Peter.

196.   Ex.3.14.

197.   As Peter is typologically identified with Moses, so here John the Son of Zebedee is identified with Elijah.

198.   Ps.46.7.

199.   cf Job.34.3.

200.   Jn.1.14.

201.   Perichoresis: John applies the Trinitarian term of the manner of relation between the hypostases to the Christology debate.

202.   Ps.88.13.

203.   John the Baptist. Hermon 9200 ft high, 12 miles NE of Caesarea Philippi, contains the source of the Jordan and is thus figuratively associated with the Baptist.

204.   Actually less than 2000 ft high.

205.   Phil.2.9.

206.   A word-play on 'anarchos', wandering or leaderless as applied to men, but when applied to Christ - without beginning, or eternal.

207.   Συγκαταβασις : the stooping down of a mother to her child.

208.   cf. I Cor.10.1-2.

209.   Lk.10.23-24.

210.   2 Kings. 24.21.

211.   Mt.16.13.

212.   Mt.14.1f.

213.   LXX Ps.63.8.

214.   Ps.32.6.

215.   Col.2.3.

216.   Jn.21.22-23.

217.   viz. Judas' remorseful suicide by hanging.

218.   cf. Ps.68.2; and Ps.37 esp.vv.10,20.

219.   cf. Deut. 17.6, 19.15.

220.   Jn.14.19.

221.   Mt.5.48.

222.   Based on Eccles. 11.2.

223.   **De Divinis Nominibus** c.1.

224.   I Cor.13.1.

225.   cf Phil.3.21.

226.   Hesychia.

227.   Lit. **Prosopon:** person/face.

228.   Ps.88.27.

229.   Lit. **Prosopon.**

230.   Ps. 88.28.

231.   Rom.8.29.

232.   Lk.10.17-20.

233.   I Kings.19.52.

234.   Jn.1.19.

235.   (LXX) Ps.77.10

236.   2 Cor.2.9.

237.   I Thess.4.9.

238.   Acts.17.28.

239.   Eccles. 3.1.

240.   viz. Heb.10.1.

241.   2 Cor.3.7.18.

242.   I Tim.3.16.

243.   ie. Joshua.

244.   I Cor.15.28.

245.   Based on Heb.1.3.

246.   Jn.13.20.

247.   Jn.6.67.

248.   Mt.13.43.

249.   cf.Mk.12.25 (I Enoch.15.6-7).

250.   Gregory Palamas: **Hom.34.** cf.PG. 151.423-436.
         Homily 35 (excerpts) (a) PG. 151.437.
                                 (b) PG.151.439.
                                 (c) PG. 151.445.
                                 (d) PG. 151.448.

See also the work of Philotheus: **Contra Gregoram Antirrheticorum Libri XI.** PG.151.1055-1110.

251. Romans 1.25.

252. The Ogdoad: The apocalyptic symbol of the fulfilment of the Creation.

253. Here he is dependent on Maximus.

254. I Cor.2.9-10.

255. Homily.21.

256. A reference to Gregory Nyssa, I think, but it is a common Patristic doctrine, based on Mt.5.8.

257. cf Gregory Nyssa. **Vita Moysi.** (Ex.34.29).

258. Mt. 13.43.

259. cf. Ps.145.13.

260. Acts.1.11 applied to the Transfiguration.

261. I Cor.15.28.

262. Rev.21.23.

263. Rev.22.5.

264. James.1.17.

265. A reference to Symeon The New Theologian. **lst Theological Discourse,** ET J. McGuckin, CS.41. Kalamazoo 1982, p.118 fn.43. The NT text on which the gloss is based would appear to be Mk.4.11.

266. Eph.4.23.

267. cf Phil.3.21.

268. Jn.12.28.

CHAPTER SIX
THE LATIN FATHERS: TEXTS IN TRANSLATION

TERTULLIAN

CYPRIAN OF CARTHAGE

HILARY OF POITIERS

AMBROSE OF MILAN

JEROME

AUGUSTINE

LEO I

GREGORY I

BEDE THE VENERABLE

AMBROSE AUTPERTUS

TERTULLIAN. c.160-220.[1]

1.   **De Praescriptione.** 21-22.

We have now given the rule of our doctrine, and it remains for us to demonstrate whether it has its origin in the tradition of the apostles, and whether all other doctrines do not necessarily proceed from falsehood.   We hold communion with the apostolic churches because our doctrine is in no way different from theirs.   This is the witness of truth.

22.   But the proof for this is easily found and if it were produced straight away there would be no more argument so let us give way for a while to our opponents to see if they can find some means of invalidating this rule, just as if we had no proof to offer. They usually tell us that the apostles did not have knowledge of everything.   But here they are driven on by the same madness that makes them defend the opposite point and tell us that the apostles certainly did know all things but did not give everything to all indiscriminately.   In either case they accuse Christ for having sent out apostles who had either too much ignorance or too little simplicity.   But what man of sound mind could possibly suppose that they were ignorant of anything whom the Lord ordained to be teachers, for he kept them constantly in his company as disciples and when they were alone he used to explain everything that was obscure, telling them that it was given to them to know the mysteries,[2] which were not given for the people to understand. Could anything be withheld from Peter's knowledge when he is called the Rock on which the Church is to be built?   Who received the keys of the Kingdom of heaven with the power of loosing and binding in heaven and on earth?   Was anything concealed from John, the Lord's most beloved disciple, who used to lean upon his breast? Who was the only one to whom the Lord pointed out Judas as the traitor, and even   commended to Mary as a son in his own place? Could he possibly   have wished them to be ignorant of anything when he even showed them his own glory from heaven, with Moses and Elijah and the Father's voice?   This was not because he disapproved of the other (disciples) but because 'by three witnesses must every word be established.'[3]

2. Adversus Praxean. 15.[4]

Paul expressly calls Christ God when he says: 'Of whom are the fathers, and of whom Christ came, according to the flesh, who is over all God blessed for ever.'[5] He also shows us that the Son of God, the Word of God that is, is visible; for he who became flesh was called Christ. But in relation to the Father he says to Timothy: 'Whom no man has ever seen or can see.' And he expands on this description even further: 'Who alone has immortality and dwells in unapproachable light.'[6] It was of the Father that he also said in a previous passage: 'To the King eternal, immortal, invisible, to the only God;[7]' and this was so that we might apply the opposite qualities to the Son himself, that is mortality and approachability. The apostle testifies of the Son that 'he died according to the scriptures'[8] and that he was seen by himself last of all[9] by means of course of that light which although it was accessible was experienced by him with great danger to his sight.[10] It was the same for Peter, James, and John who (experienced that light) at the risk of losing their reason and their mind. They were unable then to endure the glory of the Son, and if they had seen the Father, they would surely have died then and there: 'For no man shall see God and live'.[11] Since this is the case, it is evident that the one who became visible in the end must have always been the one who was seen from the beginning. The one who had never been visible from the beginning, then, did not become visible in the end. It was the Son , therefore , who was always seen[12] and the Son who always conversed with men, and the Son who has always worked with the authority and will of the Father for: 'The Son can do nothing of himself, only what he sees the Father doing;'[13] 'doing' that is in his mind and thought. For the Father acts by mind and thought[14] while the Son, who is in the Father's mind and thought,[15] gives effect and form to what he sees. So it is that all things were made by the Son and without him nothing was made.[16]

3. Adv. Marcionem. 4.22 (passim).

Marcion, you should be ashamed of yourself for allowing Christ to appear on the lonely mountain in the company of Moses and Elijah whom he had (supposedly) come to destroy. For this at least is what he wished to be understood as the meaning of the voice from heaven: This is my beloved Son. Listen to him. To him - no longer to Moses or Elijah.

But is this the way Christ shows them to be aliens - by keeping them in his own company? Is this how he shows that we should abandon them, by associating with them? Is this how he destroys them, by irradiating them with his own glory?

Peter, however, recognises their indissoluble connection with Christ and properly suggests an expedient: It is good for us to be here. That means it is good to be where Moses and Elijah are. 'Let us make three tabernacles; one for you, one for Moses and one for Elijah. But he did not know what he was saying.' How was it that he did not know? Was his ignorance the result of simple error, or was it because ecstatic rapture[18] always follows on grace? And this is the principle which we maintain in the cause of the new prophecy.[19] For when a man is rapt in the Spirit, especially when he beholds the glory of God, or when God speaks through him, he necessarily loses his sensation because he is overshadowed by the power of God: a point concerning which there is a controversy between us and the carnally-minded[20]. It is quite easy to demonstrate that Peter was in ecstasy[21] for how else could he have recognised Moses and Elijah except in the Spirit? No one had their images or statues or likenesses because the Law forbade this. So how else could he have known them except in the Spirit? And so, because it was in the Spirit that he had spoken, not in his natural senses, this was why he did not know what he had said.

But even if there is meant to be a transfer of obedient hearing from Moses and Elijah to the Christ, it is still not meant to be seen as from another God, or to another Christ; but from the Creator to his Christ, in consequence of the passing of the Old Covenant and the supervening of the New. As Isaiah says: 'It is no ambassador, no angel, that shall save them, but God himself.'[22] For it is He himself who now declares and fulfills the Law and the prophets.

But we have the entire plan of this same vision even in the prophet Habakkuk, where the Spirit through one of the apostles says: 'Lord I have heard your word and was afraid.' What word was this other than the words of the voice from heaven: 'This is my beloved son, listen to him.' It goes on: 'I considered your works and was astonished.' And when could this have happened better than the time when Peter saw his glory and did not know what he was saying? For it says: 'In the midst of two, you shall be known;'[23] which means Moses and Elijah. Zechariah saw the same two in the type of the two olive trees and the olive branches[24] and they are the ones he speaks of: 'They are the two anointed ones that stand by the Lord of the whole earth.' Again Habakkuk says: 'His glory covered the heavens' (that is with the cloud) 'and his splendour shall be like the light' (even that light which glistened in his garments).

4.   Ad Martyras. 2.8.
The prison provides the same service for the Christian as the desert did for the prophet. Our Lord himself spent much of his time in seclusion so that he might have greater liberty to pray, and that he might be rid of the world. It was in the solitude of a mountain

that he showed his glory to his disciples. So let us forget the name 'prison' and let us call it a place of retreat. Although the body is shut in, and the flesh is confined, all things are still open to the spirit. So in spirit roam abroad, and in spirit walk about; not along shady paths or long colonnades but along the way that leads to God. When you walk there in the spirit you will no longer be in chains for your legs cannot feel the chains when your mind is in the heavens, since the mind compasses the whole man and carries him where it wills. And 'where your heart shall be, there shall be your treasure also.'[25] So let our heart be there, then, where we would have our treasure.

5. De Resurrectione Carnis.[55]

But unless the flesh consistently abides throughout this altered state that is shown in the resurrection, it will of necessity be destroyed by the change that occurs. If it does not rise again it perishes. But equally it perishes even if it does rise again if one supposes that it is lost in the process of change . . .

When the Lord, in the solitude of the mountain, changed his raiment for a robe of light he nonetheless retained features that Peter could recognise. In the same vision Moses and Elijah also gave proof that the same condition of bodily existence can continue even in the state of glory; for one came in the likeness of a flesh he had not yet recovered, and the other in the reality of a flesh he had not yet put off ... In the same way it is my opinion that changes, conversions and reformations will necessarily take place in order to effect the resurrection, but the substance (of the flesh) will be preserved safe.

6. De Carne Christi. 24.3.

By declaring that his flesh is simply and absolutely true, and taken in the plain sense of its own nature, (Scripture) aims a blow at all those who make distinctions in it. In the same way when it defines Christ to be but one it shakes the fancies of those who set forth a multiform Christ: those who make Christ to be one being and Jesus another;[26] representing one as escaping out of the midst of crowds and the other as detained by them; one as appearing on a solitary mountain to three companions clothed with glory in a cloud, the other as an ordinary man subject to men; one as magnanimous but the other as timid; and finally, one as suffering death and the other as risen again. They use this event to maintain a resurrection of their own also, only it will be in another flesh. Happily, however, he who suffered will come again from heaven, and he who rose from the dead shall be seen by all men. Even those who crucified him shall see and acknowledge him then, and this in the very flesh which they treated so violently, and without which it would not be possible for him either to exist or to be seen. Let them blush with shame, therefore, who maintain that his flesh sits in heaven devoid of all sensation, like an empty covering, and that the Christ has withdrawn from it. Let them blush also who maintain that his flesh and soul are exactly the same thing, or else that his soul is all that exists now but his flesh no longer lives.

7. De Jejunio. 6

And so it was fitting that even while he was in the flesh, the Lord showed himself to (Moses) the colleague of his own fasting,[27] no less than to Elijah who also had sufficiently devoted himself to fasting, not least by the fact that he had called down a famine.[21] ... Such is the character of mere food, limited though it is, that it makes God a tent-fellow with man[29], indeed as peer with peer. For as Isaiah testifies, if the eternal God will not hunger, then this will be the time for man to be made equal with God, when he lives without food.[30]

8.   De Monogamia. 8.

When he gives the revelation of his own glory, from all the saints and prophets he prefers to have Moses and Elijah with him: one a monogamist, the other a voluntary celibate.

CYPRIAN OF CARTHAGE d.258[3]

l.   Ep.63.15.

There is no reason, dearest brother, for anyone to think that we should follow the custom of certain persons in former times who thought that only water should be offered in the Lord's chalice. We should ask whom they themselves were following in this matter. In the sacrifice which Christ offered, no one should be followed except Christ, and we should do what he himself did, and what he commanded us to do.   For he himself says in the Gospel:' If you do whatever I command you I will call you no longer servants but friends.[32]   The Father also testifies from heaven that we should listen to Christ alone, for he says:' This is my beloved son in whom I am well-pleased.   Listen to him.'   And so if we are to hear only Christ, we should not give heed to what others before us have thought should be done, but rather what Christ himself did, who is before all others.

2.   Testimonia. Ad Quirinum. l.10.

That a new Law was to be given:

In Micah: For the Law shall go forth from Sion and the word of the Lord from Jerusalem.   And he shall judge between many peoples and shall subdue and uncover strong nations.[33]

Also in Isaiah: For from Sion shall go forth the Law, and the word of the Lord from Jerusalem.   And he shall judge among the nations.[34]

Likewise in the Gospel according to Matthew: And behold a voice came out of the cloud saying: This is my beloved Son in whom I am well-pleased. Listen to him.[35]

PSEUDO-CYPRIAN.[36]

Adversus Judaeos. 5.4.

It was not without reason that God hated your ceremonies in which you destroyed his only and first-begotten son. O unfeeling day and tearful hour. O sorrowful festival and unfortunate land. O wicked city and people of the Lord bloody with slaughter. They have killed the Lord and freed a brigand. It was for this reason that the Lord was moved to make a new covenant. It was established with seven seals, and Moses and Elijah witnessed it on the mountain where he ordered that the mystery of the scripture should not be opened until the Son of Man had risen from the dead. But as soon as the Lord had risen, on the third day, he opened up the new covenant, the living covenant, and then said: Come you foreign nations my heirs; for Israel has not obeyed and therefore go, my disciples, to the ends of the earth and preach throughout the world.

HILARY OF POITIERS. c.315-367[37]

1. Comm. In Matthaeum. 17.2-3.

After six days, Peter, James and John are taken up separately to stand on the high mountain. And as they look on, the Lord is transfigured and all his garments are enwrapped in the radiance of his splendour. In this event one may find preserved system, number and analogy. For the vesture of Lordly glory is shown after six days which clearly prefigures that the honour of the heavenly kingdom will come after the span of six thousand years has been unrolled. The three who are taken up refers to the ancient three, Sem, Cham, and Japhet, which shows the future election of a people. This too is why from among all the saints Moses and Elijah come to stand with him, for Christ in the Kingdom is the mediator between the Law and the prophets. And he shall judge Israel with these witnesses through whom he first preached. Moses also stands by visibly so that we might learn that the glory of the resurrection will be determined with human bodies. But the Lord himself became brighter than the sun or the snow, clearly outstanding in the splendour of heavenly light, as we have said before. When Peter offered to build three tabernacles in that place, he did not answer him, for the time had not yet come when he would be established in this glory.

(3)   But while he was still speaking white clouds overshadowed them and they were surrounded by the Spirit of divine power. The voice from the cloud made known that this was the Son; this the beloved; this the favoured one; this the one to be heard. You see Christ is the proper author of instruction, for when he had been condemned by his generation, and chosen the Cross, and after the death of the body, he confirmed the glory of the heavenly kingdom by the example of the resurrection from the dead. After this he raised them up, terrified and afraid, and they saw only him who formerly had been standing in the middle of Moses and Elijah. Moses and Elijah stood on the mountain as an image of the future and a confirmation of the event. He ordered silence about what they had seen until after he should rise from the dead. This was so that those who recognised only the authority of his commands, but did not see this light, might be duly honoured. And so this reward of faith was kept back. Christ had sensed how weak the disciples were

when they heard the voice, and he wanted them to be witnesses
of these heavenly things only after they had been filled with the
Holy Spirit.

2. **De Trinitate.** 10.23.

And so the man Jesus Christ, only begotten God, as flesh and as
Word, at the same time Son of Man and Son of God, without ceasing
to be himself, that is God, took true humanity after the likeness
of our humanity. But when in his humanity he was struck with
blows, or wounded, or bound with ropes, or lifted up on high, then
he felt the force of suffering but without its pain. It is like an
arrow passing through water or piercing a flame or wounding the
air. It inflicts all that is in its nature to do - it passes through,
it pierces, it wounds - but all this is without effect on the things
it strikes since it is against the order of nature to make a hole in
water, or pierce flame, or wound the air, even though it is in the
nature of an arrow to make holes, to pierce and to wound ... How
is it possible to think about that flesh conceived of the Holy Spirit
by analogy with a human body? Only the body of Our Lord could
be carried by the power of his soul over the waters. Only the body
of Our Lord could walk upon the waves or pass through walls. That
flesh, that Bread, is from heaven. That humanity is from God.
He had a body to suffer, and he did suffer, but he did not have
a nature that could feel pain. His body possessed a unique nature
of its own. It was transformed into heavenly glory on the Mountain;
it put fevers to flight by its touch; it gave new vision by its spittle.

3. **De Trinitate.** 11.36-39 (passim).

The apostle, then, to make the explanation of this mystery complete,
after having said that death is the last enemy to be conquered, adds
on: 'But when it says that all things are put in subjection except
the one who put all things in subjection to him, then he himself

must be subjected to him who subjected all things to him; so that God may be all in all.[39] The first stage of the mystery is that all things are subjected to him. And then he himself is subjected to the one who subjects all things to himself. Just as we are subjected to the glory of the rule of his body, so by the same mystery, reigning in the glory of his body, is he himself subjected in his own turn to the one who subjects all things to himself. We ourselves are subjected to the glory of his body, that we may share that splendour with which he reigns in the body for we shall be conformed to his body.

(37)   The Gospels are by no means silent about the glory of his present reigning body for it is written that the Lord said:'Truly I say to you there are some of you standing here who shall not taste death until they see the Son of Man coming in his kingdom. And it happened, after six days, Jesus took with him Peter and James and John his brother, and led them up a high mountain apart. And he was transfigured before them and his face shone like the sun, and his garments became like snow.' Here, the glory of the body of Christ coming into his Kingdom was shown to the apostles. In this manner of the glorious transfiguration the Lord stood revealed in the splendour of his reigning body.

(38)   ... In the end of the world every stumbling-block shall be taken away from his Kingdom. And we shall see the Lord reigning in the splendour of his body, therefore, until that time when every stumbling-block is removed. In consequence we see ourselves conformed to the glory of his body in the Kingdom of the Father, shining with the splendour of the sun; that splendour through which he showed the apostles what his kingdom was like when he was transfigured on the mountain.

(39)   He shall deliver the Kingdom to God the Father not in the sense of laying aside his power when he hands it over but by the fact that we, being conformed to the glory of his body, shall form the Kingdom of God. It is not said: He shall deliver up **his** kingdom; rather He shall deliver up **the** kingdom; and that means

deliver up to God all of us who have been made the kingdom by the glorifying of his body ...

AMBROSE OF MILAN. 339-397[40]

1. **Ennarratio in Ps. 45. (2-3).**[41]

In the Gospel, the Lord revealed the glory of his resurrection to Peter, John and James alone, out of all the number of his disciples. He wished his secret to be a mystery and frequently admonished them not to announce to anyone what they had seen too lightly in case they should give cause for stumbling to the weak and wavering characters who could not, therefore, draw strength from the sacrament. Peter himself did not know what he should say, for he believed that three tabernacles should be built for the Lord as well as the servants. But he was unable to endure the glory of the Lord who was transfigured then, and so fell to the ground. The sons of thunder, James and John, also fell down, and the cloud overshadowed them, and they were unable to rise until Jesus came and touched them and ordered them to get up, and lay aside their fear. They entered into the cloud, then, to learn hidden and secret things; and there they heard the voice of God saying: 'This is my beloved Son in whom I am well-pleased. Listen to him.' What does this mean: My beloved son? Surely Simon it means that you should not be so mistaken as to think that the Son of God can be compared to servants. 'This is my Son.' Moses is not a son, Elijah is not a son; even though one opened the sea and the other closed the heavens. It was by the Word of the Lord that each of these overcame the natural elements as a service for him; but he alone is the one who made the waters firm and closed the heavens in a drought and when he so desired loosed them again in rain. The ministries of his servants come together when this testimony of the resurrection is given. When the glory of the risen Lord is manifested, the splendour of the servants is hidden for the risen sun obliterates the starry spheres and all their light fades before the sun of this world. How could these fleshy-stars ever be seen under the eternal sun of Justice, and in the face of that divine radiance? Where, then, are these luminaries who formerly shone in your eyes through their miracles? All things are darkness in comparison with that eternal light. All the others strive to be pleasing to God by means of their ministries but here is the one true and eternal light in whom the Father is well-pleased ...

(3)   Hear his saying 'I and the Father are one'.[42] Note that he did not say 'I and Moses are one', nor did he say that there was any bond of divine glory between himself and Elijah. So why, Peter, do you prepare three tabernacles? He does not have his tabernacle on earth but in heaven.

2.   De Fide. 1.13.

Perhaps you ask: How was the Son begotten? It was as an eternal one, as Word, as radiance of the eternal light[43] for radiance shines out from the moment of its existence - and that is the apostle's analogy not mine. So do not think, then, that there was ever a time in which God was without Wisdom, or that the light was devoid of radiance. Do not judge divine things on the basis of human, you Arian, but rather believe the divine when you do not find the human.

(80)   The pagan King saw a fourth figure in the fire, alongside the three children, that looked like an angel; and because he thought it excelled the angels he judged it to be the Son of God[44] - whom he had not read about but had believed in[45]. In the same way Abraham saw three (angels) but adored one.[46]

(81)   Peter saw Moses and Elijah on the mountain with the

Son of God and made no mistake as to their nature and glory. And he did not ask the others what he should do, only Christ. For although he was preparing to venerate all three, he nonetheless awaited the command of one. Since he had naively thought that for three persons three tabernacles should be offered, he was corrected by the authority of God the Father who said:'This is my beloved Son. Listen to him.' And this means:'Why do you associate your fellow servants with your Lord? This is my Son. Moses is not a son, Elijah is not a son, but this is the Son.' The apostle understood the correction and fell on his face, terrified by the Father's voice and the glory of the Son. But he was then raised up by the Son who is always accustomed to raise up the fallen. Then he saw only one. He saw the Son of God alone. The servants had departed so that only the Lord might be seen who alone had been designated the Son.

(82)   What then was the purpose of this vision? It was not to signify that Christ and these servants were equals, but to demonstrate a mystery: surely to make plain to us that the Law and the Prophets are in harmony with the Gospel, and reveal the Eternal Son of God whom they had announced. And therefore we too believe, when we hear that he is the Son from the womb and the Word from the heart, that he was not made by hands but begotten from the Father; not the product of a craftsman but the progeny of a parent.

3.   **Expos. In Lucam c.7.** (passim)

(1)   'There are some standing here who shall not taste death until they see the Kingdom of God.'

The Lord always brings before us the rewards that virtue will gain in the future. He teaches us to despise worldly things and even supports the infirmity of our minds by bestowing rewards on us in the present. It is indeed a hard thing to take up the cross and offer one's soul to danger and one's body to death, to deny what we are when we wish to be that which we are not. How rarely does the highest virtue lay aside present realities for the sake of those to come. How difficult it seems for men to buy hope with dangers and purchase the reward of the future by the condemnation of the present. For this reason, the good and ethical teacher offered the faithful the promise of endless life in case anyone should be worn down by desperation or weariness, in the face of the seductions of this sweet life that soften the constancy of the will. But these solaces are chilled by the fear of death, and one who loves life greatly will not prefer such flatteries of hope to the awesome salvation we desire. You have no cause for complaint, therefore, no grounds for excuse, for the Judge of all has given us a reward for virtue and a remedy for infirmity so that our infirmity may be sustained by present realities and our virtue by those to come. If you are strong, then despise death. If you are weak, then flee from it. But no one can flee from death unless life should follow after. And your life is Christ.[47] He himself is the life which does not know death.

(2)   If we wish to have no fear of death, then, let us stand where Christ is so that he may also say of us. 'There are some standing here who shall not taste death.' It is not enough to make a stand unless we stand where Christ is, for only those who are able to stand with Christ will be unable to taste death ...

(6)   How was it that Peter, James, and John did not taste death, but looked upon the glory of the resurrection? For about eight days after these words he took up only these three and led them up the mountain. What then is the meaning of this phrase 'eight days after these words'? It means that the man who hears and believes the word of Christ shall see his glory in the time of the resurrection. For the resurrection is accomplished on the eighth day. This is why so many of the psalms bear the title 'On the eighth'.[48] Perhaps it was that he might show us why he had said that the man who loses his life on account of the word of God shall

save it, since he makes good his promises in the resurrection.

(7)   But Matthew and Mark recall that they were taken up after six days. And this we could interpret as 'after six thousand years' because 'a thousand years is but a day in the sight of the Lord'.[49] But in our computations more than six thousand years have already passed and so we prefer to understand the six days symbolically, as in the six days in which the works of the world were all created, and through this symbolism of the times we can understand the works, and through the works can understand the world. And, therefore, when the times of the world have all been fulfilled the future resurrection is shown forth. He who shall rise over the world and transcend all the times of this age, for he is seated in the highest, shall look for an everlasting fruit of the future resurrection.

(8)   Let us therefore transcend the works of the world so that we might be able to see God face to face. 'Go up the mountain, you who bring good news to Sion.'[50] And if he who brings good news to Sion shall go up the mountain then how much more they who bring the good news of Christ, and Christ in risen glory. Perhaps many may see him in the body: for many of us have known Christ according to the flesh,' but now we know him so no longer.'[51]

(9)   Many of us have known him because many have seen: 'We have seen him and he had not beauty or grace'.[52] But only three, the three elect, are led up the mountain. I think that in this 'three' the whole human race is mystically encapsulated because the whole race issued from the three sons of Noah. Or perhaps it signifies that from all others only those who have confessed Christ shall be found worthy to come to the grace of resurrection, for 'the unrighteous shall not rise to judgement[53,] even though they are punished in an enduring state of condemnation. Three , then , are chosen who might ascend the mountain and two are chosen to be seen alongside the Lord. Both are sacred numbers. This perhaps means that only he who has preserved the whole mystery of the trinity, with the incorrupt sincerity of faith, will be able to see

the glory of the resurrection. Peter ascended who had received the keys of the kingdom of heaven, as did John to whom was committed the Mother of the Lord, as did James who mounted the highest throne of priesthood.

(10)   And then Moses and Elijah appeared , that is Law and Prophecy appeared with the Word. Without the Word Law cannot exist, and there can be no prophet except the one who prophesies about the Son of God. The sons of Thunder gazed upon Moses and Elijah in bodily glory, but even we see Moses beside the Son of God every day because we see the Law in the Gospel when we read: Love the Lord your God[54]. And we see Elijah with the Word of God when we read: Behold a virgin shall conceive in her womb.[55] At this point Luke adds most felicitously that 'they were talking about his death that he would accomplish in Jerusalem.'

(11)   Both teach us the mysteries of his death. Today Moses teaches us, today Elijah speaks to us, and today we can see Moses in greater glory. But who is not able to see Moses when even the Jewish people were able to see him? For 'they saw the face of Moses in glory.'[56] They wore a veil, however,[57] and did not ascend the mountain. And that was their mistake for they could see only Moses, and were unable to see the Word of God there.

(12)   So let us unveil our own faces, so that 'with faces unveiled' we may gaze on the glory of God and be refashioned into that same image.[57] Let us ascend the mountain. Let us beseech the Word of God to appear to us in his own splendour and beauty, to gain increase and to go forward to reign propitiously. These things are mysteries that have a higher significance for according to your own capacity the Word can either be increased or diminished for you. Unless you go up to the summit of a higher prudence then neither Wisdom nor the understanding of the mysteries shall be made manifest to you. You will not see how great is the glory, how great is the beauty of God the Word, but he shall only appear as once he appeared in the body having neither beauty nor grace[58]. He will appear to you as a wounded man bearing our infirmities. His

word will appear to you like the word of man, veiled in ambiguous sayings, not shining in the power of the Spirit. If, however, you study the man and come to believe that he was born of the Virgin, then little by little your faith might draw near to the understanding that he is born of the Spirit of God. It is then that you will begin to ascend the mountain. Then you will see him placed on the cross, triumphing over death, not destroyed by it. Then you will see that the earth trembles, the sun flees away, the darkness spreads over the eyes of the wicked, the tombs are opened and the dead arise. This is a sign that the Gentile nations which had been dead towards God have been illumined by the light of the cross, and rise up as if someone had unlocked their tombs. If you can see this mystery then you have ascended to the high mountain and can behold the other glories of the Word. (13)   Some of his garments are of below, and others are of above. Perhaps the garments of the Word are the words of scripture, a certain vesture of the divine intellect. And just as he appeared in a different form to Peter, John, and James with his vesture shining white, then so has the meaning of the divine scriptures become illuminated for the eyes of your mind. Thus the divine words are made like snow, a garment for the Word so white as no fuller on earth could ever make it ...

(17)   Peter saw his glory, and those with him saw it also, though they were heavy with sleep. This was because the incomprehensible splendour of the divinity weighs down our bodily senses. On the other hand, if our physical vision is unable to withstand the rays of the sun, if we look directly at it, then how could corruptible human organs sustain the glory of God? It is because in the resurrection the materiality of the vices is emptied out and a purer and more refined condition of body is formed. Perhaps also they were heavy with sleep so that they might see the appearance of the resurrection after a rest.[59]   And while they were awake they saw his majesty, for no one shall see the glory of Christ unless he stay awake.[60]   Peter falls into rapture; and thus will the man whom the allurements of this age have not trapped be taken by the grace

of the resurrection.

(18)　　　'It is good for us to be here' he said; (and Paul also says that it would be much better to be dissolved and to be with Christ[61]).　This indefatigable workman is not content merely to offer praise; he is not content with good intentions but wants to offer a more outstanding and devoted service and promises to offer a common obedience by building three tabernacles.　And even though 'he did not know what to say' he still promised this service.　It was not a reckless impudence, rather a premature devotion, the fruit of his piety.　The fact that he did not know what to say was the result of his condition; the fact that he gave the promise, the result of his devotion.　The human condition, however, does not allow us to build a tabernacle for God in this corruptible and mortal body. We should avoid searching out what it is not lawful for us to know, whether in soul or body or anything else.　But if Peter did not know how will you be able to know?　If he who made the promise did not know (he who forgot the limitations of his body because of the greatness of his soul[62]) then how can we hope to know, locked up as we are by idleness of mind within the enclosing walls of flesh? But in the end, so great a devotion was found pleasing to God.

(19)　　　'And while he was speaking a cloud came and overshadowed them.'　This is the overshadowing of the Holy Spirit which does not darken the heart of man, but reveals secret things.　And this is also seen in another place when the angel says: 'And the power of the Most High shall overshadow you.'[63]　The effect of the cloud is shown by the voice of God which says: This is my beloved son; listen to him.

(20)　　　And that means Elijah is not a son, Moses is not a son, only he is the son whom you see there alone.　For all the others had gone back when the Lord was addressed.　You see, this is perfect faith, to know the Son of God; not only for the foolish but also for the perfect, and indeed even for heavenly beings.　But I have already spoken of these things previously, so know that this cloud was not composed of misty vapours from smoke - encircled mountains, or of the pitch blackness of those oppressive atmospheres that sometime cover up the heavens with a frightening darkness. No, it is a cloud of light. It does not water us with showers of rain, or inundate us with torrential storms, but speaks to our mind, about all that God has spoken, as the dew of Faith sent out from the almighty.

(21)   And so, where there were three, there is made one. There are three in the beginning, one in the end, for being made perfect in the end they are one. And the Lord even prays to the Father for this end, that all might be one.[64] It is not only Moses and Elijah who are made one in Christ, however, for we ourselves are the body of Christ. And in the same way that they were taken into the body of Christ, so shall we be made one in Christ Jesus. Perhaps it means too that since Law and Prophecy came from the Word, then what found its origin in the Word should find its end in the Word: for 'The end of the Law is Christ, for the justification of all those who believe.'[65]

JEROME. 347-420.[66]

1.   Comm. In Matthaeum 3.17.

'Amen I say to you, there are some standing here who shall not taste death until they see the Son of Man coming in his Kingdom.' Here he wanted the apostles' dread to be healed by the hope of these promises. 'The Son of Man will come in the glory of his Father with his angels.' He will come, moreover, wielding the authority of Judge and 'will render to each according to his works.' The apostles could hardly bear such a scandal in their inmost hearts, and now you tell them that death and murder lie ahead. You promised them that you would come in the Father's glory, served by the angels, wielding the power of Judge, but this shall come about in the days to come, it lies a long way off. This is why that knower of secrets, who foresaw their objections, compensated their immediate fear with an immediate reward. And so he says to them: 'There are some standing here who shall not taste death until they see the Son of Man coming in his Kingdom.' Here he demonstrates, because of their present unbelief, what would come to pass in the future. 'And after six days taking up Peter, James and John, his brother ...' I have already spoken frequently about the reason why Peter, James and John are separated from the others in certain parts of the Gospels, and why they had privileges beyond the other apostles. Our question now is how he could have taken them up the high mountain, apart, after six days when the evangelist Luke sets the number at eight? The answer is simple, for in the former case the median number of days is stated and in the latter, the first and last days are added on. Note that Luke does not say 'after eight days Jesus took up Peter, James and John' rather 'on the eighth day ...' he led them up a high mountain apart. It is part of the Kingdom to lead the disciples to the mountain. They are led 'apart' because many are called but few are chosen.[67]

(2)   'And he was transfigured before them.' That is, there appeared to the apostles what the future would be like in the time of judgement. When it says 'He was transfigured before them' no one should suppose that he lost his former shape or appearance or that he left off his real body and assumed a spiritual or ethereal body[68]. The evangelist demonstrates how he was transfigured by saying: 'His face shone like the sun and his garments became as white as snow.' When the radiance of his face is thus manifested and the brightness of his garments described, it is not that substantiality is removed, only that the glory is altered. His face shone like the sun because the Lord was transformed into that glory in which he would come afterwards in his kingdom. The transformation increased the splendour but it did not take away his appearance. If he had been a spiritual body surely his garments would not have

been changed but they became so dazzlingly white, as another evangelist has said: 'as no fuller on earth could ever make them'. And what a fuller on earth can make is corporeal and can be touched, it is not spiritual or ethereal, something that evades the eyes and may only be glimpsed in dreams.

(3)   'And behold there appeared to them Moses and Elijah, speaking with him.' He would not give a sign to the scribes and Pharisees who tested him by asking for a sign from heaven. Then he confounded their wicked request by his wise reply[69]. But here he does give a sign from heaven in order to increase his apostles' faith. So Elijah descends from the place where he had ascended, and Moses rises up from Hades. This was prefigured through Isaiah in the case of Ahaz who was to ask for a sign for himself either from heaven or from Hades.[70] So it is written: 'There appeared to them Moses and Elijah speaking with him.' It is told in another Gospel that they told him all the things he would suffer in Jerusalem. The Law and the Prophets are shown, therefore, who with one voice announce the Passion of the Lord and his Resurrection.

(4)   'And Peter, in reply, said to Jesus: Lord it is good for us to be here.' Anyone who has ascended the mountain does not want to come down again to earthly things but always to abide in the highest things. 'If you wish let us make here three tabernacles; one for you, one for Moses and one for Elijah.' But you err, Peter, as the other evangelist witnesses, for you do not know what to say. Do not look for three tabernacles when there should only be one tabernacle of the Gospel in which the Law and the Prophets are fulfilled.[71] But if you insist on three tabernacles, do not offer them to slaves alongside the Lord but instead make three tabernacles to the Father, the Son and the Holy Spirit. But since there is only one divinity in them so there should only be one tabernacle in your heart.

(5)   'And while he was still speaking behold a bright cloud overshadowed them; and behold a voice from the cloud saying: This

is my beloved Son in whom I am well-pleased. Listen to him.'
Peter's request was an improper one and so he did not deserve a
reply from the Lord. And so the Father answered on behalf of the
Son so that the Word of the Lord might be fulfilled: 'I do not testify
to myself, but the Father who sent me himself testifies on my
behalf.'[72] The cloud appears bright and overshadows them so that
those who were looking for the fleshly tabernacle of leafy branches
or tent-skins, might instead be covered by the shelter of a bright
cloud. The voice of the Father is then heard speaking from heaven,
which both bears witness to the Son, and removes Peter's error by
teaching him the truth. Indeed it teaches the other apostles too
by means of Peter. It says: This is my beloved Son. The tabernacle
should be built for him alone. He should be obeyed for he is the
Son while the others are slaves. Moses and Elijah themselves ought
to join with you in preparing a tabernacle for the Lord in their
inmost hearts.

(6)   When the disciples heard this they fell upon their faces
and were greatly afraid. They were seized with fear for three
reasons: either because they knew they had made a mistake, or
because of the shining cloud, or because they heard the voice of
God the Father speaking and human frailty cannot bear the sight
of greater glory, and wholly seized with trembling in body and soul ,
it falls to the ground. In the degree that it seeks after what is
higher so much more does it fall to what is lower if it does not
recognise its own limitations.

(7)   'And Jesus came up and touched them.' Since they were
prostrate and unable to rise, he himself came up in kindness and
touched them so that by his touch the fear might flee, and their
feeble limbs be made strong. 'And he said to them: rise up and
do not be afraid.' He had healed them by his hand and now he
heals by his command: Do not fear. First of all he drives out fear
and then he can instil his teaching.

(8)   'And lifting their eyes, they saw no one, only Jesus.'
This was arranged so that when they looked up they would only see

Jesus; for if Moses and Elijah had remained with the Lord perhaps they would have been uncertain about whom the Father was giving this powerful witness. And so they saw Jesus standing there. The cloud had withdrawn and Moses and Elijah had vanished. For after the Law and the prophets had gone, which laid a veil over the apostles, then can the light of them both be found in the Gospel. (9) 'And while they were coming down from the mountain Jesus commanded them saying: Tell no one this vision until the Son of Man has risen from the dead.' On the mountain there had been given a foretaste of the future kingdom. The glory of the Victor was demonstrated. He does not want this to be preached to the people in case the immensity of the affair may make it sound incredible, and in case the cross following so soon after such great glory might cause scandal for unformed souls.

2. Comm. In Ep.2 Ad Cor. c.3

'But all of us with faces unveiled gaze on the glory of the Lord'. We contemplate the glory of the Lord manifestly and clearly. 'We are transformed into the same likeness' which the Lord showed on the mountain, just as it is said in another place: 'who has transfigured the body of our lowliness making it like the body of his own glory'[73]. So we are transformed daily and we press on to be transformed 'from glory to glory as though by the Spirit of the Lord'; that is we make progress for the future by means of this glory, through the working of the Spirit of the Lord.

3. Comm. In Ep. Ad Philipp. c.3.

'But our conversation is in the heavens'. This does not mean that we are completely released from earthly vices. 'Whence we expect even our Saviour, the Lord Jesus Christ', who is our head, 'who shall refashion the body of our lowliness making it like the body of his own glory' just as he demonstrated on the mountain when he refashioned one of the living and one of the dead alongside the body of his own glory. This was to show an example of the resurrection both for the dead and for the living 'according to the working of his power by which he can even subject all things to himself,' since he has not only fashioned us but has even made all things subject to his body according to the judgement whereby he has subjected all things to himself. Even this is possible to him.

4.   **Pseudo-Jerome. Comm. In Marcum** c.9.[74]

After six days, on a high mountain, he was transfigured in the presence of his disciples so that they who had seen, with their own eyes, the glory of the future resurrection, should not be afraid of the shame of the cross.

AUGUSTINE 354-430[75]

1.   **Hom. 28.**[76]

Let us now investigate and expound that vision which the Lord demonstrated on the mountain. It was of this that he had said: 'Amen I say to you, there are some standing here who shall not taste death until they see the Son of Man in his Kingdom.' Then follows the passage which we have just read: 'Six days after he had said this he took three disciples, Peter, James and John, and went up into a mountain. These are the three he had meant when he said:' There are some here who shall not taste death until they see the Son of Man in his kingdom.' This is a very difficult point, however, for that mountain was hardly the whole of his kingdom. What is a mountain to one who owns the heavens? And we have not only read that he does own them but we even see it in some sense with the eyes of our heart. In several places he calls 'his kingdom' what he refers to as the kingdom of heaven. Now the kingdom of heaven is the kingdom of the saints: 'For the heavens declare the glory of God'[77]; and it is then said in the Psalm about these same heavens: 'There is no tongue or language where their voice is not heard. Their sound goes forth through all the earth, their words to the utmost bounds of the world.'[78] Whose words are these? Surely heavenly words, words of the Apostles and all faithful preachers of the Word of God. These 'heavens', then, shall reign together with him who made the heavens. Now let us see what was done so that this might be manifested.

(2)	The Lord Jesus shone as bright as the sun and his garments became as white as snow, and Moses and Elijah spoke with him. Jesus himself shone like the sun to signify that 'He is the light that enlightens every man who comes into the world'[79]. What the sun is to the eyes of the body, so is he to the eyes of the heart; what it is to the flesh of men, he is to their heart. His garment is the Church for if a garment is not held together by the one who puts it on, then it falls off. Paul was the last border, as it were, of this garment, for as he himself says: ' I am the least of the apostles.'[80] And in another place: ' I am the last of the apostles.' In a garment, the border is the least part. And when the woman who suffered from the issue of blood touched the Lord's border, she was made whole, just as the Church, which came from the Gentiles, was made whole by the preaching of Paul. It is no wonder that the church is signified by the white garment when we hear the prophet Isaiah saying: 'Though your sins are as scarlet, I will make them as white as snow.'[81] Of what use are Moses and Elijah except when they speak with the Lord? And who would ever read them, that is the Law and the Prophets, except for the witness they give to the Lord? Note how succinctly the apostle expresses this: 'For the knowledge of sin came by the Law, but now the righteousness of God is made manifest outside the Law'.[82] So behold the Sun witnessed through the Law and the prophets , see how it now shines.

(3)   Peter sees it, and as one who enjoys the things of men he says: 'Lord it is good for us to be here.' He had been tired of the crowds and had now found a solitary mountain where he had Christ, the bread of the soul. Do you expect him to leave it again for painful labours when here he is filled with a holy love for God and enjoys this wonderful happening? He wished well for himself and so he went on: 'If you wish, let us make here three tabernacles, one for you, one for Moses and one for Elijah.' The Lord made no reply to this, but Peter still had his answer: 'For while he was still speaking behold a bright cloud came and overshadowed them'. Peter wanted three tabernacles but the heavenly response showed him that we have but one. It is human judgement that wishes to divide it. It is Christ the Word of God, the Word of God in the Law and the Word in the Prophets. Peter, why do you want to divide them? It would be more fitting for you to unite them. You look for three, so understand that they are but one.

(4)   As the cloud overshadowed them, and in this way made a single tabernacle for them, 'a voice came from the cloud saying: This is my beloved Son'. Moses was there, Elijah was there, but it was not said: These are my beloved sons. The only Son is quite different from adopted sons. He alone was praised in whom the Law and the Prophets gloried. 'This is my beloved son in whom I am well-pleased. Listen to him.' For you have heard him in the prophets and you have heard him in the Law. Where have you not heard him? 'And when they heard this, they fell to the ground'. The Kingdom of God, therefore, is shown to us in the Church. Here is the Lord, and here too the Law and the Prophets. But the Lord stands here as Lord, the Law in the person of Moses and Prophecy in Elijah. They are servants and ministers. They are vessels while he is the fountain. Moses and the prophets spoke and wrote, but

all they poured out was instilled by him.

(5)   And the Lord stretched out his hand and raised them as they lay. 'And then they saw no one only Jesus.' What does this mean? When the Apostle was being read you heard: 'For now we see through a glass darkly, but then we shall see face to face;'[83] and also that 'tongues shall cease' when what we hope and believe in shall come about. So when they fell to the ground it signified our death. As it was said to flesh : 'You are dust and to dust you shall return.'[84] And when the Lord raised them up it signified the resurrection. After the resurrection what shall the Law or prophecy be to you? This was why neither Moses or Elijah was seen then. Only he remains for you who 'in the beginning was the Word, and the Word was with God and the Word was God.'[85] He remains for you so that 'God may be all in all'.[86] Moses shall be there but no longer the Law. Elijah will also be there, but no longer the prophets; for the Law and the prophets have only witnessed of Christ that it was necessary for him to suffer and to rise again from the dead on the third day, and so to enter his glory. In this glory he fulfills the promise he made to those that love him: 'Whoever loves me shall be loved by my Father, and I myself will love him.'[87] Perhaps we can say: 'What will you give him Lord seeing that you love him?' 'I will reveal myself to him.' O great gift. Great promise. God does not keep as your reward anything of what is his, but his very self. O greedy heart why is God's promise not enough for you? You think that you are so rich, but if you do not have God, then what do you have? A man may be poor, but if he has God, what does he lack?

(6)   Come down then Peter. You wanted to stay on the mountain but come down to preach the word. 'Be constant in season and out; reprove, rebuke and exhort them with all patience as you teach.'[88] Endure your share of pain and hard toil so that you may come to possess the meaning of the white garment of the Lord through the brightness and beauty of the noble labours of love ...

2.   Ps. Augustine.   Tractatum contra V Haereses.

Christ said: 'Father glorify your Son.'[89]   And the accursed Arian
interprets it like this: 'You see how he is a lesser being and only
has that glory which he asks for from the Father?'   But hold on
fellow, do not be in such a rush.   For you are only looking at the
man and in this form he is not only less than the Father but less
than the angels too.[90]   The man lies open, the God lies hid.   You
show me the humble man but open your eyes and see the sublime
God, he who is not less than the angels but equal to the Father.
But he continues: 'that your Son may glorify you '   and see here
the equal.   We find that the Son knows the Father and he prays,
in union with him, so as not to seem ungrateful.[91]   Let us see what
the Father himself has to say about the Son.   The words of the
Gospel are: 'Jesus took up Peter and James and John his brother,
and led them up a high mountain, apart, and he was transfigured
before them.   His face shone like the sun and his garments became
as white as snow.   And behold there appeared to them Moses and
Elijah speaking with him.'   Moses and Elijah, that is the Law and
the Prophets, were speaking with him since they had often spoken
about him . They were demonstrating ,then, the one they had foretold
and manifesting the one of whom they had prophesied.   So they
were talking.   And what do you think they were talking about? -
that the Jews might be convinced, the pagans converted, the
Manicheans confounded, the heretics suppressed and the catholics
confirmed.   Here Law and Grace were speaking; harshness and
gentleness; terror and clemency; precept and assistance; the knife
and the healing; shadow and light; the herald and judge; condemnation
and mercy.   What happened then? 'Peter in reply said to Jesus:
Lord it is good for us to be here.   If you wish let us make three
tabernacles here, one for you, one for Moses and one for Elijah.'
What are you saying, holy Peter?   He brought forth the whole world
and are you now asking for some place of solitude? Do you see how
many nations have come together in unity, and you are seeking rest?
You see the darkness of the world; and do you seek to hide the

light? But 'no one lights a lantern and puts it under a bushel measure; but upon a lamp-stand so that it may illumine the whole household.'[92] The whole world is this household. The lighting of the lantern is the incarnation of the Word, and the lamp-stand is the wood of the cross. The lantern that shines on the lampstand is Christ hanging on the cross. 'No one lights a lantern and puts it under a bushel measure; but upon a lampstand so that it may illumine the whole household.' You have seen, Peter, so let us see as well. It is dark so let us not stumble with the pagans; let us not err with the heretics, but may that lantern shine upon us, may the Word in flesh teach us. Let us see what the evangelist says. (Let us see if Peter's advice is accepted.) He says: 'And while he was still speaking behold a bright cloud overshadowed them and behold a voice came from the cloud'. Let all men listen, and not close their ears. Let the mocking pagans listen; let the persecuting Jews listen; let the Manicheans with their dreaming illusions listen; let the heretics, those mistaken disputants, listen; and let the catholics listen, those faithful worshippers of God. Let them listen more carefully than any other. Let them listen for their instruction while the others listen for their correction. Let them listen so that they may never be led astray, while the others listen to their reproof. What does the voice from the cloud say? 'This is my beloved Son in whom I am well-pleased.' Where are you then who stand against the Son of God? The Father says 'This is my Son' and you say that God does not have a son? And you pagans why do you stand outside murmuring? Enter here into the school of God, open the ears of your hearts and hear the voice of the Lord, and come to know the Son of God. What are you Jews going to do, who killed that Son of God? Where shall you flee or where shall you hide yourselves? Which mountains or rocks will open up for you? 'For if you hide yourselves in the caverns of rocks, yet shall I draw you out from there, says the Lord.'[93] Nonetheless, you can come as well; enter in and listen to my advice, do not despair for 'there shall be descendants for the man of peace.'[94]

You have acted savagely, you have killed and have shed the blood of Christ. You are in danger for you have disbelieved in the Son of God. What then should you now do except believe and be baptised, and drink that blood which you shed. There is nothing here that should appal you for it is the blood of healing that is shed and it becomes a medicine for the frenzied. Why do you doubt? 'Taste and see that the Lord is sweet.'[95] And you Manicheans, how long will you dream these illusions? Wake up and see. The clouds are thundering: what is it they thunder? 'This is my beloved Son'. See on earth the Son of Man, hear from heaven that he is the Son of God. And know that both are true; that he is God and Man, one and the same Son of God and Son of Man, at once God and Man. Recognise this, man, and you will be pleasing to God. Take care you do not stumble against the rock and suffer the ruination of death; for what you dream about is emptiness but what God thunders out is the truth. Listen you Sabellians and hear the Father speaking from heaven; see the Son upon the earth and do not say that the Father and the Son are the same. Listen you Arians and do not be mistaken about the Father and the Son but follow up the matter of unity and recognise the divinity. Lord let us listen to what you say about your Son. What he says is this: This is my Son. See on earth the Son of Man, hear from heaven that he is the Son of God - 'My beloved in whom I am well-pleased'. Then what? 'Listen to him.' Thanks be to God. The divine command has thundered forth and Peter's advice is taken away. Thanks be to God. Thanks be to the one true Trinity, the one and triune truth, the one and triune unity. Thanks be to you God the Father, who have shown forth your Son and given me a teacher. Let Sabellius retreat, let Arius retreat, and so with all the other plagues. Let every wicked doctrine retreat. Let God teach not Arius; let the Son of God teach not the enemy of God. Speak my Lord Jesus; teach me that I may learn what I myself should teach.

LEO I (Pope 440-461) [96]

1.   **Hom. 51.** (passim)

(1)   The Gospel today, dearly beloved , which has struck the inner ear of our minds by the ears of the body, calls us to the comprehension of a great sacrament. By God's favourable grace we might more easily follow it if we put our minds back to those things we spoke of earlier. The saviour of the human race, Jesus Christ himself, who founded that faith which calls the wicked back to justice and the dead back to life, was engaged in training his disciples by the counsels of his teaching and his miraculous works so that they might believe that the same Christ was the only begotten Son of God and also the Son of Man. One of these without the other is not effective for salvation; for it is equally perilous to believe that Our Lord Jesus Christ is only God, not man, as it is to think that he is only man, not God. We must confess both equally. For God there was a true humanity, and likewise the true divinity was contained in the man ...

(2)   ... 'Jesus took up Peter, James and John, his brother' and when these alone had climbed with him to the top of the mountain he showed them the radiance of his glory. Although they had understood that the majesty of God was in him, they still did not know the power of his own body which covered the deity. And so he promised both accurately and clearly that some of the disciples who were then standing round him would not taste death before they had seen the Son of Man coming in his Kingdom. This is that kingly radiance which pertains especially to the nature of the assumed manhood. He wanted this to be manifested to the three disciples, for while they were still encompassed in mortal flesh it would be wholly impossible for them to gaze at or look upon the ineffable and unapproachable vision of the godhead itself.

(3)   And so the Lord revealed his glory in the presence of chosen witnesses, and showed that form which he has in common

with other bodies, but with such great splendour that his face was like the brilliance of the sun, and his garments were as white as snow. The transfiguration chiefly occurred for this end, that the scandal of the cross should be taken away from the hearts of the disciples, and so that, since they had been given the revelation of his secret majesty, the abasement of the Passion might not confound their faith. In the same providence he established the hope of the Church, so that the whole body of Christ might know what kind of transformation would be granted, and that the members might know in advance that they too would share in the honour of their Head who had been so wonderfully radiant. The Lord himself spoke about this when he talked about his coming in glory: 'Then shall the just shine like the sun in the kingdom of their Father.'[97] The blessed apostle Paul insists on the same thing when he says: 'I consider that the sufferings of this present age are not worth comparing to the future glory that shall be revealed in us.'[98] And again: 'For you are dead and your life is hidden with Christ in God. But when Christ, your life, appears then you also will appear with him in glory.'[99]

(4)   Once the apostles have been confirmed and brought to a full understanding then the instruction contained in this miracle enters upon other things as well. Moses and Elijah, doubtless the Law and the Prophets, appeared speaking with the Lord. This was so that the saying might be most truly fulfilled in the presence of five men which says: 'Every word shall stand with two or three witnesses.'[100] What can be more certain than this? What word could ever be more reliable? For in its preaching the eloquence of the Old and the New Testament rings out in harmony, and the servants of the ancient witness concur with the evangelical doctrine. The pages of both covenants agree with one another and the very one whom the ancient signs promised under the veils of mystery is now shown forth manifestly and clearly in the splendour of this glory. It is as blessed John said: 'For the Law was given through Moses, but grace and truth came through Jesus Christ.'[101] In him

the promise of the prophetic types, and the whole system of the precepts of the Law, find their fulfilment. By his presence he teaches us that prophecy is true, and he makes the commandments possible by grace.

(5)   Peter the apostle was so inspired by these revelations of mysteries that he wished to spurn and despise worldly things and his mind was taken by a kind of excessive desire for eternal things. He was so filled with the joy of this vision that he desired to dwell in that joyful place with Jesus in his revealed glory. And so he said: 'Lord it is good for us to be here. If you wish, let us make here three tabernacles, one for you, one for Moses and one for Elijah.' But the Lord made no reply to this suggestion which signifies that what he desired, though not ungodly, was not quite right. The world could not be saved except by the death of Christ, and he wanted to give believers an example here to confirm their faith, so that we might understand that although it is not right to doubt the promises of happiness, nonetheless amid the trials of life we should rather pray for endurance than glory because the joy of reigning cannot anticipate temporal suffering.

(6)   'And while he was still speaking, behold a bright cloud overshadowed them, and behold a voice came from the cloud saying: This is my beloved son in whom I am well-pleased. Listen to him.' The Father was indeed present in the Son and the essence of the Begetter was in no way separated from the only begotten in that glory of the Lord, even though allowance was made for the limited vision of the disciples . The voice came for the commendation of the proper nature of each person. And so in the vision the splendour of the body signified the Son, and in what they heard the voice from the cloud announced the Father. When they heard the voice the disciples fell upon their faces and were greatly afraid. They trembled not only at the Father's majesty but also at the Son's; for in a higher sense they understood the one deity of each person. Just as there was no hesitation in their faith, there was no distinction in their fear. This was a profound and far-reaching

testimony that was heard more in the force of the words than in the sound of the voice, for when the Father said, 'This is my beloved son in whom I am well pleased', they heard quite plainly: This is my Son who is from me and with me and who is eternally. The Begetter is not prior to the Begotten, nor the Begotten subsequent to the Begetter. This is my Beloved Son whom Godhead does not separate from me, power does not divide and eternity does not distinguish. This is my Beloved Son, not an adopted son but a true son. He is not created by another, but begotten from me; not made like me from a different nature, but from my own essence born equal to me. This is my Son through whom all things were made and without whom nothing was made.[102] All that I do, he does equally, and in whatever way I am active he too is active with me without separation and without difference. The Son is in the Father and the Father in the Son,[103] and our unity is never divided. Although I who begot him may be distinct from the one I begot, it would be wrong of you to think anything different of him from what you conceive of me. This is my Son who did not seek to grasp that equality he had with me[104], who did not presume it by usurpation, but who remained in the form of my own glory and yet bent down the changeless Godhead even to the form of a slave so that he could follow our common plan for the restoration of the human race.

(7)   This, then, is why I am well-pleased with him in all things, and why I am revealed in all his preaching. I glorify his humility. So, without hesitation, listen to him, for he is in himself both Truth and Life. He himself is my power and wisdom. Listen to the one whom the mysteries of the Law foretold, whom the mouths of the prophets proclaimed. Listen to him who has redeemed the world with his blood, who binds the devil and plunders his stock, who shatters the contracts of sin and the pacts of wickedness. Listen to him who opens the way to heaven and by the torment of the cross prepares the steps of an ascension for you to the kingdom itself. Why do you tremble to be redeemed? Why are you afraid

to be freed of your hurts? Let it be done, for my will is as that of Christ. Cast away your carnal dread and arm yourselves with faithful constancy for it is not fitting that you should fear in the Passion of the Saviour that which his grace will cause you not to fear in your own end.[105]

(8)	These things, my dear brethren, are not spoken only for the benefit of those who heard them with their own ears. For in these three apostles the whole Church learns from what they saw with their eyes and took by hearing. And in this way the faith of all is confirmed according to the preaching of the most holy Gospel, and no one is ashamed of the cross of Christ by which the world was redeemed. We are no longer afraid to suffer for the sake of righteousness, nor are we doubtful about the fulfilment of the promises made to us, for through toils we shall come to rest, and through death to life. He himself has borne the whole infirmity of our wretchedness, and if we abide in his confession and his love we too shall conquer in the way he has conquered and receive all that he has promised. Whether it is to help us keep the command-ments or to support us in our difficulties, let the voice of the Father always echo in our ears: This is my beloved Son in whom I am well-pleased. Listen to him, who lives and reigns with the Father and the Holy Spirit for ever and ever. Amen.

## 2.	Pseudo-Leo. Hom.20.[106]

Today, dearest brethren, we solemnly observe the day of him who governing all things with the Father made each day. I mean the Word, who said in the beginning: 'Let there be light. And there was light.'[107] As the Gospel text narrates, on this day his flesh was transfigured on the mountain before two prophets and three disciples. He wished to show them his face made whiter than snow, in order to give us the hope of divinity ...

(2)	If anyone wants to know why he wished to be transfigured before these two prophets and three disciples, perhaps we could recall that wonderful sermon of the Lord himself when he said to the Jews: 'It is written in your law that the testimony of two men is true.'[108] But he also brought these witnesses, together with the disciples, to look upon his glorious transfiguration in divine power, in order to demonstrate that he was the same one who said to Moses: 'I am who am. And you shall say this to the sons of Israel - He who is has sent me to you.'[109] He is the same one who sent Moses to Pharoah for the sake of the liberation of the sons of Israel; the same one who gave him the Law on Mount Sinai; the same one who carried off Elijah the prophet to the heavenly places in a chariot of fire. He called back the one from the gate of death, and the other from his translation to Paradise. Who else knew the burial place of Moses other than he who ordered it and brought him to that place? Who else knew where Elijah had gone up except he who called him there? This is the only-begotten of the Father who, for the sake of the redemption of the human race, wished to become the firstborn of a mother. Today, in his transfiguration, he wished to make a unified harmony of both scriptures. In order to demonstrate that he is the Lord of the Law and the Prophets, he wished to bring them both into the witness of the evangelists. In his transfiguration it pleased him to show the proclaimer of the Son to the proclaimer of the Father, show Peter to Moses; to show the ancient celibate to the new, that is Elijah to John. Today the disciples were able to see two suns upon the mountain; the first was in the firmament and can be seen by all men, but the other shines more splendidly than this and is seen only by the prophets and the disciples: the face of Jesus. This sun flashes on the mountain and by its power lights up that other which is in the firmament. This is the sun of Justice which shines and blazes: in its blazing it enkindles the faithful, and in its shining it illumines all men. Of this sun, John says: 'The true light which enlightens every man was coming into the world.'[110]

(3)　　　After his face had been transfigured to another form he wished his glory to be made known to us more clearly and so a bright cloud came to overshadow him and the apostles. Then he was truly glorified by the Father, who said: This is my dearest son. Listen to him. The disciples were unable to bear so great a voice and fell upon their faces. Moses and Elijah withdrew and the divine son alone remained. He lifted them up and said: Do not be afraid. Which means: let them fear who are the cruel sport of fantasies, but you who are obedient to the Father's own son, and share in his secret mysteries - why should you be afraid? And then the holy disciples looked around and saw no one, only Jesus. This was so that it might be made clear that the voice which had come did not apply to Moses or Elijah, only to the only begotten Son. In fact, in relation to this vision a most eloquent poet praised and celebrated the merit of these three apostles when he wrote:

> O wondrous merit of these three
> who in the world
> saw things beyond the world's belief.
> Though their eyes knew it not
> by heart's light they saw Elijah
> and Moses bright with virtue.
> It shall be told throughout the world
> that our faith may gain increase
> that He is the beginning and the end
> the Alpha and the O
> who stands surrounded by these radiant prophets
> One still living
> the other standing in the light of life.
> And the heavenly voice is heard:
> This is my Son.
> The Father's voice shows Christ begotten by Word.[111]

(4) Now the Lord also says: 'When I shall pass by, you will see my nether parts, but my face you are not able to see.'[112] This is because the face of the Lord is the incomprehensible Godhead, but his nether parts are believed to be the assumed humanity of the

Son. By 'face' is doubtless meant the divinity which is before all ages, since face is the foremost part of the body; but the nether parts are the humanity of Christ which has come to us in these end times through the inviolate Mary. On this day the Father has faithfully accomplished what he promised to Moses his servant.[113] It was about the solemnity of this day that David said: You have put on glory and majesty, clothed in light as in a robe.'[114] Christ is clothed with glory and honour when he is glorified with the glory of the Father's voice. He is clothed in light as in a robe when he shows the disciples his face that shines with the splendour of the sun ...

GREGORY I (Pope 590-596) [115]

1. **Moralium in Job. 40. Lib.32.6.8.**

God is clothed in beautiful garments for he has taken round him the chorus of the holy angels, which he created for his own glory, and he has revealed the Church as a glorious garment for himself, having neither spot nor blemish[116]. And so the prophet says of him: 'You have put on confession and beauty: clothed in light as in a robe.'[117] Here he has truly put on confession, there beauty; because those whom here he makes confess through penance, there he reveals as shining through the beauty of righteousness. And so, he is clothed in light as in a robe because he is clothed with eternal glory in the company of all the saints, of whom it is said: 'You are the light of the world.'[118] This is why it is said in the Gospel that when the Lord was transfigured on the mountain his garments became as white as snow. In this transfiguration what else is announced other than the glory of the final resurrection? On the mountain his garments became as white as snow because on the mountain top of heavenly brightness all the saints cling to him who shine with the light of righteousness.

2. In Primum Regium Expositio. Lib.5.29-30.

What is the beauty of his face other than the comeliness of sanctity?
What is the beauty of his face other than the splendour of his
incomparable speech? For in everything he ever did he shone with
an incomparable light of grace. The psalmist admires the beauty
of this face when he says: 'Your appearance is beautiful beyond
the sons of men, for grace is poured out upon your lips.'[119] Paul
preaches the same: 'He who is the splendour of his glory and the
figure of his substance, upholding all things by the word of his
power, making a purification of sins, he sat down at the right hand
of the majesty on high having become as much superior to the
angels as the name he has inherited is more excellent than theirs.
For to what angel did God ever say: You are my Son, today I have
begotten you?'[120] It was of him then that the prophet was rightly
ordered: 'Rise and anoint him for this is the one.'[121]

(30)   The apostle Peter, moreover, not only a prophet but also
chief patriarch, saw the ineffable light pouring down from on high
when the cloud overshadowed him and the Father's voice cried out:
'This is my beloved Son in whom I am well pleased.' There it is
said:' For this is the one.' Here it is said: 'This is my beloved Son.'
There, when it is said 'This is the one' it was as if it was shown
in a type, as if something far off had been discerned. But here,
when it is said:' This is my beloved Son in whom I am well-pleased,'
it is discerned more immediately since his radiance had already been
revealed. This is the one to be anointed, therefore, this is the one
to be praised and honoured with everlasting glories. But who can
give worthy praise who cannot even look upon the glory of that
which he is praising? Why is it that Peter falls down when he hears
the voice sending forth such great commendations? He was weak
and yet he saw what was beyond him to see. He saw, but in seeing
he fell down as a sign that he was not able to attain to that which

he was granted to see: 'For no one can say Jesus is Lord except in the Holy Spirit.'[122] Peter had not yet received that fullness of the Spirit and so being a weak man he was not strong enough to preach Jesus. He is first ordered to rise up, then, and tell no one what he had seen until Jesus had risen from the dead. Indeed after the resurrection he would receive the Holy Spirit. Of this it is written: 'For the Spirit had not yet been given since Jesus had not yet been glorified.'[123] This was why it was not right for Peter to tell of the vision before the resurrection because although he had indeed seen, before he had the Spirit he had not understood.

BEDE THE VENERABLE   673-735.[124]

Hom. 28. (passim)

Our Lord and Redeemer has determined to bring in his elect through the toils of this life, to that which knows no toil: the life of future beatitude. And sometimes in his Gospel he depicts the labours of temporal struggles, and other times the palm of eternal rewards. We therefore hear about the necessity of pains and understand that we cannot seek for rest in this life. And yet when we hear of the sweetness of the future reward perhaps these passing evils seem all the lighter since they have this hope of being compensated by eternal joys. A little earlier Jesus had reminded his disciples that they were all destined to suffer, and now he immediately adds on this saying which we have just heard read out: 'For the Son of Man shall come in his Father's glory, with his angels and then he shall recompense each one according to his works.'[125] He fittingly calls this the day of the Last Judgement when he comes in great power and majesty to judge the world, the same who had come formerly in humility and abjection to be judged by the world. On that day he shall stand in the severity of a judge to require

the harvest of good works from those to whom he had formerly given, in merciful kindness, the grace of his own gifts. When he gives to each one according to their works he will lead the elect into the kingdom of his Father but will cast out the wicked with the devil into everlasting fire. How beautifully it is said: 'The Son of Man shall come in the glory of God the Father.' For he who is less than the Father in the nature of man, the self same, true man, in divinity is of one and the same glory as the Father, true God through all ... 'I tell you solemnly there are some standing here who shall not taste death until they see the Son of Man coming in his Kingdom.' The disciples truly saw him coming into his kingdom when they saw him shining in glory on the mountain. This is that glory in which he shall be seen by all the saints in his kingdom, once the judgement is over. The eyes of the disciples were still mortal and corruptible and could not endure the sight; but in that day the Church of all the saints shall have already been made incorruptible by the resurrection and it shall mightily behold. Of which it is written: 'His eyes shall see the King in his splendour.'[126]
'And after six days Jesus took up Peter, James and John ...'
In order to show his glory to his disciples he led them up a high mountain. This was to teach all of us who desire to see his glory, not to lie in the lowest pleasures or to serve carnal allurements, or to cling to earthly desires, but always to be lifted up to heavenly things, in love with what is eternal. We must always be bent on imitating a life of justice, angelic purity, piety, peace and love, as far as it is possible for mortal beings; in accordance with him who said: 'For our conversation is in heaven whence we expect Our Lord and Saviour Jesus Christ.'[127] In order to show the glory of his majesty he led the disciples up the mountain so that they might learn, and anyone else who thirsts to see this might also learn, that they are not to seek glory in the depths of this age but in the Kingdom of heavenly happiness. And when it says 'He led them up a high mountain', how fittingly it adds 'by themselves' for now the just are constrained in the company of the wicked, though they

are separated from them with their whole mind and heart and faith, but then in the future they will be utterly separated from them, 'by themselves' when he shall shelter them in the shade of his face from all the assaults of men[128] and protect them in his tabernacle from lying mouths ...

'And he was transfigured before them ...'

When the Lord was transfigured before his disciples, he revealed to them the glory of his own body which was to be manifested through the resurrection. He shows how great will be the splendour of the future bodies of the elect after the resurrection. On this matter he says elsewhere: 'then shall the just shine like the sun in the kingdom of their Father.'[129] And here, as a sign of his own future splendour, his face is as radiant as the sun ...

'And Peter said, Lord it is good for us to be here ...'

Peter was right to say this for in truth it is man's only good to enter into the glory of his Lord and to stand forever in his contemplation. It is right to think that if, by his own fault, a man has never been able to see the face of his creator then he has never had anything that is truly good. But if the blessed Peter is overcome with such great joy when he contemplates the glorified humanity of Christ that he never wants to be separated from this vision ever again, then what should we think, my dear brethren, is the happiness of those who have merited to see the immensity of his deity? If the beauty of the transfigured human Christ on the mountain with only two of his saints was enough to make Peter think that this was the greatest good, then what tongue could tell, what mind could ever grasp how great must be the joys of the righteous when they come to Mount Sion and the city of the living God, Jerusalem; where the thousands of angels throng and where we shall see the founder and builder of that city, not as at present as if in a shadow or through a glass, but face to face ...

AMBROSE AUTPERTUS died c.779.[130]

Hom De Transfiguratione.

(1)   It is not an unusual thing, indeed it is almost commonplace that in the homes of Kings and princes any base and contemptible man is chosen to clean up the gold or silver dishes. And what indeed are the hearts of the elect in the holy church other than these regal vessels I have just mentioned? Paul witnesses to this when he says that in a great house there are not only gold and silver vessels but also those made of wood and earthenware. And some are used for honourable purposes and some for dishonourable (Rom.9.21). Whoever shall cleanse himself from dishonour, then, shall be a vessel made holy and honourable, useful for the Lord, and ready for every good work. You, then, my dearest brethren, you are the vessels of the eternal King shining like precious metal in the reverence of holy religion. But keep in mind that as long as you live on earth you shall never be wholly free from the stains of vice. This is why John, the one the Lord loved especially, said in his Epistle: 'If we say that we have no sin we deceive ourselves and the truth is not in us.' (I Jn.l.8.) And so, in case the tarnish of sin should eat away the vessels of God, it is necessary that this hand of holy preaching should daily be busy polishing. Let every man here know that this office of cleaning has been entrused to me who am clearly one of the unworthiest servants of God. But do not, I beg you, let the defilements of this paltry man affront you as long as there is the slightest chance that this office of preaching might perhaps serve to rub any stains of sin from out of your hearts. This is why I take it upon myself to expound the reading of the Holy Gospel in which Our Lord is shown transfigured in the presence of the three disciples. I will expound on the secret mysteries of this text as far as my ability allows; not as if the text has not been elucidated by others before me, but because there is something in this which has not yet been spoken and which has been reserved for me to announce. So, my dear brethren, as you

have just heard, before our Redeemer ascended the mountain to be transfigured, he said to the apostles: 'There are some of those now standing here who will not taste death until they see the Son of Man coming in his Kingdom.' (Mt.16.28.) Some of the commentators have understood this to refer to the condition of the church in the near future. The following context of the reading, however, shows that the Lord said this about his own transformation, for the evangelist continues:

'And after six days Jesus took up Peter, James, and John his brother, and led them up a high mountain by themselves, and was transfigured before them.' (Mt.17.1.) Indeed these three apostles are the ones he said would not taste death until they saw him transformed in glory. Yet in this transformation there is also demonstrated what the future condition of the church will be for the saints in the heavenly fatherland. First of all we must enquire why it is that when Matthew predicts the Saviour's transfiguration after six days, Luke shows that it happened after eight days. Surely it cannot be the case that they disagree with one another, and one of them, therefore, deviates from the truth? We should know that Matthew reckons the whole from the whole, when mentioning the number of days, and Luke the part from the whole. For it was on the evening of that day when the Lord spoke these things, a fact which Matthew undoubtedly overlooked, but which Luke reckoned in as if it were a whole day. Likewise it was early morning when he was transfigured on the mountain and while Matthew subtracts this from the total, so does Luke add it on. In consequence Matthew signifying the whole from the whole, introduces only the six days interlude, whereas Luke, signifying the whole from the part, has also reckoned in the evening of the first day and the morning of the eighth. We are meant, then, to understand in this that noble figure of speech which the Greeks call Synedoche and which in Latin is called either 'whole from part' or 'part from whole'. To know that this occurs often in the sacred writings solves many of our difficulties. It unravels, for example, that particular problem wherein the Lord of Heaven is said to have lain in the tomb for three days and three nights, while it is evident that daylight was already waning on the sixth day, for it was the ninth hour when he sent forth his spirit, and yet he rose again on the Sunday before dawn.

(3)   We would also ask ourselves why he climbed the mountain to pray with only these three disciples, and why only manifest the glory of his majesty to them? Surely his intention was not deliberately to hide the mysteries of his revelation from the other apostles? For sacred authority witnesses that he said to them: 'To you is given to know the mystery of the Kingdom of God.'(Lk.8.10.); and again: 'All things whatsoever I have heard from my Father I have made known to you.' (Jn.15.15.) Let us suppose, then, that it was because these three were the leaders, being the 'pillars' among the other apostles, just as Paul says: 'Peter, James, and John, who were seen to be the pillars.' (cf. Gal.2.9.). This was the reason why the Lord revealed his secrets to these rather than to the others. For to these alone did he reveal the sorrow of his heart over the treachery of Judas and the Jews when all was soon to happen to him, as his Passion drew close. But on all accounts we must not presume that there is no other mystery hidden here for us. Peter, James, and John are taken up also as a sacrament of prefiguration looking to the great glory of the Redeemer. Peter takes his name, as it were, from the word 'rock'. But as the apostle Paul taught: 'That rock was Christ' (I Cor.10.4.). To this rock, then, Peter says 'You are the Christ, the Son of the living God.' (Mt.16.16.) And truly in these words the faith of the entire church is professed. How fittingly does the rock reply to Peter: 'And I say to you that you are Peter, and on this rock I will build my church.' (Mt.16.18.) Meaning, as we can evidently see: 'I shall build you upon me.' And this applies also to you who bear the figure of his church built in you, built upon Christ himself. It is as the selfsame blessed Peter says, using the prophetic witness: 'Behold I am laying in Zion a cornerstone, extremely precious, set as a foundation.' (I Peter 2.6.) And then he added: 'And like living stones be yourselves built up

into spiritual dwellings.' (1 Peter 2.5) Paul also comments on this when he says : ' No man can lay any other foundation beyond that which is already set, which is Christ Jesus.' (1 Cor. 3.11) And he goes on :' Let each one see how he shall build upon it.' (1 Cor.3.10) So when we speak of Peter being set in place by building upon this foundation , it certainly signifies the whole church being built up on Christ. Also in our language 'James' is translated as meaning 'supplantor'.[131]   But supplantor of what ?   Surely the vices ? And truly, in the person of James, let us all supplant them by the birthright of the virtues.[132]   Let us win through by holy application to our prayers. The psalmist speaks about this supplanting of the vices when he says :'Blessed is he who shall seize and dash his children against the rock.' (Ps.137.9) But, in addition, 'John' is translated as 'dove',[133] which doubtless symbolises those who are within the holy church of God and kindled with the love of their neighbour. In the figure of the dove the Holy Spirit is designated, who is demonstrated to be the love of the Father and the Son. It is also written :'The love of God is poured out in our hearts, through the Holy Spirit who is given to us.'(Rom.5.5)   In short, the faith is shown forth in Peter, the working of the virtues in James, and love in the apostle John. On this account it was fitting that only these three should have climbed the mountain with the Lord, for they bear in their persons the figure of all the saints. And now, pondering the words of the reading, let us interpret them individually.

(4)   'Jesus took up Peter, James and John, and led them up a high mountain, by themselves, and was transfigured before them.' (Mt.17.1) Anyone who is transfigured is changed to a different form. Luke expresses this very thing when he says :'And while he prayed the aspect of his face was changed.' (Lk.9.2a)   From this we immediately learn to shun the madness of those heretics who think that human bodies shall be changed into a different nature after Judgement Day.[134] For the same mediator between God and Man, the man Jesus Christ, who as the apostle tells us has reformed

the body of our lowliness conforming it to his own glorious body, appeared in the locked room to his disciples after his resurrection and said to them: 'Touch and see, for a spirit does not have flesh and bones as you see I have.' (Lk.24.59.). What else is given us to understand by these words except that the body he offered to their touch was of a different glory, but not of a different nature, and that he came in through the locked doors in true flesh, and with true bones. So when it is said: 'He was transfigured' (Mt.17.2.), it means that he was changed to a different form - not of nature, but of glory. And then it immediately continues:

(5)   'And his face shone like the sun.' (Mt.17.2.) This indeed was a transformation, a different appearance to his countenance, when he who was visible in flesh so suddenly appeared radiant in majesty. But what is so strange if we should speak like this about so much majesty suddenly radiating in the body, when it is a daily figure of speech among us to talk of a transformation when we see someone either after he has just cleansed himself of dirt, or become joyful again after sorrow. 'He is not the same man as he was', we say, 'he is a different man altogether.' We should notice, however, that prayer precedes this glorification of the Redeemer. And Luke tells us that he climbed the mountain for this very reason, that he might pray. By this he evidently demonstrates how ceaseless prayer is essential for all who would strive to behold his glory; and not only praying in the depths, but always on the mountain. Only they can do this ceaselessly who do not succumb to earthly desires and the pleasures of vices, but rather, bound fast in celestial love, look only to the things of heaven. Thus Paul, bound in the chains of oppression, said: 'But our abode is in heaven.' (Phil.3.20.) And the Lord also teaches us this same thing in other places by his own example. For when he could find no quiet during the day, even to have time to eat, he still spent the whole night on the mountain though he was tired. By this behaviour he surely reveals to us what his expectations are, and teaches that some degree of solitude is necessary for whoever wishes to pray, and that a man who speaks

with God will find a greater intimacy when no disturbances press round him. But how should we wretched men respond to this who are weighed down with countless burdens of sins? We anticipate the night's work (of prayer) by falling asleep. But our God and Lord who was conceived and born without sin, and even led to an undeserved death, on some nights only allowed himself a little sleep and on others none at all. In this he offered himself as an example to sinners. With oft-repeated sighs and laments he also frequently spent all the watches of the night on bended knee weeping as if he were guilty of mortal vices, though the wonder of it was that he was wholly innocent and did all this for our sakes. He came to die for us, and so was carrying our sins and interceding for us with the Father, even as if he were a sinner himself. This was how he offered himself as an example for us to imitate. And we learn two things in this, first that he intercedes with the Father on our behalf, and second that he never ceases from prayer, for even to this present time he who came as the Image of God intercedes for us all. Let us therefore cast aside laziness and sloth and let this wonderful example of the Lord spur us on. He himself, as we have said, had no sins of his own that needed atonement but when his blessed passion drew close he prayed all the more earnestly and abundantly and struggled so mightily that instead of his body's sweat there flowed down drops of blood. As the evangelist tells us: 'He was in an agony, and prayed all the more abundantly, and his sweat became like blood dropping on the ground.' (Lk.22.44.) And so, my dear brethren, let us always remember these things in case we should ever be swayed by indolence and become neglectful of the sacred vigils and prayers. For how great a work it is to close the door on temptation and shun all the assaults of evil. As the Lord tells us: 'Pray that you may not enter into temptation.' (Lk.22.46.) and again: 'Keep watch, praying at all times that you may be worthy to escape all these things that are to happen, and stand before the Son of Man.' (Lk.21.36.) And again: 'One ought always to pray and not lose heart.' (Lk.18.1.)

(6)   Since we know that it is written of the saints: 'Then shall
the just shine like the sun in the kingdom of their Father,' (Mt.13.43.)
how is it that in this text the face of Christ is compared to the
sun's glory? Surely it would be impious to suggest that the just
have as much glory in the kingdom of the Father as he who has
justified them? Who would say this except a heretic? But it seems
to me that there are possibly four reasons why the text speaks like
this. Possibly it was because he was still mortal and the very
mortality of the flesh did not allow the glory of his divinity to be
shown forth in its full reality. Possibly he tempered the force of
his own radiance so that the eyes of the beholders would be able
to look upon it. Possibly he only manifested that form which by
his pre-knowledge he knew would be manifested on the Day of
Judgement, both to the elect and to the damned. Or finally, and
indeed this is both more likely and more salutary, perhaps because
in his own glory he was showing what manner of form his members
would possess when, as has been said, in the future they themselves
will shine out. The text now continues:

(7)   'And his garments became as white as snow.' (Mt.17.2.)
This glory, my dear brethren, flowing externally through the very
garments of Christ, proceeded from that inner light of his which
no corporeal eye of human kind is ever able to behold, as it is
written: 'No man has ever seen God,' (Jn.1.18.) or again: 'For no
man shall see me and live.' (Ex.33.20.) Not even the angels see
this light as it is, even though they look upon it every day, they
perceive only in so far as it is given to them to see. For as sacred
scripture witnesses (Mt.18.10.) the angels look upon the face of the
Father daily, and are consumed with longing to be able to behold.
How great the force and power of this inner light must be that
sheds so much light on the outside that it even grants such glory
of radiant majesty to the very clothes themselves. Dearly beloved,
from that light are illumined all things which shine with light, even
the sun and moon and stars, in an external sense, and the angels

and human souls, in an internal sense. (Let us therefore stand in wonder before the Lord on the mountain who shines in this external way. But let us have even greater wonder before the godhead within which here flashes forth. (Let us venerate the manner in which he appeared on the mountain in the presence of the three disciples, and let us long for this ourselves, the manner he shall appear in heaven to all the pure in heart.) For in truth, as he appeared on the mountain externally, so shall he appear in the future and even the wicked shall behold it. But what he was internally, that he has remained, and none but the blessed shall behold this.

(8)   (The church of the just is figured in the vesture of the Redeemer, in the shining brightness of snow. Not as the church is now, for here it is not free from sin, but as it shall be in the future when it will no longer be capable of sin.) In the brightness of snow the brightness of purity is designated and the heat of vices is shown to be utterly extinguished, for snow is both snowy-bright and devoid of all heat. It is just so with the elect of God for when they attain to the glory of God they shall obtain the brilliance of purity and no longer feel any heat from corrupt flesh. It then continues:

(9)   'And behold there appeared to them Moses and Elijah speaking with him.' (Mt.17.3.) Some believe that Moses in company with Elijah prefigure the last coming of Christ, and for this reason both of them appear in this, his transfiguration. Others, however, have understood better who have said that Enoch would come with Elijah in order then to die for Christ's sake, since as yet they had not paid the debt of death in the flesh. For the apostle teaches us that Enoch was translated so that he should not see death, and Elijah was lifted up to heaven to remain alive there until the day that he appeared again in some part of the earth.

So Moses did not appear with Elijah in glory in order to come and suffer beside him, but rather that the Gospel of eternal salvation should receive the testimony of the Law and the Prophets. We notice that both Moses and Elijah had fasted forty days. The Lord too fasted forty days. But we cannot wonder that the Lord should in every way surpass his servants. Let us see, then, whether a great sacrament does not lie hidden in this number of forty days? It surely would not have been difficult for the Lord to have extended his fast to a hundred or a thousand days, when he had granted to his servants that they might pass forty days without the sustenance of bodily food? Surely we all recognise in this that the Lord is able to fast more than the servant, but in choosing the same number of days he wishes to signify not so much a miracle of endurance but more a sacrament of virtue. For who does not know that the Mosaic law is two-fold, divided into a spiritual decalogue, and the offering of sacrificial victims? The commands of the law are two-fold, and here it is made clear for us that the whole law is perfected in the first but not at all in the second of those parts. And David says to the Lord: 'I have run in the way of your command-ments' (Ps.118.32.) and 'I have not swayed from your ordinances.' (Ps. 118.157.) See in this the fulfilment of the law, doubtless referring to the spiritual aspect of the decalogue, according to which the Apostle also says: 'The law is holy and its ordinance is holy and just and good ' (Rom.7.12.) and accordingly whoever observes it shall live in this state. But on the other hand Peter says: 'Why do you tempt God, placing a yoke on the necks of disciples which neither we nor our fathers have ever been able to bear?' (Acts 15.10.) We see here how the law is rendered null. But surely this refers to the carnal aspect of the law's ritual, according to that saying: 'I have given them precepts which are not good, in which they shall not live.' (gloss on Vulg. Neh.9.14.16.) And the apostle also says: 'The law has led no-one to perfection.' (Heb.7.19.) We also knew this because that part of the law which is spiritual, and able to be observed, the Decalogue, has in the fullness of time passed over into the care of the New Testament. But that part which was carnal, unsupportable, that is the offering of victims, has ceased to be observed since the Lord's death on the cross. So the law is spiritual in the commandments of the decalogue, and carnal in the offering of victims; in the one it is like a sacred fast, in the other a drunken banquet. But we have rejected completely the gluttony of carnal sacrifice, and it now remains that we say something about the fast of the spiritual law.

(10)   For what else is it to say: 'You shall not kill, you shall not steal, you shall not speak false witness, you shall not covet your neighbour's property, or desire his wife or his slave or his maid or ox or sheep or donkey or anything which is his,' - what else is it than to impose a kind of fasting upon the soul? For does not that man truly fast who turns away from evil that he might hold to the good? But before this fast of the decalogue could rise forth as a forty-fold fast, it had to wait long ages for the precepts of the New Testament before it could run to the Gospel. So then let Moses and Elijah come to the Lord, like the law and the prophets coming to the Gospel so that a fourfold decalogue might be made. Let it embrace all the elect and enclose the whole orbit of the earth in its preaching even to the four corners of the heavens. Let it appear that the fast of forty days has been sanctified in each Testament from the beginning to the end. For whoever spiritually observes the law in the four books of the holy Gospel, by loving God and his neighbour, he it is who mystically fasts the forty days and keeps the commandments of love. Hence it is written: 'Love is the fulfilment of the law.' (Rom.13.10.) The lord adds to this when he says in the Gospel: 'Love the Lord your God with your whole heart and your whole mind and your whole strength. For this is the first and greatest commandment of the law and the second is like it: You shall love your neighbour as yourself.' For then he immediately added that on these two precepts hung the entire law and prophets. (Mt.22.37.) But when a man shrinks back from all that would lead his soul into the desires of the flesh, only then does he keep these two supreme and central commandments. For as John says: 'Whoever loves the world, the love of the Father is not in

him, for all that is in the world is the concupiscence of the flesh, the concupiscence of the eyes and the pride of life.' (I Jn.2.15.) And so the Lord rightly brought forth Moses and Elijah in his own transformation, since he had made them like himself in fasting. He did this to indicate what the future would be for them, and in so far as he reconciles both testaments he also shows forth , as we have previously indicated, the future state of all those pre-destined for life, those who have passed through the desert as pilgrims keeping the forty day fast in the way they summed up the law in the double precept of love shown in the Gospel. For it is our constant duty always and without ceasing to cling to what is good, and ever to shun what is evil.

(11) We should not pass over in silence the fact that Moses, Elijah, and the Lord all fasted in the desert. This doubtless signifies the pilgrimage of life, for as the blessed Job indicates, this life is a time of trial. Also in the desert are bitter waters and fiery serpents. After forty years, as if it were forty days, the sons of Israel completed their fast in the wilderness and arrived at a land flowing with milk and honey. So it is that we too, forty days before the resurrection, in the observance of abstinence, attain to the Jubilee (cf. Jerome. In.Is. 16.58.6f.) which is the year of remission, and full of delight.

(12) It is interesting to investigate what the bitter waters in the desert signify, or even the fiery serpents. And in the first place I think that we might fittingly believe that in just the same way as the manna which fed the Jewish people did not offer the same taste to all who ate it, as holy scripture witnesses, since for some it was an increase for others a loss in their salvation, then so did the waters seem sweet to some but bitter to others. Whoever was able to comprehend the remedy of the saving wood tasted no bitterness in these waters, but they who tried the water without faith sensed all the bitterness. Likewise only they were healed from

the serpents' bites who looked upon the serpent and expected the mystery with deeper faith. For sacred scripture announces that not every man who looked upon it was thereby healed. In short, they were not saved by that which was revealed externally, in the letters, but by that which was hidden within, in a sacrament. What else do the bitter waters signify, then, other than the trials of this age. And the only one to drink of these undeservedly was he who 'drank from the stream by the wayside' (Ps.2.) that he might thence sit down at the right hand of the Father and assume dominion. This was why the Lord was given gall to eat and vinegar to drink. So the loving creator eats and drinks what is bitter and then cries out: 'It is fulfilled.' (Jn.19.30.) How else could the bitter waters be turned to sweetness except by the mixing in of the wood of salvation? And finally, when the people of Israel complained because of the bitterness of the water, Moses cried out to the Lord who then showed him the wood, and when he had put this in the waters they were turned to sweetness. This is indeed the wood of the tree of life in God's paradise, the very one planted beside the running waters, none other than the Lord Jesus Christ, perfect God and Man. It was of him that Solomon said: 'Blessed is the man who finds wisdom, for those who touch it, it is the wood of life and whoever holds on to it is blessed.' (Prov.3.18.) When the wood was put into the bitter waters, whatever had been bitter was soon turned to sweetness, and so it is that when the passion of the blessed Mediator is mixed in our tribulations the weight of their burden is taken away. But let us enquire, according to the limits of my poor understanding, why it was that the waters still tasted bitter for some, while for others they were sweet. It is because some seek after, but others shrink away from, the one same chalice of the passion. They seek after it who find its bitterness sweet, and they shrink back who find the bitterness distasteful. They seek after it who tread the narrow path, and they shrink back who run with pleasure along the broad and spacious highroads of the world. But the man who draws from within his soul the sweetness of the wood and mixes this in the waters, he alone shall taste no bitterness. For the sweetness within covers all sense of bitterness. When a man drinks to the dregs all the sweetness that lies hid in the secret of the cross, then all things, even bitter things, seem sweet to him. This is what sacred scripture means when it says: 'To a thirsty soul even bitter things seem sweet.' (Prov.27.7.) Who is there so ungrateful as would not follow after the cross of the Master in a secret martyrdom, if not a public one, especially when we remember the scripture: 'If we do not suffer with him, we shall not reign with him.' (2 Tim.2.12.) Peter also encourages us when he says: 'Christ suffered for us, leaving you an example that you should follow in his steps.' (2 Peter 2.21.) Paul found these things to be true among the Hebrews, to whom he wrote: 'Looking to Jesus the author and perfecter of faith, who for the joy set before him, bore the cross and despised the shame.' (Heb.12.2.) He also wished it to be true for those to whom he wrote the following: 'Know that as you share in his passion, so shall you share in the consolation,' (2 Cor.1.7.) for he said this to turn the bitterness of their sufferings into sweetness. When we speak in this manner we must always distinguish the two covenants; how the waters seemed bitter in the one, and sweet in the other. The waters were certainly bitter for those of whom Moses spoke: 'The Egyptians hated the sons of Israel, and afflicted them with derision. They reduced their lives to bitterness by hard labours in clay and bricks, and they and all their families were laden down with toil in this land.' (Ex.1.12.) Things were also bitter for those to whom Jeremiah spoke using the type of a woman: 'My stomach turns over, my heart sinks within me, for I am full of bitterness ' (Lam.1.20.) and again: 'He has made me overflow with bitterness, and made me drunk with wormwood.' And: 'Gall and sorrows have surrounded me.' (Lam.3.15.) But today all these things are turned to sweetness by mingling in the wood of salvation and Luke witnesses this when he says: 'For the apostles went out from the sight of the council rejoicing that they had been found worthy to suffer disgrace for the sake of his name.' (AA.5.41)

Things remained bitter for Moses, however, when sorrow overwhelmed him: 'Why Lord have you afflicted your servant? Why do I not find grace in your presence? Why have you laid the burden of this whole people upon me? I cannot support this nation myself for it is burdensome for me. If you will not agree, then I pray that you would bring my life to an end that I may find grace in your eyes, and no longer be visited by so many evils, for fear rains down upon me.' (cf. Num.11.11f.) Things were also bitter for Elijah when he was fleeing through the desert from the persecutions of Jezebel. In great distress and pain he cried out: 'It is enough Lord, take away my life I beseech you, for I am no better than my fathers.' (I K.19.4.) But again, through mingling in the sacred wood these very things become sweet for Paul when he says to the faithful: 'Now I rejoice in all my tribulations for your sake.'(Rom.5.3.) And: 'For me to live is Christ, and to die is gain.' (Phil.1.21.); or again: 'I am ready not only for imprisonment, but even for death at Jerusalem for the sake of the name of the Lord Jesus.' (Acts 21.13.)

(13) Our fathers also taught another significance of the bitter waters when they suggested that it referred to the bitterness of the circumcision of the flesh, and the retributive punishments of those who had been condemned. But in each case the power of the wood turns the bitterness of the water to sweetness, because our Redeemer brings upon his innocent head the full severity of the law, at the same time fulfilling it and making its decrees henceforth null. All that was harsh in the commandments he has changed to gracefulness in the leniency of the New Testament. What else do the fiery serpents symbolise other than the death-dealing suggestions of our ancient enemy? Paul agrees with this opinion when he says: 'Take up the shield of faith by which you shall be able to quench the fiery darts of the evil one.' (Eph.6.16.) Those who have been struck down are commanded to look upon the brazen serpent as their chief and only remedy. Here it is not my own

interpretation which is stretching the symbolism, but it is the Lord's own exegesis which confirms this interpretation, for he says: 'Just as Moses lifted up the serpent in the wilderness, so the Son of Man must be lifted up, so that all who believe in him may not die, but have eternal life.' (Jn.3.14-15) And behold how the secret adversary suggests all manner of evil in your minds. If you give your consent, then the serpent has bitten you; but so that you may not be totally lost look at the bronze serpent, that is the Lord hanging upon the cross. For if you contemplate his passion then it will quench all the evil of sin within us. But you only contemplate it well if you attempt to imitate it, and if you do this then there will be no deadly sin that can ever overcome you. It is as Paul says: 'For those who are of Christ have crucified their flesh with its sins and desires.' (Gal.5.24.) And I ask you, what pleasures of sin have ever been able to seduce men like this? If a man is crucified then the pain of his death means that he can never feel the bite of any venomous serpent ever after. What dead man can ever feel the bite of a snake? The same great preacher says as much to the faithful: 'You are dead, and your life is hidden with Christ in God.' (Col.3.3.)

(14)   Let us see, at least if we can briefly allude to it, why the Lord revealed Moses and Elijah in the Transfiguration, his faithful servants whom he had as his companions in the mystery of fasting. How fitting it was that he brought them before the eyes of Peter and John. Here we have, without doubt, two witnesses on each side of the Testament to their harmonious agreement in fact and symbol. For Moses parted the sea so that he could come to the feeding with manna, and Peter walked upon the sea so that he could come to Christ who is the true and heavenly manna. Elijah ascended in a fiery chariot so that he could seek those things which are above, and John lay back on the burning heart of Christ so that he could enter into the secrets of the Word. What should we make, then, of James? Do we separate him out from this symbol of harmony as if he were less of a type than Peter and John whom we have

judged to agree with the figures of Moses and Elijah? James, as we have already said, means 'He who trips up' and this is seen to relate fully to Moses and Elijah. The one killed the Egyptian who attacked a Hebrew, and then hid in the desert. The other made mockery of Baal and slaughtered the prophets by the river. As the authority of the fathers teaches us, all these things refer to the extinction of the vices. Let us now enquire what it was the Lawgiver and the prophet said to the Lord of them both. If I had wanted to expound this, it might have been thought a rash thing, or at least any empty presumption, if I had not already been told by another evangelist what that conversation was.

(15)   And he tells us: 'Behold two men were talking with him. They were Moses and Elijah, and they spoke about his passing which he was to accomplish in Jerusalem.' (Lk.9.31.) This 'passing' is nothing other than the undeserved torments of the passion which he had already inaugurated for the life of the world but had not yet consummated. For he had already begun to suffer our wretched condition but had not yet arrived at the punishment of the cross. Let us see if we can understand what the substance of the conversation was that they had with him. It was something like this: 'You have come, you who were sent, born of the virgin. You grew, you hungered and thirsted and sat down weary, but you have not yet handed over your spirit in dire punishment and so you have started but not yet completed your perfect consummation, loving creator, when you hang upon the cross.' We might also understand this same word 'passing' to mean that what was begun in the prophets was not fulfilled in them. Thus even the Lord says: 'You have filled up the measure of your fathers.' (Mt.23.32.) And what he meant was that their fathers had killed the prophets, but that was not the full measure, for they themselves wanted to kill the Lord of prophets, and then the measure of their fathers would be filled up. For all the sufferings of the just are consummated in the passion of their Lord. And where else could this passing be

fulfilled except in Jerusalem ? For he himself says : 'It is not fitting for a prophet to die outside Jerusalem.' (Lk.13.33) O wretched and damnable Jerusalem that reached this climax of damnation that all the blood of the prophets was shed in your walls. For indeed all the innocent blood of the prophets was poured out within your walls. Indeed all the innocent blood that has ever been shed upon the earth, from the blood of the just Abel to the blood of Zechariah son of Barach which you cruelly spilt between the Temple and the altar (Mt.22.35), all has fallen upon you, and all because you cried out before Pilate :'The blood of this man be upon us and upon our children,' (Mt.27.25) and so it has been upon your heads and those of your descendants. But what great merit you gained for the world by this heinous and wicked crime of yours, as one of your own number unconsciously prophesied : 'It is fitting that one man should die for the people rather than let the whole nation perish.' (Jn.18.14) The text then continues :

(16)   'Peter said to Jesus in reply , Lord it is good for us to be here. If you wish let us make three tabernacles, one for you, one for Moses, and one for Elijah.' (Mt.17.4) I beseech you , blessed Peter, that the boldness of this wretched slave who takes you to task over this may not displease you, for there is no servile arrogance intended in my remarks. I ask you this with a free humility, and I also ask it of you, my hearers. Tell me, then, were you brought up the mountain for the sake of building tabernacles and possessing the Lord for yourself, with a few companions ? How was it that having seen this glory of his body, only a little time passed before he came to the chains, the scourge, the spitting, the blows, the torments of the cross, and his burial, but still you denied that this man was God, and betrayed your master ? But now the glorified face of Christ pleases you so much that you do not want to come down off the mountain. Wait only a short while and you will certainly forget these things. In the presence of a low-born slave you will even deny that you know him. And when that hour

draws near then is the saying of the prophet fulfilled: 'He has no splendour or beauty; and we saw him and there was nothing in his appearance, and his face was as if hidden and cast down. And so we did not reckon him.' (Is.53.2.) What should you have said then? You should have asked the Lord that he would hasten the time when all that had been written about him would be fulfilled so that he could reveal his face to you as he passed into his glory, not as he is now, but as he truly is. Jesus, however, must make allowances for you since you are so sleepy when you say these things. This is what the evangelist says about you and your companions: 'But Peter and those who were with him were heavy with sleep.'(Lk.9.32.) It was a sleep, doubtless, of the mind, not of the flesh. So it was that you and your companions forgot about the Lord and were concerned with Moses and Elijah, saying: 'Let us make three tabernacles here, one for you, one for Moses and one for Elijah.' But look how the Lord shines out in the radiance of the sun while the bright cloud puts Moses and Elijah in the shade. What use is a tabernacle then? Is it for yourself? but you have no part in these things. Is it for the ones who have been graced to share in this event? What are you and your colleagues thinking about? Do you want to be associated with them by means of the tabernacles so that they can be lords and you the three servants of the lords in their respective shrines? But who among you will be the servant of the Lord? Who the servant of Moses or Elijah? It would indeed have been more acceptable if you had said: 'Lord let us make here one tabernacle so that Moses, Elijah, myself, James and John might all serve you in the one shrine.'

(17)   But, my dearest brethren, although we cannot follow Peter's ignorance in saying this, we still pay homage to the outstanding love he showed to the Lord. And that worthy disciple did not merely hide this in his heart, he showed it openly with signs of his affection. So it is that when the Lord himself asked the twelve: 'Who do you say that I am?' It was he who first replied: 'You are

the Christ, the Son of the living God.' (Mt.10.15.) But then, because he did not wish his master to suffer, he denounced the passion and argued with him saying: 'Far be it from you Lord. This must not happen.' (Mt.10.22.) And when the hour of the passion arrived the Lord himself said: 'You will all be scandalised in me this night.' (Mt.26.31.) But while all the others were distressed, the intrepid Peter replied: 'They may all be scandalised in you, but I shall never be scandalised.' And he even added: 'Even if I have to die with you I will not deny you.' And so it was that when Christ was already arrested Peter drew his sword and with a random blow cut off the ear of a persecutor. Afterwards, having seen Christ on the shore, Peter came to him as the very first of them all because he threw himself into the sea. The Lord confirmed this love he had after he rose from the dead and deliberately asked him: 'Simon son of John do you love me more than these others?' And he replied then: 'Lord you know that I love you.' (Jn.21.15.) In this present episode he sees the radiance of the Lord's face and because of his love he does not wish to come down again; even though, as the evangelist tells us, he did not know what he should say. Peter had spurned the glory of this age and despised what is pleasing to this world. After he had seen the face of Christ so radiant with the brilliance of the sun, nothing else was pleasing to him. What should we learn from this? Well, if this vision was so delightful to him while yet in a mortal body, what must he now behold when he has cast off his mortality? And he not only disdained the earth beneath him, but even the heavens above him for he wanted only to remain on the mountain with his Lord. But Peter did have to come down from the mountain, and in the meanwhile the poor Lord had to be followed, he who said to them: 'The foxes have lairs, and the birds of heaven have their nests but the Son of Man has nowhere to lay his head.' (Mt.8.20.) And Peter did come to imitate him, even to the torment of the cross. This was how he came to gaze eternally on the face of Christ with no more temporal interruptions, which he was unable to do on the mountain. For when he asked the Lord what was his will in regard to the making of the tabernacles he had said: 'Lord, if you wish, let us make here three tabernacles.' And one sees that he has implicitly accepted the consequence: 'If you do not wish, then we will go down again.' The Gospel text continues:

(18)   'While he was still speaking a bright cloud overshadowed them and behold there came a voice from the cloud saying: This is my beloved Son in whom I am well pleased. Listen to him.' (Mt.17.5.) Go then, blessed Peter, your task of building tabernacles is taken from you. Moses has departed, Elijah has gone away; the very ones you wanted to enshrine. But they were slaves, not lords. They had not come to exercise dominion, but rather to hear revelation so that all justice might be fulfilled. He alone who remains is Lord. Your master is the only beloved Son. In him alone is the Father well-pleased. And even though Moses can be called a son of God, as can Elijah; and even though Moses was also beloved of God, as was Elijah; and even though God was pleased with Moses, as he was with Elijah; nonetheless if we should compare them with Christ who is born from the substance of the Father, then Moses is no son, neither is Elijah and nor are they the beloved or the accepted ones of God. As the voice of the Father has taught us: ' Here is my beloved Son in whom I am well pleased.' So do not listen to Moses or Elijah, listen to him. Moses ordered tabernacles to be made, but Christ orders the church to be built. So listen to him, venerable Peter, for he has not appointed you as a tent maker but as a shepherd of his sheep. What, brethren, are we to think   the bright cloud signifies, other than the grace of the New Testament? For it is written that before the advent of the Mediator there was to be 'darkness, clouds and mist', which means the obscure under-standing of the words of the law and the prophets. But now the teaching of the New Testament is not in a dark cloud but the voice of the Father thunders out through a bright cloud. We also note how this bright cloud overshadows Moses and Elijah. It removes and hides them, and then it is not they who speak from the cloud

that conceals them, only the Father speaks through it. The bright cloud, then, only expresses the Father's voice. This symbolises how the grace of the New Testament overshadows, contains, hides, yet retains, the law and the prophets. For it overshadows it in the letter, yet retains it in the spirit. It hides it in figures, and yet it retains it in mysteries. And so it comes to pass that whatever the law and prophets spoke about is still received, though now it is spiritually observed. Before the advent of the Redeemer in flesh, when there was only darkness, clouds, and mist, how many things to do with the future grace of the New Testament the law and the prophets spoke of. But now he has come and the bright cloud overshadows Moses and Elijah. Moses is silent, Elijah keeps quiet. The Father's voice alone responds through the bright cloud:' This is my beloved Son in whom I am well pleased. Listen to him.'

(19)   'And when the disciples heard it, they fell on their faces to the ground, and were filled with a great fear. But lifting up their eyes they saw no-one only Jesus.' (Mt.17.6.) So that the disciples could hear this either the Lord himself had set the elements in motion through this cloud, or had used some intermediary angel. But in any case a voice sounded through the cloud, and since it came from this source it appeared like thunder and this is why the   disciples fell to the ground. A similar thing happened when the passion was imminent and the Son said to the Father: 'Now is my soul troubled, and what shall I say, Father? Save me from this hour? For it is for this hour that I came Father glorify thy name. And then there came a voice from heaven: I have glorified it and I shall glorify it again. The crowd which was standing by heard this and said: It was a thunderclap.' (Jn.ll.27.) Why was it that when the crowd heard this thundering voice, on that occasion it did not fall down, but here the disciples did fall on their faces? Doubtless because in the one example we see arrogant pride and in the other trembling humility. And not without cause did they tremble. But they received their reward in this , for the Lord himself came to

them straightway and touched them, teling them to rise up and not be afraid. These events give us some indications of the charisms of spiritual grace. The Lord could have told them that if the voice had ordered them to listen to Moses, or to imitate Elijah then they really would have had good cause to be afraid. For the first had slaughtered twenty three thousand sinners on one day not sparing a single one (I Cor.10.8. on Num.25.1-9.) while the other strangled, without mercy, all the prophets of Baal and incinerated two companies of men with heavenly fire, no less than a hundred altogether. But no, the voice proclaimed that I, the Christ, am to be listened to. I who justify the repentant tax collector in the Temple, I who receive the apostle who denied me. I who free the adultress about to be stoned. I who sanctify the thief repenting upon his cross. Why then are you so needlessly afraid? In the law there is fear. But in the Gospel there is love. And love has no fear: 'For perfect love casts out fear.' (I Jn.4.18.) The text continues:

(20)   'And coming down from the mountain Jesus ordered them to tell no-one about the vision until the Son of Man had risen from the dead.' (Lk.17.8.) After Moses and Elijah had been taken from the sight of the Lord and his apostles, they did not immediately come down the mountain, but as the other evangelist tells us, they remained there the rest of that night and then on the following day they came down to the plain where the crowd was waiting. But, my dear brethren, I do not know if they were even aware of night since they had merited to see so great a light. And although it was taken away from the material eyes of their bodies, it nonetheless remained in their hearts where incorporeal realities cannot suffer any sunset. The same was true of the blessed Moses who gazed for forty days and nights at the spiritual light within him, and was no longer conscious of hunger or thirst or darkness. The inner light had expanded the vision of the inner man so much that he was even able to see that which God had made in the

beginning. This is the light which shines in the darkness, which the darkness cannot overcome. (Jn.1.5.) But what of the fact that men have loved the darkness more than they have loved the light? (Jn.3.19.) The persecutors of Christ were not able to see this light. This was why they pressed blindly on with his execution. 'For if they had known, they would never have crucified the Lord of glory.' (I Cor.2.8.) And they would have learned who he was if they had been able to witness the events on the mountain. But if this had happened then the whole reason Christ was born for us would have been rendered pointless. This is why the disciples are most forcefully warned not to let anyone know of this vision until after his resurrection. When the passion of the loving Redeemer eventually came, Pilate heard him say: 'My Kingdom is not of this world' (Jn. 18.36.) and again: 'He who is of the truth listens to my voice.' (Jn.18.37.) Even from these signs Pilate began to think that he was the Son of God, and from then on frequently tried to rescue him and set him free. This was why he ordered Jesus to be scourged, dressed in purple, and crowned with thorns so that he might satisfy the bloodlust of the Jews by presenting this mockery before them. He intended to save Jesus from death. But if this is what he does after receiving such small verbal signs of Christ's power, becoming so circumspect and using many powerful arguments to let him go free, what do you think he would have done if he had been aware of the manner in which Christ appeared to the disciples on the mountain? I am sure that the power of Caesar he so greatly feared would have become as nothing to him. This was why the loving Redeemer forbade his disciples to reveal to any man what they knew him in reality to be. He wanted to come as an unknown figure and thus be despised, arrested, bound, scourged, spat upon, struck with fists, crowned with thorns, crucified, made to suffer death, and buried. Then just as the lost sheep was sought after and found, and when found, placed on the shoulders of the loving shepherd, so it was that when the shepherd rose from the dead the sheep is found and carried with the shepherd to heaven. This is he who lives and reigns with the Father and the Holy Spirit, God for ever and ever. Amen.

NOTES TO CHAPTER SIX

1. Tertullian: For a selection of his works in ET cf. **ANCL**, Vols. 7, 11, 15.

> De Praescriptione Haereticorum 21-22 (which is paralleled by **Scorpiace** 12.1) cf. PL.2.38-40.
> Adv. Praxean. 15. cf PL.2.196-7.
> Adv. Marcionem. 4.22 cf PL.2.442-444.
> Ad Martyras 2.8.cf PL.1.695-7.
> De Resurrectione Carnis 55. cf PL.2.924.
> De Carne Christi 24.3. cf PL.836.
> De Jejunio.6. cf PL.2.1012.
> De Monogamia.8. cf PL.2.990.

2. Mt.13.11.

3. Deut.19.15. 2.Cor.13.1.

4. This theologically parallels the argument of **Adv. Prax.** 14 which has a direct relationship to Irenaeus **Adv. Haer.** 4.20.9. qv. in previous chapter. The terms of this theology are also found in Novatian **De Trinitate.** 18.1, although this latter text has no direct bearing on the Transfiguration narrative and so is not included here.

5. Rom.9.5.

6. I Tim.6.16.

7. I Tim.1.17.

8. I Cor.15.3.

9. I Cor.15.8.

10. Acts.22.11.

11. Ex.33.20.

12. viz. in the Theophanies of the OT.

13.   Jn.5.9.

14.   **in sensu.**

15.   Ms. variant reads (as opposed to **in sensu**) **in sinu** viz in the Father's bosom (Jn.1.18)

16.   Jn.1.3.

17.   Marcion defined the God of the OT as utterly different and opposed to the God of the New Covenant, the Father of Jesus.

18.   Tertullian in his last period believed that true prophecy would be an ecstatic rapture (amentia) ie. trance-like. cf **De Anima.**21 & 45.

19.   ie. Montanism

20.   **Psychicos:** this refers to the Catholics as opposed to the Montanists who were the so-called **Pneumaticos.** cf. I Cor.2.14.

21.   **Amentia.**

22.   LXX Is.63.9.

23.   Hab.3.2f (LXX) (cf Augustine **De Civ. Dei.** 2.32)

24.   Zech.4.3,14.

25.   Mt.6.21.

26.   A doctrine associated with Cerinthus.

27.   Moses fasts 40 days cf. Ex.24.18 & 34.28; Deut.9.11,25. Augustine parallels the terms of this exegesis in his **Homily 75.** ET **NPNF.** vol.6. p.480.

28.   I K.17.

29.   referring to the 3 tabernacles Peter wished to build for the three greatest fasters.

30.   Fasting in the Fathers is an eschatological sign (Apatheia) of the next age when the saints will see God and become like him, transcending all bodily needs and limitations.

31.   Cyprian: **Ep.63.14.** cf PL.4.396-7. (ET cf. LF.17, 1844).   **Testimonia Ad Quirinum** cf PL.4.712.   **Adversus Judaeos** (Ps Cyprian) cf PL 4.999f.

32.   Jn.15.14-15.

33.   Micah.4.2-5.

34.   Is.2.3-4.

35.   An exegesis probably based on Tertullian's **Adv. Marcionem,** 4.22.

36.   The anonymous author was writing sometime before 260 AD. The work depends heavily on the Homily **De Passione** of Melito of Sardis. cf. J. Quasten. **Patrology;** Vol 2, Antwerp, 1975, p.370.

37.   Hilary of Poitiers: **In Matthaeum** 17.2-3 cf PL.9.1012-15. Select Works: **De Trinitate .** 10.23. cf PL.10.361-4. NPNF.9. **De Trinitate .** 11.36-39. cf PL 10. 423-4.

38.   By the time of the fifth century such views are highly suspect. Eutyches is condemned at Chalcedon for holding substantially the same opinion. Hilary wishes to exempt Jesus from the weaknesses which he sees as the peculiar penalty of sin. Jesus' apatheia for Hilary is the result of his sinlessness. This is substantially in agreement with Nicene Credal orthodoxy.

39.   cf I Cor.15.26.

40.   Ambrose of Milan: **Ennarratio in Ps.45.** cf PL 14.1187-90. **De Fide.** 1.13. cf PL.16.569-70. **In Lucam.7.**1-21 (passim) cf. PL.15.1785-92. See also his references in **Com. In Ep.Ad Phil.**3.20-21, in PL.17.441; and also **Enn. In Ps.**43, 87-90 in PL 14.1185-6.

41.   An exegesis based on the Manuscript title of the Psalm: 'A Psalm of David for the Sons of Core; for the Secrets.' The last phrase originally referred to the tone to which it was sung in the Temple, but by the time of the Fathers it seemed a strange introduction. Ambrose develops greatly on the theme of 'secret initiation' in his exegesis.

42.   Jn.10.30.

43.   Heb.1.3.

44.   Dan.3.25.

45.   cf Dan.3.92.

46.   Gen 18.2f. The three lords of the narrative are addressed as (singular) 'Lord' by Abraham. This was taken in patristic literature as a type of the Trinity. The most graphic example of this is the famous Rublev Icon of the Trinity at the Oak of Mamre.

47.   cf Col.3.3-4.

48.   eg, Pss. 8 or 12. 'On the eighth' which is here given a mystical and eschatological interpretation (since the 8th day was the symbol of the New Age) meant originally 'for the eight stringed harp' of the Temple musicians.

49.   Ps.89.4.

50.   Is.40.9.

51.   2 Cor.5.16.

52.   Is.53.3.

53.   Ps.1.5. For the ancient Judaic idea of only the just rising again cf Luke 14.14.

54.   Deut.6.5. Mt.22.37.

55.   ie. seeing Elijah as a symbol of Prophecy, particularised by Isaiah: Is.7.14; Mt.1.23.

56.   Ex.34.30.

57.   cf 2 Cor.3.12-18.

58.   Is.53.2.

59.   ie. after the 'rest' or sleep of death, the Resurrection is intimated.

60.   cf. Lk.12.37.

61.   Phil.1.23.

62.   A reference to Peter's walking on the sea. Mt.14.28f.

63.   Lk.1.35.

64.   Jn.17.21.

65.   Rom.10.4.

66.   Jerome: **Com. In Matthaeum** 3.17,1-9, cf PL 26.121-124.

Com In Ep.2 Ad Cor.c.3 cf PL.30.780.
Com In Ep. Ad Phil.c.3 cf PL.30.850.
In Marcum 9 (Ps. Jerome) cf PL.30.614.

67. Mt.20.16; 22.14.

68. Jerome is attacking Origen here.

69. Mt.12.39.

70. Is.7.10f.

71. Here he is directly dependent on Origen's exegesis.

72. Jn.5.37; 8.18.

73. Phil.3.21.

74. The sentiment is expressed again by Leo in terms very reminiscent of this passage.

75. Augustine: **Hom.28** cf PL.38.490-93.
     Tractatus contra V.Haereses (Ps.Aug.) PL.42.1101f.

76, Homily number 78 in the Benedictine version. A much abbreviated version of the exegesis is given in the subsequent homily 29/79. ET.**NPNF** vol.6. p.349.

77. Ps.19.1.

78. Ps.19.3-4.

79. Jn.1.9.

80. cf I Cor.15.9.

81. Is.1.18. He gives a parallel exegesis of this Ecclesial typology in the **Ennarratio In Ps.147** (He giveth snow like wool) ET **NPNF** vol.8. pp.670-671.

82. cf Romans. 3.20-21.

83. I Cor.13.12. (which was the first reading of the liturgy of the day).

84. Gen.3.19.

85. Jn.1.1.

86. I Cor.15.28.

87.   Jn.14.21.

88.   2 Tim.4.2.

89.   Jn.17.1.

90.   Ps.8.6.

91.   viz. Jn.11.41-42.

92.   Mt.5.15.

93.   Jer.49.16.

94.   Ps.37.37.

95.   Ps.34.8.

96.   Leo the Great: **Hom.51.1-8** (passim) cf PL.54.308-313.
       (Ps Leo)   **Hom. 20 .** cf PL.54.520-522.
       See fn. 106 below.

97.   Mt.13-43.

98.   Rom.8.18.

99.   Col.3.3-4.

100.   Dt.19.15; Mt.18.16; 2 Cor.13.1; Heb.10.28; Jn 8.17 et al.

101.   Jn.1.17.

102.   Jn.1.3.

103.   Jn.10.38.

104.   Phil.2.6f.

105.   The idiom is a little involved. The last two paragraphs
       have been envisaged by Leo as the voice of God addressing
       the disciples. Here we have a reference to the courage
       they will show later in the face of their martyrdoms.
       The discourse was evidently preached and scribally
       recorded.

106.   The opening phrases of the homily perhaps suggest the
       author to be Caesarius: **Hodie fratres charissimi solemnitur
       colimus.** cf **Initia Patristica.** CC 104.

107.   Gen.1.3.

108.   Jn.8.17

109.   Ex.3.14.

110.   Jn.1.9.

111.   Sedulius. Carmina 50.3 vv.284f.

112.   Ex.33.23.

113.   viz. that he should see the face of God.

114.   Ps.104.2.

115.   Gregory : **Moralium in Job** 40, Lib.32.6.8, cf. PL 76.639-40. **In Primum Regium Expositio.** 5.29-30, PL. 79.465-8.

116.   Eph.5.27.

117.   Ps.104.2 (Vulg.)

118.   Mt.5.14.

119.   Ps.44.3

120.   Heb.1.3.

121.   1 Sam.16.12. 1st Samuel is that '1st Kings' on which Gregory is commenting; not on our '1st Kings' which for him would be '3rd Kings'.

122.   1 Cor.12.3.

123.   Jn.7.39.

124.   Bede the Venerable : **Hom.28, Quia Dominus Ac Redemptor.** Text in CC 122 (1955) pp.170f.

125.   Mt.16.27.

126.   Is.33.17.

127.   Phil.3.20.

128.   Bede's monastery at Jarrow on the river Tyne in North-East England was particularly susceptible to Viking raids. Impressive ruins still remain.

129.   Mt. 13.43.

130.   Ambrose Autpertus :**Hom.De Transfiguratione.** cf PL 89,1305-1320, also CC (Continuatio Mediaevalis) 27B,pars III,pp.1003-24.

TRANSFIGURATION BIBLIOGRAPHY

M. Aubineau.   Une homelie Grecque inédite sur la Transfiguration. Analecta Bollandiana, 85,1967, 401-427.

B. W. Bacon.   The Transfiguration Story. AJT.6.1902, 236-65.

F. J. Badcock.   The Transfiguration. JTS 22,1921,321-6.

D. Balfour.   St Gregory the Sinaite: Discourse on the Transfiguration. (Editio Princeps with ET). Theologia, Athens 1982.

H. Baltensweiler.   Die Verklärung Jesu. Abhandlungen zur Theologie des Alten und Neuen Testaments. No.33. Zurich. 1959.

G. D. Barry.   The Transfiguration of Christ. London 1911.

J. B Bernardin.   The Transfiguration. JBL.52,1933,181-189.

P. T. Bilianuk.   A Theological Meditation on the mystery of Transfiguration. Diakonia. vol.8, No.4. 1973, 306-331.

J. Blinzler.   Die Neutestamentlichen Berichte über die Verklärung Jesu. Diss. Munster-Aschendorff. 1937.

G. H. Boobyer.   St Mark and the Transfiguration Story. Edinburgh 1942.

W. C. Braithwaite.   The Teaching of the Transfiguration. Expository Times. 17,1905-6, 372-5.

G. B. Caird.   The Transfiguration. Expository Times. 67,1955-6, 291-294.

C. E. Carlston.   Transfiguration and Resurrection. JBL.80,1961, 233-240.

B. D. Chilton.   The Transfiguration: Dominical assurance and Apostolic vision. NTS 27.1. 1981,115-124.

L. P. Crawford.   The Transfiguration. A Manifestation of God in Man. London 1912.

E. Dabrowski.	**La Transfiguration de Jesus.** Scripta Pontif. Inst. Bibl. no.85. Rome. 1939.
R. de Feraudy.	**l'Icone de la Transfiguration.** Spiritualité Orientale. Abbaye de Bellefontaine, Begrolles, 1978, No.23. 117-119.
C. H. Dodd.	**The appearances of the Risen Christ,** in **Studies in the Gospels,** pp.25f Oxford 1955.
M. Eichinger.	**Die Verklärung Christi bei Origenes: die Bedeutung des 'Menschen Jesus' in seiner Christologie.** WBzT,24,1969.
A. Feuillet.	**Les perspectives propres à chacque évangeliste dans les récits de la Transfiguration.** Biblica 39,1958,281-301.
W. Gerber.	**Die Metamorphose Jesu: Mark.9.2f.** TZ 23,1967,385-395.
T. F. Glasson.	**Greek influence in Jewish Eschatology.** SPCK Biblical Monographs. London. 1961.
M. Goguel.	**Notes d'histoire évangelique. 2. Esquisse d'une interpretation du récit de la Transfiguration.** RHR 81,1920,145-157.
G. Habra.	**La Transfiguration selon les Pères Grecs.** Paris 1973.
A. von Harnack.	**Die Verklärungsgeschichte Jesu.** Sitzungsberichte der Preussischen Akademie der Wissenschaften. 1922, pp.62-80. (English synopsis in C G Montefiore: The Synoptic Gospels vol.1. p.205f).
E. Hennecke.	**New Testament Apocrypha.** vol.1, London 1973, vol 2, London 1975.
J. Holler.	**Die Verklärung Jesu. Eine Auslegung der Neutestamentlichen Berichte.** Freiburg.1937.
R. Holmes.	**The purpose of the Transfiguration.** JTS. 6. July. 1903.
M. R. James.	**The Apocryphal New Testament.** Oxford 1926.

P. Jensen.	Die Verklärungsbergszene und Nachbarepisoden in einem Chinesischen Marchen? TSK 104, 1932, 229-237; also ibid 105, 1933,330-336.
H. Kennedy.	The purpose of the Transfiguration. JTS vol.4. Jan. 1903 270-273.
A. Kenny.	The Transfiguration and the Agony in the Garden. CBQ.19,1957,444-452.
X. Leon-Dufour.	Études d'Évangile. Paris.1965 (pp.83-122).
W. L. Liefeld.	Theological motifs in the Transfiguration Narrative. In: R Longenecker and M Tenny (Eds) New Dimensions in NT Study. 1974 (pp.162-179).
E. Lohmeyer.	Die Verklärung Jesu nach dem Markus Evangelium. ZNW.21.1922, 185-215.
S.Losch.	Deitas Jesu und Antike Apotheose. Rottenburg. 1933
H. P. Muller.	Die Verklärung Jesu. ZNW.51,1960,56-64.
U. B. Muller.	Die Christologie Absicht des Markusevangeliums und die Verklärungsgeschichte. ZNW.64,1973, 159-193.
J. M. Nutzel.	Die Verklärungserzahlung im Markus evangelium .1973
R. W. Pfaff.	New Liturgical Feasts in later Medieval England. OTM 1970,13-39.
A. M. Ramsey.	The Glory of God and The Transfiguration of Christ. London. 1949.
R. Reitzenstein.	Hellenistic Mystery Religions. (ET) Pittsburgh, 1978.
H. Riesenfeld.	Jesus Transfiguré. L'Arrière Plan du récit évangelique de la Transfiguration de Notre Seigneur. Acta Seminarii Neotestamentici Upsaliensis. No.16. Copenhagen 1947.
L. Rivera.	Interpretatio Transfigurationis Jesu in redactione evangelii Marci. Verbum Domini 4,1968,9-104.

M. Sabbe. La redaction du récit de la Transfiguration: La Venue du Messie. RB No.6. Bruges 1962,65-100.

W. Schmithals. Der Markusschluss die Verklärungsgeschichte und die Aussendung der Zwölf. ZTK 69,1972,379f.

H. Smith. The Ante Nicene Exegesis of the Gospels. London 1927, vol.3. pp.182-203.

R. H. Stein. Is the Transfiguration a misplaced Resurrection account? JBL.95, 1976, 79-96.

V. Taylor. The Gospel According to S. Mark. London. 1957,386-92.

W. Teasdale. The Spiritual Significance of the Transfiguration. Diakonia vol.14. No.3. 1979,203-212.

M. E. Thrall. Elijah and Moses in Mark's account of the Transfiguration. NTS.16. 1969-1970, 305-317.

J. Tomajean. La Fête de La Transfiguration, 6 Août. L'Orient Syrien. No.5., 1960,479-82.

J. M. Voste. De Baptismo, Tentatione et Transfiguratione Jesu. Studia Biblica Neotestamentica. vol.2. Rome.1934.

A SELECT BIBLIOGRAPHY ON RESURRECTION

R. M. Achard. **From Death to Life: A study of the development of the doctrine of the Resurrection in the OT.** (ET J. Smith). Edinburgh.1960.

H. C. C. Cavallin. **Life after Death.** 1974.

C. F. Evans. **Resurrection and the NT.** SBT 12. London.1970.

R. H. Fuller. **The Formation of the Resurrection Narratives.** London (Revised Edn.) 1980.

M. J. Harris. **Raised Immortal.** London 1983.

C. D. F. Moule (ED) **The Significance of the Message of the Resurrection for Faith in Jesus Christ.** SBT 8. London . 1968.

G. W. E. Nickelsburg. **Resurrection, Immortality, and Eternal Life In Intertestamental Judaism.** London 1972.

N. Perrin. **The Resurrection Narratives.** London. 1977.

A. Rodriguez. **Targum y Resureccion.** Estudio de los textos del Targum Palestinense sobre la resureccion. Carmona Biblioteca Teologica Granadina. Granada. 1978.

A. F. Segal. **Heavenly Ascent in Hellenistic Judaism, Early Christianity and the Environment.** Aufstieg und Niedergan der romischen welt. Bd.23.2, Berlin 1980, pp.1333-1394.

G. Stemberger. **Der Leib der Auferstehung.** 1972.

K. Stendhal (Ed) **Immortality and Resurrection.** New York. 1965.

U. Wilckens. **Resurrection.** Edinburgh. 1977.

INDEX